HEARING CHRIST'S VOICE

Living and Proclaiming
the Gospel in
an Embattled World

KELLY MALONE

HANNIBAL BOOKS
www.hannibalbooks.com

Today's church overflows with resources—human, financial, technological, and methodological. Yet it falls behind in its missiological task. Kelly Malone reminds us of Christ's challenge to complete that task as we let His presence transform us into instruments of world-changing service.

—Ray Franklin, Associate Professor of Missions
Ouachita Baptist University

To truly address the increasing lostness of this world, believers must become radical witnesses in both word and lifestyle—radically changed by the indwelling of Christ. Dr. Malone uses the model of Christ's life as described in the Gospel of John to clearly communicate how all Christ-followers can proclaim their grace-full salvation in everyday living. Having had the privilege of ministering in Japan beside Dr. Malone, I know that he writes out of his own vital relationship with Jesus as lived out in his own life and ministry.

—Mark Edlund
Former Missionary to Japan
Executive Director, Colorado Baptist General Convention

Dr. Kelly Malone's *Hearing Christ's Voice* is a wonderful blend of spiritual insight, biblical scholarship, and practical application in the best Evangelical tradition. Malone reminds us that the secret to sharing Christ in an embattled world is found in the person and life of Christ Himself.

—David Garrison
Missionary and author, *Church Planting Movements*

Hearing Christ's Voice allows the reader to peer through the window of our Lord Jesus Christ as the model for evangelistic living. This book needs to be required reading in all missions classes and for anyone serious about evangelism.

—Wade Akins, Missions Professor
Mid-America Baptist Theological Seminary
Global Evangelist and Church-Planting Trainer

Printed in the United States of America
by Lightning Source, Inc.
Cover design by Greg Crull

Library of Congress Control Number: 2006926038
ISBN 0-929292-42-1

Hannibal Books
P.O. Box 461592
Garland, Texas 75046
1-800-747-0738
www.hannibalbooks.com

TO ORDER ADDITIONAL COPIES, SEE PAGE 251

Dedicated
to

Molly, Maggie, and Kevin—
God's precious gifts

Acknowledgements

I would not have completed *Hearing Christ's Voice* without encouragement and assistance from so many who helped bring this book to fruition. A special word of thanks goes to Dr. Timothy George, dean of Beeson Divinity School at Samford University in Birmingham, AL. During the 1999-2000 school year Dr. George allowed me to work at his fine institution as a visiting scholar. This is when I initiated research for this book.

Also I wish to thank missionary colleagues Rich McLaughlin, Scott Parish, and Gary Fujino, who read portions of the manuscript and suggested helpful improvements to the overall quality. I bear responsibility for any remaining weaknesses. I give thanks to the many missionaries who encouraged me.

I am most grateful for Louis and Kay Moore of Hannibal Books, Garland, TX, for their willingness to publish my book. Their expertise makes up for so many of my shortcomings.

Finally thanks to my wife, Molly, and children, Maggie and Kevin, who often wondered, "What kind of book is Dad writing?" while I sat in front of the computer for hours on end. In these pages you finally have an answer.

I pray that my book will encourage readers to live and proclaim the good news of Jesus Christ to a world full of people who need Him so much.

God's richest blessings,
Kelly Malone

Contents

Foreword

Frequently authors of books about missions are more theoreticians than they are practitioners. They know about missions through reading books on missiology, periodic visits to mission fields, and serious studies of culture. But they basically are theoreticians.

This book is authored not by a theoretician but by a practitioner. Kelly Malone is training strategist for the International Mission Board of the Southern Baptist Convention for a crucial and heavily populated part of Asia. He knows missions from the standpoint of a missionary. His book is an optimistic, yet realistic, appraisal of the status of missions in our 21st-century world.

Using the Gospel of John as a backdrop, Dr. Malone points out that missions is the natural outflow of a relationship with Jesus, the ultimate missionary. In this sense this is a book about Him. Missionary motivation springs from the life of Jesus' indwelling flowing through the believer. Jesus is our primary resource for igniting passion for missions. The object of this book is to help you reignite passion for missions in your life.

Roy J. Fish
Distinguished Professor of Evangelism
Roy Fish School of Evangelism and Missions
Southwestern Baptist Theological Seminary
Fort Worth, TX 76122

Preface

He Knocks, but Do We Hear His Voice?

"Hear I am! I stand at the door and knock. If anyone hears my voice and opens the door, I will come in and eat with him, and he with me" (Rev. 3:20).

What Does Jesus Most Want Us to Do?

As we proceed into the 21st century and the third millennium, many Christians ask whether we live in the final age of world history. After all, Jesus said, "*this gospel of the kingdom will be preached in the whole world as a testimony to all nations, and then the end will come"* (Matt. 24:14). For the first time since Christ was born on earth, the church seems to have the resources to complete the Christ-given task to preach the gospel to all nations (Matt. 28:18-20).

Now more than two billion people—about one-third of the earth's population—claim to be Christians. This is more than at any time in history. In Asia and Africa a growing number of people daily convert to Christianity. Statistics show that the number of Christians in Asia and Africa outnumber those in Europe and North America. Not only are Asian and African churches growing, they also have become seedbeds for future church growth. Nations such as China, South Korea, and the Philippines in Asia, and Nigeria and Kenya in Africa now send significant numbers of missionaries to other countries, including North America and Europe. Surely this vast army of witnesses, armed with the Word of God, will have a significant impact reaching the last corner of the world with the good news of Jesus Christ.

Besides increased membership the church now also has more funds. Utilizing television, publishing, and the Internet, Evangelical Christians in North America each year spend vast sums to spread the gospel. Thousands now gather together in one place to worship God as mega churches continually show up in major cities. Millions of dollars pass through mission agencies to assist churches already rapidly growing in other lands.

Also churches have access to more technology than ever before. With the miracles of electronic communication and cybernetic technology we can transmit messages across the world in a matter of seconds. Through distance-learning students in Nairobi and Tokyo simultaneously can participate in seminary classes situated in Los Angeles. By using innovative computer programs we now can translate the Bible into any language.

Finally the church has superior methodology. Missiology, developed in the 20th century, uses insights from Scripture, church history, the social sciences, and present missionary and Evangelical work to capture the most effective means for making Christ's disciples among the people of the world. Scholars measure the church's effectiveness by numbers of believers, spiritual maturity of believers, number and quality of church leaders, number and size of churches produced, and ability of churches to stand on their own without outside support.

When we reflect on the vast human, financial, technological, and methodological resources now available to the church, we may be tempted to say, along with the church at Laodicea, "*I am rich; I have acquired wealth and do not need a thing*" (Rev. 3:17). We easily could expound on this statement by saying, "God has given us everything we need to make the gospel known to the people of all nations. The end is in sight. The Lord soon will return."

On the other hand, the church also faces unprecedented challenges in its quest to make disciples of all nations. We have not kept up the pace with the general population explosion now taking place in Third World countries. Moreover Islam, mysticism, and occult religions continue to grow as people increasingly renew interest in spirituality. For example in Great Britain the number of people who attend mosque on Friday exceeds that of those who attend church on Sunday. In Japan, a nation long resistant to the gospel, hundreds of new religions spring up each year, as people attempt to meet their spiritual needs by experimenting with an ever-increasing variety of options.

Although greater financial resources are available than ever before, much is misused. Nations of the world spend billions each year on armaments but don't provide food for the starving masses. This year Americans spent more money on entertainment and leisure than to help tsunami victims. Film and sports stars are paid millions to entertain people, while those who make important decisions affecting our lives get by with less. Ten percent of the world population uses the majority of energy, food, and natural resources available, while the remaining 90 percent lives without. No wonder other countries are disgusted by Americans' lifestyles.

Technological use now involves ethical decision-making. Misuses of technological devices can lead to destruction. Modern weapons can decimate the earth. Genetic research, designed to heal and prolong life, now can be used to objectify human life. The Internet can be used to send obscene, pornographic, or otherwise indecent materials across national borders into homes and offices around the world. The same can be said for cable television. An increased number of channels does not always lead to an increase in decent programming.

Some now overanalyze methodology to the point at which they view people as objects for coercion and manipulation rather than as humans. Increasingly societies believe the world is part of one great machine. According to this view individuals either act as cogs to make the system go or as a crust to be crushed, sanded down, and thrown away. Now productivity determines human value. People are valued and devalued based on their ability to create rather than because God created them in His image. Now, when the church has unprecedented resources available, Christians shrink away and feel inadequate. When we are confronted by a needy world, we quickly realize we really are *wretched, pitiful, poor, blind, and naked* (Rev. 3:17).

Jesus reaches out to this world and this church. He stands knocking at the door and waits to enter. He says, *"If anyone hears my voice and opens the door, I will come in and eat with him, and he with me"* (Rev. 3:20).

This book is about the One Who stands at the door and knocks. Not only does Jesus bring a message from God, He **is** the message. Jesus is the *Word of God* Who takes on flesh and lives among us (John 1:1, 14). Since God's message to us was enfleshed as a human being, this message no only is *heard* but also is *seen with the eyes and touched with the hands* (1 John 1:1). This message from God includes the total work of God in Christ. This begins with His birth and includes Jesus' teaching, His miracles, His death on the cross, His resurrection, and His ascension to the Father. God continues to speak to us through the exalted Christ, Who sends the Holy Spirit, intercedes for us in heaven before God the Father, and one day will return to declare the final victory of God's kingdom over the powers of evil (1 Cor. 15:24-25; Rev. 20:7-15). At that time God will establish a new heaven and a new earth in which God's people will be with Him forever (Rev. 21-22). Because God has spoken to us in this way through His Son, when we look at Jesus, we see God Himself in all His glory (John 1:14).

Jesus is God's message to our world. The world is overpopulated by hungry, diseased, tired, discouraged, and distraught people. Many either entrap themselves in wealth or enslave themselves in poverty. People spend their lives operating and repairing technology designed to set them free. Methodology depicts people merely as a means to an end rather than an end supported by the means. Jesus brings to this world life, love, and freedom. Jesus brings all of God's blessings to a world needing them.

Jesus is God's message to an embattled world. The battle between light and dark, good and evil, truth and falsehood rages. The battle between God and Satan continues since the dawn of time when the angel, Lucifer, in envy desired to become God. The *son of the dawn* said in his heart,

"I will ascend to heaven; I will raise my throne above the stars of God; I will sit enthroned on the mount of the assembly, on the utmost heights of the sacred mountain. I will ascend above the tops of the clouds; I will make myself like the Most High" (Isa. 14:13-14).

And there was war in heaven. Michael and his angels fought against the dragon, and the dragon and his angels fought back. But he was not strong enough, and they lost their place in heaven. The great dragon was hurled down—the ancient serpent called the devil or Satan, who leads the whole world astray. He was hurled to the earth, and his angels with him (Rev. 12:7-9).

Jesus stands at the door of our embattled hearts and speaks profound, sometimes unbelievable, words—words that contradict what the world tells us about God. The world says either God does not exist or, if He does, we cannot know Him. The world reduces God to a distant, impersonal subject which we study, philosophize about, and discuss rather than view Him as a person. Contrasting this modern, non-theistic mythology, Jesus says, "I stand at the door and knock. If anyone opens the doors I will enter in." Jesus is near. We can know Him. He longs for us personally and daily to commune with Him. Jesus says doing so signifies two people sharing a meal together. Communion warrants that people share time, location, substance, thought, feeling, word, and deed. In short when we intimately know Jesus, we experience the true and living God.

Jesus' words also run contrary to the experience of our everyday lives. Each day we experience illness, pain, earthquakes, and volcanoes as well as human-made disasters such as war and famine. People cannot insulate themselves from worldwide suffering. Yet Jesus says, "Satan, the Prince of Darkness, has been defeated. The evil power has been overcome. You have been set free from bondage to sin and death. Your salvation has been won!"

In John's Gospel, Jesus transforms those who, by seeing, hearing, and touching Jesus, realize He is the Word of God. Nicodemus experiences new spiritual birth which results in eternal life through faith in Jesus (John 3:1-18). The Samaritan woman meets the

Messiah (John 4:25), Who tells her *everything she ever did* (John 4:39). As a result of her testimony, her whole community begins to believe in Jesus as the *Savior of the world* (John 4:42). When the crowds turn away from Jesus, because He refuses to entertain them with miracles, Peter refuses to follow the crowd. Rather Peter bears witness to the disciples' faith in Jesus: "*Lord, to whom shall we go? You have the words of eternal life. We believe and know that you are the Holy One of God*" (John 6:68-69). Martha realizes Jesus not only has the power to overcome sickness but also has the power to defeat death. When Jesus challenges Martha by saying, "*I am the resurrection and the life. He who believes in me will live, even though he dies; and whoever lives and believes in me will never die,*" in faith she responds, "*Yes, Lord, I believe that you are the Christ, the Son of God, who was to come into the world*" (John 11:25-27). When Thomas meets the resurrected Christ, this disciple experiences a life-changing transformation from doubt to faith. As he falls on his knees before Jesus, Thomas commits himself to serve Jesus as Lord and to worship Jesus as God (John 20:24-28).

In Revelation 3:20 Jesus knocks on the church's, not the world's, door. The world needs God's Word, but the church needs Him more. The church is wealthy in terms of people, money, technology, and methodology. But we impoverish ourselves by depending on those resources and shutting out the Lord, Jesus Christ. We labor in Christ's Name as His Body and with His Message. When we do not allow Jesus to hold the proper place in the church and in our lives, all of this is peripheral and ineffective. We forget John's testimony that what God has provided for us through Christ is complete. He alone has the power to transform the human condition and free us from slavery to sin and death and give us a new, free, and powerful life as God's children in His kingdom. Often we do not let Christ dwell in the innermost part of our beings. We do not allow Him to transform us completely through the power of His Word.

Jesus stands at the church's door and knocks. As those who call ourselves believers in Jesus Christ, open the door and allow Jesus His rightful place in our individual lives and in the church. Only then can Jesus, the Word of God Who became flesh, work through us to redeem and transform the spiritual battleground which we call our world.

Jesus stands at the door and knocks. Do you hear His voice?

Responding to His Voice

1. Have you allowed anything to take priority over your relationship with Jesus?

2. Has your message to the world focused on Jesus or on something else?

3. In your daily life and ministry have you allowed another resource to become more important than Jesus?

Chapter 1

He Came to His Own

In the beginning was the Word, and the Word was with God, and the Word was God . . . He was in the world, and though the world was made through him, the world did not recognize him. He came to that which was his own, but his own did not receive him. Yet to all who received him, to those who believed in his name, he gave the right to become children of God (John 1:1, 10-12).

Why Was Jesus Sent to Earth?

Because I have served as a missionary to Japan for more than a decade, I often cannot return to my small hometown of Royse City, TX. When I say small town, I emphasize the word ***small.*** Before the expansion of the Dallas-Fort Worth Metroplex began including my hometown, Royse City had only one main street with one bank, one pharmacy, and 10 or so churches. When Royse City was the little, two-stoplight town in which I grew up, everyone knew me. In fact everyone knew everyone. When I do get to visit, I always ask myself, **"Will anyone know me?"** This is my town with my streets and my people. I belong to this town, because part of my identity stems from Royse City. When people in Tokyo ask where my hometown is, I usually mumble, "near Dallas," because almost no one ever knows of Royse City. But if they press for specifics and ask, "Where near Dallas?", the truth surfaces. I say, "I'm from Royse City," to which they respond, "Oh. I've never heard of it." I'm afraid one day I will walk down Main Street to find **no one welcoming me home.**

Think of how Jesus felt. John tells us that Jesus created the world and that the world belongs to Him, yet when He arrived, the *world did not recognize him* (John 1:10.) We can't feel the full impact of this statement unless we know Who Jesus is, how He relates to the world, and how the world is to relate to Him.

We only really know who we are, how we relate to the world, and how to relate to Jesus when we know Who He is. Did you catch that? The key is knowing not **how the world is to relate to us**, but **how we are to relate to Jesus**. When we have a proper relationship with Him, everything is right. When our relationship with Him is not right, nothing else is either.

God Speaks

John begins his Gospel by identifying his subject as *the Word.* Although this term means little to us, it meant a great deal to John's initial readers. In the first century the definition of *Word*, or *Logos* in the original Greek, was packed with meaning. In the Stoic philosophy among educated Gentiles during that period *Logos* was the underlying law or principle governing everything in the universe, including human intelligence. Similarly Platonism defined *Logos* as what is real or ideal.[1] In either case *Logos* was abstract.

Among ancient-world Jews *Logos* connected with the Old-Testament understanding of the Word of God. According to Genesis 1, *God spoke* the world into existence. In other words God through His Word brought the world into existence. Through the Old Testament God continually reveals Himself to people through His word.[2] *God spoke*, identifying Himself as God, and then commissioned the person He spoke to for a specific task. *God spoke* to Noah and told him to build an ark to save from the flood his family and two of every kind of animal (Gen. 6:13-21). *God spoke* to Abraham and told him to go to a new country in which he and his descendants would become a great nation and a blessing for all the peoples of the earth (Gen. 12:1-3). *God spoke* to Jacob and promised to multiply his descendants and bless all peoples on earth through them (Gen. 28:13-15). *God spoke* to Moses and sent him to free the Hebrew people from slavery in Egypt (Ex. 3-4). *God spoke* to Joshua and sent him to lead Israel in the conquest of Canaan (Jos. 1:1-11). *God spoke* to Gideon and sent him to lead Israel in the defeat of the Midianites (Judg. 6:12-16). *God spoke* to David and told him that his descendant would build a house for God and rule over a kingdom that will last forever (1 Chr. 17:3-14). *God spoke* to Isaiah (Isa. 6:1-13), Jeremiah (Jer. 1:4-19), Ezekiel (Ezek. 2:1-3:11), and the other prophets and sent them to call God's people to repentance and to share His promise of salvation through the Messiah.

When John writes about the *Word,* or *Logos*, He wants us to realize that God speaks to us. However now God speaks to us differently. Hebrew 1:1-3 highlights this contrast:

> *In the past* ***God spoke*** *to our forefathers through the prophets at many times and in various ways, but in these last days* ***he has spoken to us by His Son****, whom he appointed heir of all things, and through whom he made the universe. The Son is the radiance of God's glory and the exact representation of his being, sustaining all things through his powerful word. After he provided purification for our sins, he sat down at the right hand of the Majesty in heaven* (emphasis added).

Before this time God spoke to people through audible words, visions, dreams, and angelic representatives.[3] Now God speaks to us through Himself. God expresses Himself to us in a way only He can.

God's capacity for self-expression is difficult for us to grasp. As humans we cannot express ourselves in the same way God can. We only can express ourselves through words and actions. We convey thoughts and feelings by speaking words with our mouths, writing them with our hands, or typing them on a typewriter or computer. Through actions we sometimes convey thoughts of anger through fighting, covetousness by stealing, lust through pornography or sexual deviance, and pride with arrogant acts of showmanship. We have a great capacity for self-expression but not compared to God's ability to express Himself. When God wants to communicate with us, He does not send a letter or do something so we will know His thoughts and feelings. When God wanted to communicate with us so we would understand Him clearly and completely, He sent Himself. When God communicates with us, He involves all of Himself.

John simply explains, *"The Word was God"* (John 1:1). The human language capacity limits John's ability to adequately express the things of God. Ray Summers succinctly stated what John intended: "The Word was as 'divine' as God was 'divine.' The Word was deity as God was deity."[4] This is the key to understanding John's entire Gospel. John intends for us to understand that the "deeds and words of Jesus are the deeds and words of God."[5]

Gordon H. Clark tells of his friend who handed a Jehovah's Witness a copy of a Greek New Testament after his statement that, on the basis of the Greek grammar, John 1:1 translates, "Originally the Word was, and the Word was with God, and the Word was a god." The Jehovah's Witness carefully examined it, turned it upside down, examined it again, and then, turning it on its side, looked at it a third time before asking, "What is this?" Clark's friend replied, "That is a Greek New Testament about which you have been talking." Clark goes on to say,

> The Deity of Christ is . . . the main message of the Gospel of John. To mistranslate the first verse is to misconstrue the whole book. Yet the first verse of John is not by any means the only passage where the Deity of Christ is taught.[6]

In John's Gospel, Jesus claimed to be God and refers to Exodus 3:14. In Exodus 3, God commanded Moses to return to Egypt to lead the Hebrew people out of slavery. Moses did not think he was up to the task. He began to express doubts. He asked,

> *"Suppose I go to the Israelites and say to them, 'The God of your fathers has sent me to you,' and they ask me, 'What*

is his name? Then what shall I tell them?" In response God said, *"I AM WHO I AM. This is what you are to say to the Israelites: 'I AM has sent me to you'"* (Ex. 3:13-14).

The Hebrew word, translated *I AM* here, literally means the **One Who was, Who is,** and **Who will be**. God was saying to Moses, "I am the One Who always has been here and Who always will be here. I am the eternal One." The meaning is much like Jesus' words about Himself in Revelation 22:13: *"I am the Alpha and the Omega, the First and the Last, the Beginning and the End."* The Bible teaches that One true God, Who is now and Who always will be, existed before all things. In John's Gospel Jesus claimed to be this God by repeatedly referring to Himself as "*I am*." Whenever Jesus said, "*I am"*, He claimed to be and do something only God could be and do. By saying He was "*I am"*, Jesus claimed to be:

The Source of Eternal Life

"I am the bread of life . . . I am the living bread that came down from heaven. If anyone eats of this bread, he will live forever. This bread is my flesh, which I will give for the life of the world" (John 6:48, 51).

The One Who Knows God

"You know me, and you know where I am from. I am not here on my own, but he who sent me is true. You do not know him, but I know him because I am from him and he sent me" (John 7:28, 29).

The One with Unlimited Access to God

"I am with you for only a short time, and then I go to the one who sent me. You will look for me, but you will not find me; and where I am, you cannot come" (John 7:33, 34).

The One Who Enables Us to Clearly See the Way to Live

"I am the light of the world. Whoever follows me will never walk in darkness, but will have the light of life" (John 8:12).

The Eternal One

"Your father Abraham rejoiced at the thought of seeing my day; he saw it and was glad . . . I tell you the truth . . . before Abraham was born, I am" (John 8:56, 58).

The Way of Salvation

"I am the gate; whoever enters through me will be saved" (John 10:9).

The One Who Truly Knows Us

"I am the good shepherd; I know my sheep and my sheep know me—just as the Father knows me and I know the Father" (John 10:14, 15).

The One Who Defeats Death

"I am the resurrection and the life. He who believes in me will live, even though he dies; and whoever lives and believes in me will never die" (John 11:25, 26).

The One Who Overpowered Satan

"Now is the time for judgment on this world; now the prince of this world will be driven out. But I, when I am lifted up from the earth, will draw all men to myself" (John 12:31, 32).

The Only Way to God

"I am the way and the truth and the life. No one comes to the Father except through me" (John 14:6).

The Source of a Fruitful and Abundant Life

"I am the vine; you are the branches. If a man remains in me and I in him, he will bear much fruit; apart from me you can do

nothing . . . If you remain in me and my words remain in you, ask whatever you wish, and it will be given you. This is my Father's glory, that you bear much fruit, showing yourselves to be my disciples" (John 15:5, 7-8).

When we hear the Word of God as Jesus, He is no less than God. This is what sets apart the *Logos* of John's Gospel from the *Logos* of ancient Greek philosophy. The philosophical *Logos* merely is a thing. So often, even among Christians, people tend to reduce God to a topic for discussion. We talk about God as though He is something we can analyze under a microscope. But the *Logos* of the gospel is not merely an object of study. **The Word of God** is a person to know and love. More importantly **He is a person Who loves us, created us,** and **longs to transform us, through His power, into eternal children of God.**

He Came to His Own

The world belongs to God. God created the world through His Word. In the Scriptures we see remarkable agreement on this point. According to Genesis 1, **God spoke** the universe into existence. In 11 instances through Genesis the Scriptures read, *God said.* Eight are acts of creation (Gen. 1:3, 6, 9, 11, 14, 20, 24, 26). The remaining three (Gen. 1:22, 28, 29) are blessings God gives His creation. Psalm 33: 6-9 tells us,

> *By* ***the word*** *of the Lord were the heavens made, their starry hosts by the breath of his mouth. He gathers the waters of the sea into jars; he puts the deep into storehouses. Let all of the earth fear the Lord; let all of the people of the world revere him. For* ***he spoke****, and it came to be; he commanded, and it stood firm* (emphasis added).

The New Testament clarifies that the Word, through which God created the world, is none other than the Son of God, Jesus Christ.

John 1:3 tells us, *Through him, all things were made; without him nothing was made that has been made.* Paul's writing clarifies Christ's role in creation.

> *For us there is but one God, the Father, from whom all things came and for whom we live; and there is but one Lord, Jesus Christ, through whom all things came and through whom we live* (1 Cor. 8:6).

While life exists through and because of the Father, we were brought into being and live through the Son. John's Gospel carries this theme throughout. Allow me to call attention to another point. John 1:4 says, *In him was life, and that life was the light of men.* Leon Morris writes,

> It is only because there is life in the **Logos** that there is life in anything on earth at all. Life does not exist in its own right. It is not even spoken of as made "by" or "through" the Word, but as existing "in" Him.[7]

To fully feel the impact of these words, expand on the first two. "*In Him*", **in relationship to Christ** Who is the Word of God, life exists. Christ is the means through which God gives life. Without Him life doesn't exist.

Surely, you say, life exists apart from Christ, because many people in the world have no relationship with Jesus and still live. At least physically they live for a while. Not so, for Jesus Christ provides physical and spiritual life. Remember that Jesus is the eternal Word through which God created the world. On the sixth day of creation, the Word brought forth men and women created in the *image* and *likeness* of God (Gen. 1:26-27).

The Lord God formed the man of the dust of the ground and breathed into his nostrils the breath of life, and the man became a living being (Gen. 2:7).

Some may assume this ***breath of life*** is the air we breathe to sustain life. No doubt God provided us air, along with water, food, clothing, the sun's heat, and everything else necessary to sustain life.[8] But the passage intends more. The Hebrew word *neshama*, translated *breath*, also rendered *spirit*, is synonymous with the presence of life.[9] So life exists only where the Spirit is present. God provides the Spirit to us. *Jesus said, "It is finished." With that, he bowed his head and gave up his spirit* (John 19:30). At this point Jesus died. The Spirit's departure is synonymous with death. Physical elements which constitute the body return to their natural state: *"For dust you are and to dust you will return"* (Gen. 3:19).

We are here and alive as a result of God's creative work through His Word, Jesus Christ.[10] However this relationship to God through Christ is not limited to people. Regarding Christ Paul writes,

> *For by him all things are created: things in heaven and on earth, visible and invisible, whether thrones or powers or rulers or authorities; all things were created by him and for him. He is before all things, and in him all things hold together* (Col. 1:16-17).

Christ created, sustains, and fulfills everything. Everything in the universe, whether physical or spiritual, completely depends on Him. The Word of God created the universe and will sustain it until His creation is complete.

This is why the Word came to *his own* (John 1:11). His purpose was to fulfill what He long ago began when He said, "Let us create . . . ." At long last, when everything was ready, the Word—God's Son, Jesus—was sent to that which belonged to Him. After all, He made it and holds it together. He was sent to complete what He intended millennia before He made the world, placed the stars in the sky, and caused the planets to orbit around the sun. He was sent to finish what He planned when He separated the water from the land and filled both with life. He returned to clean up the mess we made when we decided to turn our backs on Him, for "even a fallen, alienated creation is His."[11] Turn your attention to this fallen creation.

His Own Did Not Receive Him

God created the world through His Word. However the world does not know Him. This point is so significant, John states it three different ways. First he says, *The light shines in darkness, but the darkness has not understood it* (John 1:5). You may wonder how anyone fails to understand light—something that is a part of the everyday human experience.

To better understand this, suppose we discovered a race of human beings living in caves a thousand miles below the earth's surface. When explorers first encounter these people, the cave-dwellers are shocked because the explorers brought flashlights—basic tools for exploration. The cave-dwellers are shocked because they always have lived in perpetual darkness, with no knowledge that such a thing as light even existed. If the explorers only described light to the cave-dwellers, they immediately would have dismissed the description as myth, legend, or fantasy—certainly not something believed to be literally true. Though the cave-dwellers only have lived in darkness, they cannot even understand it. This is because only darkness can be understood to exist in contrast with its opposite—light.

Those living in spiritual and moral darkness reject the light because it does not fit into their own experience. They even question the possibility that such a thing as light exists. This is what Jesus points to when He says,

> *"This is the verdict: Light has come into the world, but men loved the darkness instead of the light because their deeds were evil. Everyone who does evil hates the light, and will not come into the light for fear that his deeds will be exposed. But whoever lives by the truth comes into the light, so that it may be seen plainly that what he has done has been done through God"* (John 3:19-21).

Rejection of Christianity in the form of reason or science actually is rooted in humans' desire to hide in their hearts spiritual darkness. Fredrikson writes, "If the light unmasks and reveals true darkness then the darkness will not remain passive but will fight back."[12] People reason that if God does not exist, light does not exist and so neither does darkness. However they will cover up the desire to remain in darkness by claiming, "scientific investigation and philosophical inquiry do not support the existence of God." But this acts only as a smokescreen to hide the hideous, inner darkness haunting their souls. What complicates the matter is that the results of these scientific and philosophical speculations fall on a world filled with people eager for a means to conceal darkness in their own hearts.

Allow one example to suffice. A few years ago I knew of a prominent Japanese scientist who, on the basis of the theory of evolution, debunked the idea of creation and God as Creator. However the real reason he refused to acknowledge God's existence is because he knew God would hold him accountable for his immorality. He refused to admit the existence of the ***Light*** because he preferred to continue his own dark existence. The theory of evolution merely was an alternate, godless explanation of reality which allowed him to continue living in **darkness** without having to acknowledge the existence of the ***Light***.

Second, *He was in the world, and though the world was made through him, the world did not recognize him* (John 1:10). People often reject the Creator out of the desire to create and control their reality. This brings to mind a Japanese student who once told a friend of mine who taught her Bible class at a Japanese college, "I decide what is god. If I say that this pencil is my god, it is." Paul writes,

> *For although they knew God, they neither glorified him as God nor gave thanks to him, but their thinking became futile and their foolish hearts were darkened. Although they claimed to be wise, they became fools and exchanged the glory of the immortal God for images made to look like mortal man and birds and reptiles* (Rom. 1:21-23).

Shall we add to Paul's list inanimate objects such as money, automobiles, houses, computers, and even pencils? God provides life through his Word. So, as a result of serving a lifeless god, people become like what they worship. As the psalmist writes, *Those who make them will be like them, and so will all who trust in them* (Ps. 115:8). The things of this world, whether alive or not, do not have the power to give life. The gods of this world may bring temporary satisfaction and pleasure. In some cases they even may sustain and extend life. But total dependence on something other than God, Who created and sustains us through His Word, ultimately results in death.

Third, *He came to that which was his own, but his own did not receive him* (John 1:11). Jesus "did not come as an outsider, but as One Who belonged."[13] In one sense this speaks of the Jewish people. Long ago God promised a Messiah would be born among the Jews, save them from oppression, and be a blessing to the nations. Jesus was born of a Jewish mother and was, by blood, a descendent of King David and of the patriarchs Abraham, Isaac, and Jacob. For example,

> *And now the Lord says—he who formed in the womb to be his servant to bring Jacob back to him and gather Israel to himself, for I am honored in the eyes of the Lord and my God has been my strength—he says: "It is too small a thing for you to be my servant to restore the tribes of Jacob and bring back those of Israel I have kept. I will also make you a light for the Gentiles, that you may bring my salvation to the ends of the earth." This is what the Lord says—the Redeemer and Holy One of Israel—to him who was despised and abhorred by the nation, to the servant of rulers: "Kings will see you and rise up, princes will see and bow down, because of the Lord, who is faithful, the Holy One of Israel, who has chosen you"* (Isa. 49:5-7).

When the Messiah returns, not only will He restore Israel to its proper relationship with God but also to its proper place among the nations. The restoration of the **tribes of Jacob** alone is too small a task for Him to accomplish. Also the Messiah will ***"bring . . . salvation to the ends of the earth."*** So great will be His accomplishment that the rulers of the nations will bow before Him as Lord and King.

Yet if Jesus is both the Word through whom God created the nations and the Lord and King Who will return to rule over them, then ***his own***, to which John 1:11 refers, surely speaks of more than only the Jews. It also refers to every person created by Him whom He wants to call Jesus *Lord*. Jesus arrived for all of us—to every man, woman, boy, and girl of every people and tribe, language, and culture, in the whole world. But, for the most part, Jesus had been, and continues to be, misunderstood, unrecognized, and rejected. Many different explanations of Jesus exist: a great moral and religious teacher, a social reformer, a political liberator, a liar, or a misguided sage, even as one of many Who has pointed the way to God. At the beginning of the third millennium, since the birth of Christ, no more than 10 percent of the world's population (about 600 million) believe in Jesus as God the Son, Savior, and Lord.

Every person determines how he or she will respond to Jesus.[14] This is because, while Jesus was sent for the **whole** world, He is here for each one of us. When anyone preaches, teaches, or talks about the Word of God, He speaks to us. Jesus brings the power of the Holy Spirit to transform us. This transformation is radical. It begins in our hearts—the innermost part of us. This transformation not only is a one-time, quick fix but a slow, painstaking process. The second a person recognizes Who Jesus is and believes in Him, the process begins and continues until each of us meets Him face to face. That is what Christ's hope is all about. One day we will meet Jesus. On that day *we shall be like him, for we shall see him as he is* (1 John 3:2). Whether or not we experience this life-transforming power depends on how we respond to Jesus.

Becoming God's Children

Through His Word God created us to have a relationship with us. Now, although the vast majority of people reject Jesus and live as though no true God exists, His purpose does not change. The God Who created us continues to love and desires to have a relationship with us. Also, the means by which God intends to have a relationship with us has not changed. We have been created **through God's Word** in order to have a relationship with Him. He intends to have a relationship with us **through His Word**. Most people have not recognized or received God's Word (John 1:10-11), *yet to all who received him, to those who believed in his name, he gave the right to become children of God* (John 1:12).

God has given those who believe in Christ the "authority, or privilege, or power to become children of God . . . They did not previously have this power. It was a gift [from] God."[15] Through God's self-revelation as a child, taking on human flesh, we can understand His purpose for us in terms of a Father-child relationship.[16] Through God's Spirit those who believe in Christ experience a new birth into His family (John 3:5-8). Through the external work of God's Son and the internal work of His Spirit we are able to call God "Father" (Rom. 8:1-2, 11-17; Gal. 4:4-7).[17]

Belief in Christ cannot be overstated. That belief brings about spiritual change. According to John without belief in Christ people are "children of the devil" (John 8:44) who "cannot know the truth" (John 8:32). They are "slaves to sin" (John 8:34) who only can be set free by the Son of God (John 8:36).[18] Belief in Christ turns people into God's children. Elsewhere in John belief in Christ results in eternal life (John 3:15-16; 5:24; 6:40; 11:25-26), the gift of the Holy Spirit (John 7:39), forgiveness of sins (John 8:24), knowing the way to God (John 14:1-6), and spiritual fruitfulness and joy (John 15:5-11). Belief in Christ is so important that John says this is the reason he wrote his Gospel:

> *Jesus did many other miraculous signs in the presence of his disciples, which are not written in this book. But these*

> *are written that you may believe that Jesus is the Christ, the Son of God, and that by believing you may have life in his name* (John 20:30-31).[19]

John's purpose is not to tell us everything about Jesus. John left out a lot. Instead he **focuses on what we need to know to believe in Jesus**. When you talk with people about Jesus, always encourage them to believe in Him. John did not write his Gospel so people only **know** Jesus is the Christ. John wrote so people would **believe** Jesus is the Christ. People do not become God's children by **knowing** about Jesus. People become God's children by **believing** in Jesus.

With Christianity knowledge is secondary and faith is primary. This does not mean knowledge is not important. Some knowledge is essential for belief in Jesus. However accumulated knowledge without accompanied accumulated faith can be dangerous. This is because knowledge, when not entrusted to God, leads to pride. I have met people who studied the Bible all their lives but do not believe in Jesus. In some extreme cases they try to use the Bible to prove why belief in Jesus is unnecessary. Their vast knowledge has become a barrier to, rather than a means of, faith.

Belief in Christ, which causes us to become God's children and brings about such blessings as forgiveness of sin and eternal life, is faith in God's Word, Jesus Christ. God gives us the opportunity to believe in Jesus by sending Him to us as a gift. *"For God so loved the world that he gave his one and only Son, that whoever believes in him shall not perish but have eternal life"* (John 3:16). God sent His Son to us so we could believe in Him and have eternal life through Him. So not only is the Son God's gift; God's gift also is faith and eternal life.

Consequently, faith comes from hearing the message, and the message is heard through the word of Christ (Rom. 10:17). The message here is the gospel message. To experience salvation, believe this message and hear it. Paul says we only hear this message **through the Word of Christ**. We have a gospel message to preach and teach, to hear and understand, to believe and to be saved because Christ was sent to us. This **message** is God's Word in the form of Jesus Christ. God's gift of salvation is Christ. No other means of salvation exists apart from faith in Jesus. When we, by faith, receive Jesus, whom God sent, we become children of God.

The Word in Human Flesh

Some reinterpret Jesus to make Him palatable to contemporary human thinking. Dissatisfied with claims that Jesus actually is God in human form, some interpret Him as a moral teacher, a political liberator, a social reformer, or one of many Who provides a way to God. As we have seen, all of these views clearly contradict what Jesus tells us about Himself. In this regard C.S. Lewis writes,

> I am trying here to prevent anyone from saying the really foolish thing that people often say about Him: "I'm ready to accept Jesus as a great moral teacher, but I don't accept His claim to be God." That is the one thing that we must not say. A man who was merely a man and says the sort of things Jesus said would not be a great moral teacher. He would either be a lunatic . . . or else he would be the Devil of Hell. You must make your choice. Either this man was, and is, the Son of God: or else a madman or something worse. You can shut Him up for a fool, you can spit at Him and kill Him as a demon; or you can fall at His feet and call Him Lord and God. But let us not come with any patronizing nonsense about His being a great human being. He has not left that open to us. He did not intend to.[20]

When we bring the incarnation to the foreground in our understanding of Jesus, everything falls into place. Everything Jesus does, we expect God to be able to do—calm storms, walk on water, heal the sick, and raise the dead. Surely, if an all-powerful God created the universe, He can do such things. The unexpected thing is that He does these things within the limitations of human flesh.

Jewish religious leaders who met Jesus understood this issue. Sometimes we think lightly of these Jews because they did not fall down and worship Jesus as God. Let's give them some credit. They saw this man named Jesus from Nazareth heal the sick, the blind, and the lame and asked Him where He received His power. Nicodemus voiced the opinion of all when he said, *"Rabbi, we know that you are a teacher who has come from God. For no one could perform the miraculous signs you are doing if God were not with him"* (John 3:2). However to say Jesus is from God is not enough. Not only is Jesus **from** God; **He is God**. Jesus said, *"The one who sent me is with me; he has not left me alone, for I always do what pleases him"* (John 8:29). *"Anyone who has seen me has seen the Father"* (John 14:9). Alister McGrath writes,

> As Jesus acts as God and for God in every context of importance, we should conclude that, for all intents and purposes, Jesus is God. Thus when we worship Jesus, we worship God; when we know Jesus, we know God; when we hear the promises of Jesus, we hear the promises of God; when we encounter Jesus, we encounter none other than the living God. The idea of the incarnation is the climax of Christian reflection on the mystery of Christ—the recognition that Jesus revealed God; that Jesus represented God; that Jesus speaks as God and for God; that Jesus acted as God and for God; that Jesus was God.[21]

What can impress us here is the extent to which God is willing to go so we may know Him, believe in Him, and have a relationship with Him. Read the words of Paul: *God was reconciling the world to himself in Christ* (2 Cor. 5:19). Through Jesus Christ, God personally is involved in bringing us to Himself.

Jesus has done this by living *for a while among us* (John 1:14). This literally means dwelling in a tent. This reminds us of the tabernacle God ordered Moses to build as God's dwelling place (Ex. 25:8) while the people of Israel were in the wilderness. When Moses completed it, the *glory of the Lord filled the tabernacle* (Ex.

40:35), but this "glory was partial, unfulfilled, and even sporadic."[22] The glory of the tabernacle, and later the temple, might be described as **reflected glory**. In other words, the glory of these places of worship was not their own glory but, rather, **the glory of another reflected through them**. The writer of Hebrews tells us the function of the tabernacle and the related sacrificial system is to point beyond themselves to Christ, the Great High Priest, Who made a sacrifice once for all our sins (Heb. 9:1-10:18).

By thinking about the light of the moon we can illustrate how the tabernacle in Exodus reflects the glory of Christ. The moon has no light of its own. Left on its own the moon only would be a dark, cold rock in space.

This is what happens when the moon is cut off from the source of light. For example when a lunar eclipse occurs, the earth passes in a direct line between the sun and the moon. The moon no longer has any light to reflect. As a result it becomes dark and almost invisible to the naked eye.

In much the same way the glory of the tabernacle in the wilderness is not its own glory but, rather, the glory of Jesus Christ. His is the glory of the *One and Only, who came from the Father, full of grace and truth* (John 1:14).

God's glory reveals itself when Christ humbles Himself, lives among human beings, and suffers for them.[23] God's glory through Christ has two characteristics. The first is grace. This is God's undeserved, self-giving love which results in God sending His Son to us so we can have eternal life and forgiveness of sin through Him.

> *This is how God showed his love among us: He sent his one and only Son into the world that we might live through him. This is love: not that we loved God, but that he loved us and sent his Son as an atoning sacrifice for our sins* (1 John 4:9-10).

The second characteristic of God's glory revealed in Christ is truth. God sent Jesus Christ in order to show us God as He really is.[24] You don't have to speculate about God or imagine what He might be like. We now have clear *knowledge of the glory of God in the face of Christ* (2 Cor. 4:6).

For the Word of God—God became flesh—to fully affect us, He leaves His imprint on us. Just as the tabernacle in the wilderness reflected Jesus Christ's glory, He also made us to reflect His glory. Indeed, *we have this treasure in jars of clay to show that this all-surpassing power is from God and not from us* (2 Cor. 4:7). The Word of God formed us out of the dust of the ground and enlivened us with His Spirit so He could reveal His glory in us. Many times the New Testament parallels Jesus to those who believe in Him. Jesus is the Son of God. Through faith in Him we become God's children (John 1:12). Jesus took on a body (John 1:14). Together believers form the *Body of Christ* (1 Cor. 12:27). Jesus is the *"light of the world"* (John 9:5) as we also are if our good deeds bring glory to the heavenly Father (Matt. 5:14-16). Jesus bore the cross for us. *Take up* [your own] *cross daily* (Luke 9:23) and *follow in his steps* (1 Pet. 2:21).

Allow the Word of God to fully impact you. He made us to reflect His glory. We were made in such a way that God the Son could become **enfleshed in us**. I do not refer to a literal incarnation, because God, the Son, assumed human form in the person of Jesus Christ. What I mean is believing in Christ, trusting Him for our salvation, and yielding to Him so He can accomplish His will through us. When we do that, God's Word to us becomes God's Word **through us to the world**. As a result, when we talk, Jesus speaks through us; when we act, Jesus works through us; when we walk or drive or fly, Jesus goes through us. He transforms the world to reflect His image to the glory of God the Father.

Responding to His Voice

1. When has God spoken to you? What has He sent you to do?

2. Have you received or rejected the Word of God? What are the results of your response to God's Word?

3. What do you need to do for God's Word to enflesh Himself in you?

Chapter 2

God's Dwelling Place

Jesus answered them, "Destroy this temple, and I will raise it again in three days." The Jews replied, "It has taken forty-six years to build this temple, and you are going to raise it in three days?" But the temple he had spoken of was his body. After he was raised from the dead, his disciples recalled what he had said. Then they believed the Scripture and the words that Jesus had spoken (John 2:19-22).

Experience God's Presence and Power

At the stroke of midnight on December 31 temple bells across Japan begin to toll to welcome the New Year. Millions of Japanese people walk out of their houses and make their way to the neighborhood Buddhist temple. At the temple they follow a few simple, prescribed rituals. By tossing salt on them the priest purifies them of past-year misdeeds. He then prays for their good luck and happiness during the New Year. Finally the people buy some sort of good-luck charm as evidence that the Buddha has blessed them for the year ahead. Then they make their way home.

During my more than 10 years in Japan, as I repeatedly watched these rituals unfold before my eyes, I asked myself, "Why do the Japanese do it?" What compels them to leave their houses early in the morning on January 1? What draws them to follow religious traditions of their ancestors? Fear of possible harm for failure to receive the Buddha's blessing through their local priest? The reason may be some combination of these motives and more I failed to mention. Motives for going to the temple at each new year are as varied as are the people who observe the ritual.

One thing weaves a common thread through all of these motivations. They go to the temple to meet with the deity. Buddha is at the temple. The temple is his house—his holy ground. They go to his place to be where he is.

This kind of thinking is not unique to Buddhism in Japan. Rather, all of the world's religions share this theme. Each religion has holy places. Many times these holy places are dwelling places for one or more deities. They may have an elaborate temple, as in Buddhism or Hinduism, or a natural phenomenon such as a tree, waterfall, or mountain, as in animism. In other cases the deity does not dwell at the holy place. Nevertheless the holy place is where people go to meet their god. Examples include mosques in Islam, synagogues in Judaism, and the church building in Christianity.

In John 2 Jesus confronts Jewish leaders with their inadequate understanding of the temple—God's dwelling place. For the Jews the temple was a place in Jerusalem at which they went "to meet with God, to be forgiven, delivered, and restored as His people."[1] But when Jesus said to them, "*Destroy this temple . . .*" (John 2:19), He did not refer to a place. He referred neither to a geographic location nor to a building. Jesus referred to His own body as God's dwelling place. In chapter one, God, in the person of Jesus, arrived as the *tabernacle* among us (John 1:14). Jesus is the one to whom all people go to meet God. We go to Jesus to be purified from sin and to receive God's blessings.

This House Is Not for Sale

Jesus's interchange with the Jewish leaders is rather dramatic. He traveled from Capernaum on the north shore of the Sea of Galilee to Jerusalem to participate in the Passover (John 2:12-13). When Jesus arrived in Jerusalem, He found that the temple, which He long had regarded to be His *"Father's house"* (Luke 2:49; John 2:16), had been reduced to a place of commerce. *In the temple courts he found men selling cattle, sheep and doves, and others sitting at tables exchanging money* (John 2:14).

The Jewish leaders in charge of the temple conducted commercial activity as a matter of convenience and profit. Pilgrims traveled great distances throughout the Roman Empire to participate in the Passover. Each family was required to have an animal sacrifice (Ex. 12:5). Since not everyone could bring sacrificial animals with them, such animals were sold in Jerusalem as a convenience for the pilgrims. What could be more convenient than to sell animals at the temple in which sacrifices took place?[2]

Additionally every Jewish male older than 19 had to pay a half-shekel annual temple tax—the equivalent of two days' wages. Most currency at the time was considered unacceptable for paying the temple tax.[3] This may have been because many bore the image of foreign rulers or deities and thus was considered unclean for sacred purposes. Another reason may have been because the weights of various coins did not measure up precisely to the required weight of a half-shekel.[4] Whatever the reason a fee was exacted from those who needed to exchange money on temple grounds. The people in charge made huge profits.[5]

Jesus reacted quickly and decisively. *He made a whip out of cords* to drive everyone and everything out of the temple area. John is specific on this point. Jesus drove out **all** of the *sheep and cattle* as well the merchants and those who exchanged money (John 2:16). *To those who sold the doves he said, "Get those out of here! How dare you turn my Father's house into a market!"* (John 2:16).

Notice His words. Jesus was not responding to what was being done. He never condemned the animal merchants and moneychangers for carrying on their trade. These activities were necessary if the temple tax and sacrificial system were to continue at the time. Jesus responded to the issue of where these activities took place. He was upset that animals were sold and money was exchanged in the temple.[6]

The temple was God's house—the place to meet with and worship with God. The temple was to be a place to receive forgiveness of sins and experience spiritual renewal. But these men reduced the temple to a place of business and a means of profit. This was why Jesus was in an uproar.

When we apply what Jesus said and did here to the situation of contemporary Christianity, our Lord is not pleased. No doubt economic activity is a necessary part of Christianity. Bibles, books, music, CD's, and DVD's produced and sold provide essential assistance for contemporary Christians in evangelism, missions, spiritual growth, and worship. These items are just as important to us as animals and money exchange were to Passover pilgrims in first-century Jerusalem. The problem lies not with commercial activity but with the **place** it occupies.

I am not thinking of place, such as a building or geographical location, in a physical sense. The issue does not involve setting up a booth or bookstore for the benefit of those participating in worship, such as at a Christian concert. Rather a place, in the spiritual sense, is **located in the heart**. I am concerned that too often we reduce events meant to worship God and lift up Jesus to occasions dedicated to making a profit. We change the event's purpose from meeting God to getting something for ourselves. The place intended for God's worship becomes a place to fulfill ulterior motives.

What do you think Jesus would have done if He found only a few moneychangers in a small corner of the temple? What if only one or two men sold sheep there? Would He have said, "They only are taking up a small corner and are not disrupting the primary purpose of the temple. People still can meet God and worship Him here. The moneychangers and merchants aren't too disruptive. And they actually are providing a valuable service for some worshipers, even if they are making a little money for themselves, so I will just leave them alone." No, Jesus would have thrown them out.

Jesus is concerned with the **place** God occupies in our hearts. Jesus said we are to love *"God with all of* [our] *heart*[s]*"* (Mark 12:30). This means **all of our hearts** belong to God for His habitation. God doesn't want to share with something else any portion—not even a small corner—of our hearts. When we allow profitability, or some other worldly motive, to occupy even a small corner of the place God intended for Himself, we have a serious problem.

Remember Jesus drove the merchants, the animals, and the money-changers out of the temple. His message to them was, "This is my Father's house; this house is not for sale."

"This Is My Father's House"

Jesus said the reason He cleared the temple was because the temple was His *"Father's house"* (John 2:16). This statement raised a serious question for Jewish leaders: *"What miraculous sign can you show us to prove your authority to do all of this?"* (John 2:18). The temple occupied a very special place in the Jewish world at that time. If Jesus was going to make the claim that this temple was **His Father's house**, He was going to have to back up His words.

In Jewish understanding, while "God dwelt in heaven" (Gen. 11:5; Ex. 19:11; 1 Kings 8:27), he chose "particular places where He would meet with His people."[7] For example Jacob named *Bethel* the place in which God appeared to him in a dream. *Bethel* means house of God (Gen. 28:10-22). Mount Sinai became a sacred area after the Lord appeared to Moses and gave him the law. God instructed Moses to build the *Tent of Meeting* (Ex. 40:6), in which God met with the priests who would represent Him before the people of Israel. Finally, the temple replaced the tabernacle as the place to go to meet God.[8] When the priest entered the innermost part of the temple—the Holy of Holies—he was the representative of the Jewish people into the very presence of God.[9]

In order to fully understand the significance of the temple for first-century Jews, get past the Christian belief that a person can meet with God in many places. At the time Jews understood that God chose to meet with His people in **one place**—the temple.

People began regarding the temple as God's dwelling place and a replica of God's dwelling place in heaven.[10] Some of this imagery is in the Old Testament. For example in Isaiah 6:2-6 the temple is a place in which God is enthroned as the ruler of the nations. In Isaiah 6:1 the prophet has a vision of the holiness of the Lord *seated on a throne, high and exalted, and the train of his robe filled the temple.* Perhaps the most exalted vision of the temple as God's dwelling place is found below.

> *The glory of the Lord entered the temple through the gate facing east. Then the Spirit lifted me up and brought me into the inner court, and the glory of the Lord filled the temple. While the man was standing beside me, I heard someone speaking to me from inside the temple. He said: "Son of man, this is the place of my throne and the place for the soles of my feet. This is where I will live among the Israelites forever . . ."* (Ezek. 43:4-7).

The Jews also regarded the temple as the center of the universe—the place in which earth linked to heaven above and the underworld below as well as the geographic center of the world. Everyone and everything was defined in relationship to the temple. For example, social order determined the extent to which people could enter the temple: the high priest entered into the Holy of Holies, the priests into the Holy Place, Jewish men into the inner court, then Jewish women, and then Gentiles. The sick and handicapped, seen as unclean, entirely were excluded from temple worship and Jewish social life. The annual calendar also revolved around major events of temple worship—the New Year, the Day of Atonement, the feasts of Booths, Passover, and Pentecost.[11]

For the Jews, when Jesus said the temple was His Father's house, He claimed the center of the universe. Jesus laid claim to the temple as His rightful place of authority. He replaced the corrupt system of sacrifice and rituals[12] with a complete, perfect sacrifice. As the writer of Hebrews tells us:

> *Now there have been many of those priests, since death prevented them from continuing in office; but because Jesus lives forever, he has a permanent priesthood. Therefore he is able to save completely those who come to God through him, because he always lives to intercede for them. Such a high priest meets our needs—one who is holy, blameless,*

pure, set apart from sinners, exalted about the heavens. Unlike the other high priests, he does not need to offer sacrifices day after day, first for his own sins, and then for the sins of the people. He sacrificed for their sins once for all when he offered himself (Heb. 7:23-27).

Jesus sacrificed Himself **once** and provided the opportunity for **all** people to meet God, experience His forgiveness, and have a relationship with Him. The old temple does not allow for this opportunity.

For the Jews, Jesus' testimony that the temple was His Father's house was earth-shattering news. If the temple, at the center of the universe, belonged to Jesus' Father, then the rest of the universe also does. How could any man claim to have such immense power and authority? The Jews needed some evidence to believe His claim.

Many struggle with this. Jesus entered into their world from the outside, entered their hearts—the very center of their universe—and basically said, "This is my Father's house. You have corrupted, defiled, and used it for your own purposes long enough. I have arrived to clean it up and set it aside for the purpose God intended." When Jesus moves to the center of the universe, people realize, if He speaks truthfully, change is inevitable. Change begins by redefining the understanding of the world. People realize God—not themselves—is the center of the universe. God has authority over their lives. Through His Son, Jesus Christ, He lays claim to His place and authority . But, before any redefining begins, people want to know if Jesus really is Who He says. People ask, "What miraculous sign can you show us to prove your authority to do all of this?"

"Destroy This House, and I Will Build it Again"

Jesus responded to the demand for a miraculous sign, *"Destroy this temple, and I will build it again in three days"* (John 2:19). The Jews had no idea what Jesus meant. The temple was a place in

Jerusalem which had taken 46 years to build. How could Jesus rebuild the temple in three days? (John 2:20) The Jews didn't understand, because their religious experience limited their vision. As they looked at the temple around them, they were limited by what they could see with physical eyes.[13]

With the advantage of hindsight we understand what Jesus meant. John writes,

> *But the temple he had spoken of was his body. After he was raised from the dead, his disciples recalled what he had said. Then they believed the Scripture and the words that Jesus had spoken* (John 2:21-22).

No one in the temple that day, not even His disciples, knew what Jesus meant. John tells us that only **after** Jesus' resurrection did His disciples recall His words and understand what He meant. Also the disciples only believed Jesus' Word and what the Scriptures (i.e. the Old Testament prophecies) said about Him when they looked back at everything **through Jesus' resurrection**.

The Jews wanted proof of Jesus' authority over the temple. Jesus responded by pointing to His resurrection from the dead. The resurrection is proof of Jesus' divine authority. Ravi Zacharias states this point so clearly.

> Jesus gave the greatest proof of His authority by accurately predicting His death and the time of His bodily resurrection. Temple authorities should have been alert to His promise, but they never believed it actually would happen. The fulfillment of that prediction reveals the uniqueness of Jesus among all contenders.[14]

New Testament writers repeatedly emphasize the relationship between Jesus' resurrection and His authority. For example Jesus tells His disciples, *"All authority on heaven and earth has been given to me"* (Matt. 28:18). In John 2 the resurrected Christ exercises God's authority over all things.

Luke's writing depicts Jesus' resurrection as in conjunction with His empowerment of the disciples through sending the Holy Spirit.

In Luke 24:48-49 Jesus says, *"You are my witnesses of these things. I am going to send you what my Father has promised; but stay in the city until you have been clothed with power from on high."* Jesus reiterates this point: *"But you will receive power when the Holy Spirit comes upon you; and you will be my witness . . ."* (Acts 1:8). However in Luke's writings the clearest statement of the connection between Jesus' resurrection and sending the Holy Spirit is found in Peter's sermon on the day of Pentecost.

> *God has raised this Jesus to life, and we are all witnesses of the fact. Exalted to the right hand of God, he has received from the Father the promised Holy Spirit and has poured out what you now see and hear* (Acts 2:32-33).

Paul writes that Christ, who was raised from the dead (1 Cor. 15:20), has the authority to make alive all who believe in Him (1 Cor. 15:22, 57). This is because the authority of His kingdom extends to *all dominion, authority and power,* including the power of death itself (1 Cor. 15:24-26). In Philippians 2 Paul sequentially relates Jesus' authority to His death on the cross. Jesus *became obedient to death—even death on a cross.* As a result *God exalted him* (Phil. 2:8, 9). Paul does not explicitly mention the resurrection here but implies it, since Jesus' exaltation follows His crucifixion. As a result of this exaltation Jesus is endowed with kingly authority over all things.

> *That at the name of Jesus every knee should bow, in heaven and on earth and under the earth, and every tongue confess that Jesus Christ is Lord, to the glory of God the Father* (Phil. 2:10-11).

The implication of the resurrection is that Jesus has authority over all things. However whether people accept this authority hinges on how they respond to the resurrection. Some like what they hear about Jesus but cannot believe in His resurrection. Denial of the resurrection reduces Jesus to a human being admired and perhaps imitated but not trusted in as the way of salvation.

However, when belief in the resurrection of Jesus does occur, it inevitably leads to the conclusion that Jesus is God Who lived a sinless life on earth as a human, died on the cross for our sins, and now is the risen and living Savior and Lord. When people take the next step and act on their mental belief in Jesus to actually trust in Him as their Savior and Lord, tremendous spiritual power is at work in their lives. This power is the result of the innerworking of the Holy Spirit. The result of the Spirit's work has been described using such words as *transformational* and *life-changing*. Paul says that the result of the Spirit's work is that a person becomes a *new creation* (2 Cor. 5:17). Jesus calls it a new birth (John 3:6-7). We can see what resurrection faith is like by seeing how it changed the lives of those who knew Jesus and witnessed His resurrection firsthand.

Resurrection Faith

John writes that after Jesus *was raised from the dead, his disciples recalled what he had said. Then they believed the Scripture and the words that Jesus had spoken* (John 2:22). This really is the point of the whole story. Not only does John want us to know about how Jesus threw the merchants and moneychangers out of the temple. Not only does John want us to know what Jesus said to the Jewish leaders when they questioned His authority. Rather John wants us to look, through the lens of His resurrection, at what Jesus did and said that day in the temple. When we do this, we understand that only the One with the divine power Jesus had could have done what He did. Only the One with the divine authority Jesus had could have said what He said. These were the acts and words of Jesus—the Son of God, the ruler of heaven and earth.

The purpose of focusing the lens of Jesus' resurrection on the John 2 events that occurred in the temple is not simply so we can know about them. John wants us to recognize Who Jesus is. He does not want us merely to be awestruck by His divine power and authority. Rather, the purpose in all this is so we may **believe** in Jesus. In chapter one of this book I already have pointed out the purpose of John's Gospel: *These things are written that you may believe that Jesus is the Christ, the Son of God, and that by believing you may have life in his name* (John 20:31).

John knew about the results of faith in the resurrected Christ because he experienced it firsthand. He also had seen the results of this faith in the lives of other people. John was with Simon Peter on Sunday morning, the third day after Jesus died on the cross, when Mary Magdalene arrived with the news, "*They have taken the Lord out of the tomb, and I don't know where they have put him!"* (John 20:2). On hearing this shocking news the two disciples began to run. They ran all the way to the tomb where Jesus had been buried. John says that when he reached the tomb and went inside, *he saw and believed* (John 20:8). While scholars dispute what John actually believed at this point, his words below leave little doubt about his faith in the resurrected Jesus and the impact of this faith on his life.

> *That which was from the beginning, which we have heard, which we have seen with our eyes, which we have looked at and our hands have touched—this we proclaim concerning the Word of life. The life appeared; we have seen it and testify to it, and we proclaim to you the eternal life, which was with the Father and has appeared to us* (1 John 1:1-2).

Based on what John saw, heard, and touched, he believed in the *life who appeared*—in Jesus Who was dead but is now alive and Who will live forever. Because of John's faith in Jesus he experienced eternal life.

Mary Magdalene stood and wept outside the tomb when a man, whom she mistook to be the gardener, said to her, *"Woman, why are you crying? Who is it that you are looking for?"* Mary said to Him, *"Sir, if you have carried him away, tell me where you have put him, and I will get him"* (John 20:15). Mary's grief may have prevented her from recognizing Jesus.[15] Or perhaps because Mary had the usual human mindset to interpret death as the end, she failed to recognize the possibility of life beyond the grave. Whatever the case all of that changed in an instant when Jesus said her name, *"Mary."*

In that instant Mary turned toward Him and cried out, *"Rabonni!" (which means Teacher)* (John 20:16). Then she fell at His feet and grasped Him with her hands. We can imagine Mary still weeping with tears of great joy in place of bitter sorrow.

Jesus said to Mary, *"Do not hold on to me, for I have not yet returned to my Father. Go instead to my brothers and tell them, 'I am returning to my Father and your Father, to my God and your God'"* (John 20:17). Mary turned to Jesus, but He turned her back around and sent her into the world. He said to her, *"Do not hold on to me, for I have not yet returned to the Father. Go instead to my brothers and tell them, 'I am returning to my Father and your Father, to my God and your God.'"* So Mary went to the disciples and told them her news, *"I have seen the Lord!"* (John 20:18).

That evening the disciples huddled together in the upper room where only a few days before they had celebrated the Lord's Supper with Jesus. I am sure they rehashed recent events and tried to make sense of everything that had happened. Just a few days before, Jesus had entered Jerusalem in triumph as He rode on a donkey. People seemed ready to make Him King. Then suddenly Jesus was arrested, tried, and crucified. The disciples' ecstasy was replaced by agony, their hopes dashed, their future dreams of glory brought to a screeching halt at the end of three, very large Roman nails.

In the morning Peter and John returned from the garden tomb and said Jesus' body was missing but His graveclothes were not. Someone would not have taken the body and left the wrapping. Who would want the body, anyway? **Jesus appeared to have just gotten up and walked out of the tomb!** But dead men don't walk or talk. Jesus was dead. Or, at least, Jesus had been dead. A short time later Mary brought news that she saw **Jesus alive** and not dead.

As the gathered disciples contemplated all of these things, Jesus spoke these words,

> *"Peace be with you! As the Father has sent me, I am sending you . . . Receive the Holy Spirit. If you forgive anyone his sins, they are forgiven; if you do not forgive them, they are not forgiven"* (John 20:21, 22).

These words are the closest thing in John's writings we have to the Great Commission. William Banks points out that Jesus gave them His peace so they could become messengers of the gospel of peace.

> In a worn, torn world full of hatred and bitterness, the disciples of Christ are to possess the peace of Christ, for the very message of the church is Christ, the Prince of Peace. The preacher must possess what he preaches![16]

Thomas was not there when Jesus appeared to the other disciples. When Thomas heard the news, he responded in accordance with his character as a human being: he doubted. Thomas said, *"Unless I see the nail marks in his hands and put my fingers where the nails were, and put my hand into his side, I will not believe it"* (John 20:25).

Thomas gets a bum rap. To be fair to Thomas the other disciples also doubted until they saw Jesus with their own eyes. And so also with Thomas. When he saw Jesus—resurrected and alive—with his own eyes and heard Jesus' words, "*Peace be with you . . . Stop doubting and believe"* (John 20:26, 27), Thomas was transformed. His doubt was changed to faith as he cried out to Jesus, "*My Lord and my God!"* (John 20:28).

These simple words Thomas cried summarize the meaning of the Christian faith. A Christian is someone who bows a knee to Jesus as Lord and worships Jesus as God. Both are important. On the one hand, if a person only commits to follow Jesus, He is reduced to a great human being, a moral example, and a religious teacher. On the other hand, when Jesus is thought of only as God, He often becomes a distant, unknowable, philosophical concept rather than someone with whom we can have a relationship.

Let's again look at resurrection faith through the experience of Jesus' first followers. First, resurrection faith is based on a **personal encounter** with Jesus, Who is resurrected and alive. Jesus shows He is interested in an intensely personal relationship with us. Jesus cares about us and wants to be involved in our everyday lives. Second, **resurrection faith draws us to Jesus**, Who enables us to know God as Father. As Jesus said, *"Anyone who has seen me has seen the Father"* (John 14:9). Third, resurrection faith brings about the **recognition that Jesus is both Lord and God**. Thomas' statement of faith becomes our own. Fourth, resurrection faith **results in internal peace**. As Paul writes, through Jesus Christ our hearts and minds are filled with the *peace of God which transcends all understanding* (Phil. 4:7). Finally, those who have this resurrection faith are **sent by Jesus into the world** as messengers of the Good News about Jesus.

If people in the contemporary world are to meet God, they cannot meet Him by going to a place. They cannot meet God by going to a temple constructed by human hands. They cannot meet God by going to a mosque or a cathedral. **They can meet God only by meeting the resurrected Jesus.** They can be transformed only by God's power through faith in the living Christ. Now that Jesus has ascended into heaven to be with God the Father, how can people meet Him? How can they see Jesus, be touched by Him, and be transformed by His power?

We Are His Temple

If the world is to meet Jesus, this will happen through us. We are the temple of God's Spirit Who dwells in us. As Paul writes,

> *Don't you know that you yourselves are God's temple and that God's Spirit lives in you? If anyone destroys God's temple, God will destroy him; for God's temple is sacred, and you yourself are that temple* (1 Cor. 3:16-17).

The presence of the living God can bring about a sharp contrast between God's people and the world in which we live. Gordon Fee ably points out this contrast in the context of the Corinthian church to which Paul addressed his letter.

> In contrast to the "gods many and lords many" of pagan religion with their multiplied temples and shrines, a temple of the living God now was in Corinth—and they did not so much as have a building; they were the building . . . What made it God's alternative, his temple in Corinth, was his own presence in and among the people.[17]

In this temple, we, *like living stones, are being built into a spiritual house to be a holy priesthood, offering spiritual sacrifices acceptable to God through Jesus Christ* (1 Pet. 2:5). For the temple to be complete, all of these stones had to fit together. Each stone is important. None can be left out. As Ravi Zacharias writes,

> The Christian does not go to the temple to worship. The Christian takes the temple with him or her. Jesus lifts us beyond the building and pays the human body the highest compliment by making it His dwelling place, the place where He meets with us.[18]

The New Testament explains, in many ways, the idea of God's presence within Christians. Jesus related His living within us by sending the Holy Spirit so that when the Spirit lives within, so does Jesus (John 14:16-20). Matthew 28:20 in conjunction with Acts 1:8 portrays the same idea. In Matthew 28:20 Jesus promises to be with us. In Acts 1:8 He promises to send the Holy Spirit. In other words, Jesus wants to dwell within us as the Holy Spirit. Paul's writings also describe this relationship between Jesus and the Holy Spirit. For example Paul writes, *God sent the Spirit of his Son into our hearts* (Gal. 4:6). Also he refers to the *Spirit of Jesus Christ* (Phil. 1:19).

This does not mean the Son of God and the Spirit of God are one and the same. According to the doctrine of the Trinity one God exists as three persons. However such a unity between the Father, Son, and the Holy Spirit exists that they always act together in complete harmony. Jesus said of God the Father, "*The one who sent me is with me; he has not left me alone, for I always do what pleases him*" (John 8:29). While Jesus was on earth, He always perfectly carried out the will of God the Father. In the same way we can expect the Spirit's work in us always to be in accordance with the will of the Father and Son. In this regard Jesus said, "*But the Counselor, the Holy Spirit, whom the Father will send in my name, will teach you all things and will remind you of everything I have said to you*" (John 14:26).

When we conform to what the Holy Spirit teaches, we also conform to the will of God, just as Jesus did. In this way **our response to the Spirit's work produces Christ's work in us.** When this happens, our tongues speak the words of Christ, our hands do the work of Christ, and our feet carry Christ's love and compassion to a lost and needy world. We become, as Paul says, the *Body of Christ* (1 Cor. 12:27).

As the church, act as Christ for the world. The Body of Christ refers to the whole church made up of a variety of people with a variety of spiritual gifts (1 Cor. 12:1-31). Only when all of these people use all of their spiritual gifts for the service of Christ can the church reach its full potential. Only then will the world have the maximum opportunity to meet Jesus. Fee writes,

> The church desperately needs to recapture this vision of what it is by grace, and therefore also what God intends it to be. In most Protestant circles one tends to take the local parish altogether too lightly. Seldom does one sense that it is, or can be, experienced as a community that is so powerfully indwelt by the Spirit that it functions as a genuine alternative to the pagan world in which it is found.[19]

Jesus is everywhere His feet take Him. He is everywhere Christians go carrying the message of the gospel and acting in His name. "Every square inch of the world, every split second of time, belongs to Jesus, by right of creation and by right of redeeming love."[20] As Christians go into the entire world, Jesus goes with them and acts through them to reclaim the world for Himself.

Responding to His Voice

1. Through whom did you meet Jesus? What about that person's life made you aware that Jesus was present in that person?

2. What is your own testimony of **resurrection faith**? How did you meet the Living Christ? How did meeting Jesus change you?

3. Have you given over any part of your temple for another purpose other than the worship and glorification of God? If so, what will you do about it?

Chapter 3

The Giver of Life

"Flesh gives birth to flesh, but the Spirit gives birth to spirit. You should not be surprised at my saying, 'You must be born again.' The wind blows wherever it pleases. You hear its sound, but you cannot tell where it comes from or where it is going. So it is with everyone born of the Spirit . . . For God so loved the world that he gave his one and only Son, that whoever believes in him shall not perish but have eternal life" (John 3:6-8, 16).

Who Is the Source of Life?

I know a husband and wife who desperately wanted to have a baby. After a series of physical examinations, a doctor told them the possibility of the wife conceiving a child was unlikely. Yet since they believed the angel Gabriel's words to Mary, *"nothing is impossible with God"* (Luke 1:37), they continued hoping. For six years they prayed for God to give them a child. They considered all options—from artificial insemination to adoption—available for contemporary couples desiring to parent a child. Because of economic factors and preparing for missionary service overseas none of these options seemed feasible. Then suddenly, quite unexpectedly, the couple discovered the wife was expecting her first child. Soon they found out they were going to have a baby girl whom they named Hannah. They chose the name Hannah because, like the biblical Hannah described in 1 Samuel 1, they believed God provided them with a child in answer to their prayers. Before the baby was born, the couple had a change of heart and chose another name. But the conviction that God answered their prayers and gave them a child hasn't changed. In fact that same conviction persists to this very day. This couple now has two children. Pictures of their children are separated by a plaque which reads, "**Prayer changes things.**"

I know this couple quite well. Every morning I look at Maggie's and Kevin's baby pictures that hang on my bedroom wall and read those words, "**Prayer changes things**." From this experience my wife, Molly, and I learned that life, whether physical or spiritual, is God's supreme gift to us. Cherish, nourish, and enjoy this divine gift. I cannot understand those who take life lightly and would choose to snuff it out without considering the One Who gave the gift.

The evening in which Nicodemus visited with Jesus, he did not realize Who Jesus was. Nicodemus took Jesus only to be a *"teacher who* [had] *come from God"* (John 3:2) rather than God Himself.[1] Nicodemus was amazed when Jesus began to talk about the need for new birth and spiritual life. I think Nicodemus wondered how any person, even a godly teacher, could know such things. After all Nicodemus was a Pharisee, a member of the Jewish ruling council (John 3:1), and a religious teacher in Israel (John 3:10). He knew the Old Testament teachings. He knew what God's law required. And, as a Pharisee, he did his best to live in accordance with these standards. For his era, or any era, Nicodemus was an upright, moral person. He was a religious person. He was a man of faith.

Yet Nicodemus had failed to realize that the One seated across from him was different from any man he ever had met. This One was no mere human being; He was God in human flesh. **Jesus spoke from personal experience**. *The Lord God formed the man from the dust of the ground and breathed into his nostrils the breath of life, and the man became a living being* (Gen. 2:7). Jesus knows if God does not breathe life into a person, no life exists.

What is true of physical life is true of spiritual life. Jesus knew unless he gave Nicodemus spiritual life, he would have none. In essence Jesus said to Nicodemus, "You sought me to know what you do to have eternal life. Don't **do** anything. Indeed, you **cannot do** anything. The only way you can have spiritual life is if you are reborn through the work of God's Spirit. And God's Spirit only gives spiritual life to those who believe in me."

The more I think about what Jesus said to Nicodemus that night, the more amazed I am. Nicodemus wanted to meet someone whom he thought could throw new light on the meaning of God. Instead he met God Himself. Nicodemus wanted to meet the One Whom he thought could tell him about life but instead met *the Life* (John 14:6). He wanted to meet the One Whom he thought could tell him how to live. Instead he met the only One Who could make him really alive. Like Nicodemus did, take some time with Jesus, the One Who gives new life to those who believe in Him.

"*Flesh Gives Birth to Flesh*"

In the last few years a remarkable melding together of Western rationalism and Eastern mysticism has developed. Formerly these were considered two incongruent streams. Western rationalism consisted of a **search for truth** based on logic and analysis of sensory data. If people could understand the facts about something, then they could know the truth. In Western thought truth was absolute. Only one truth exists, while other claims to the truth were mere pretenders dismissed when all facts were known.

On the other hand Eastern mysticism was more passive. Rather than people searching for truth, **truth found them.** But, with this belief, you could not understand or know truth. Truth was subjective rather than objective. Indeed mysticism says that no such thing as truth in the absolute sense exists. Rather someone became aware of truth as it entered his or her experience. The meaning of truth varied from one person to the next.

I have mentioned the story of a missionary colleague of mine who tried to point out to his college class rational proof for God's existence. One of his students objected, "If I say that this pencil is my god, it is my god." This is a good example of what I am talking about. For the American missionary only one God existed. The missionary could provide rational evidence for God's existence. But for his Japanese student, rational evidence to the contrary, truth entirely depended on a person's viewpoint, feelings, and experience. No absolute truth about God or anything else exists.

Although Western rationalism and Eastern mysticism are quite different, their shared belief in evolution merges the two. In the West this begins from a rationalistic bent—scientific evolutionary theory, survival of the fittest, biological determinism, social determinism, and, finally, genetic determinism. In the East, where mysticism is supreme, human evolution is determined internally. A person advances to higher orders of existence by overcoming internal weaknesses—character flaws, ignorance, and vice. If in this life the person doesn't advance toward perfection, he or she can try again in another. In Hinduism and Buddhism this gives rise to belief in reincarnation.

The recent blend of Eastern and Western thought especially is seen in contemporary psychology, which emphasizes personal advancement (i.e. evolution) through overcoming internal problems. This extends back in an Eastern direction, because some claim many psychological and emotional issues with which we now deal stem from previous generations—our **ancestors**, you might say. This is remarkably similar to the doctrine of **karma** found in Hinduism and Buddhism.

What lies behind Eastern mysticism, Western rationalism, and their common belief in evolution is the human attempt at spiritual advancement without God's assistance. They believe that, in some way, **flesh gives birth to spirit**. Through our own efforts human beings can achieve a new, higher order of existence. This kind of thinking even seeps into many Christians' lives. As Fredrikson points out,

> They may go through the motions of religion, but there is no reality in it. We have asked people to repeat the "right words," and we have been running in circles, doing things, taking on more projects, and desperately trying to behave "right." But at the center of existence, in their deepest selves, people have been untouched and unchanged. Then

> we have covered up the old, unconverted self with churchy language. We say, "Of course, he was baptized." "Yes, she's been a member here for over 20 years." "You know what a great job she has done handling the committee." "They are about the best givers we have." And all the time, many of these people are empty and needy, spiritually bankrupt. Little wonder much of what we do in church is unredeemed and ego-centered.[2]

Jesus responded to this kind of thinking when He said to Nicodemus, "*Flesh gives birth to flesh*" (John 3:6). To paraphrase, **flesh cannot give birth to spirit. Flesh only gives birth to flesh**. What begins as "earthy" always remains "earthy."[3] The spirit cannot simply "evolve upward" to a new, higher, spiritual plain of existence without some divine assistance.[4]

Although we can do much about our existence in the present world, we are "helpless" regarding the issue of entering into the new world.[5] We can cleanse or "adorn" ourselves externally, but for internal spiritual transformation the power of God's Spirit brings about regeneration.[6]

This is what the natural person, whether east or west, cannot accept. He or she cannot accept his or her complete helplessness to overcome the limitations of human nature. "Certainly," the person reasons, "problems arise. I have to overcome insurmountable obstacles. But I have gotten this far. Surely I can do something." He can go about perfecting human nature. He can improve the conditions of his present life with better food, water, housing, and medical care. He can lengthen his life; he can delay death, but he cannot defeat it. And he has no say so about what will happen to him the second after he takes his final breath.

He fails to recognize that he would not have gotten this far if not for the grace of God. He cannot accept his need for God. So he remains, without God's Spirit intervening, a human trapped by the constraints of life in the present world.

Spirit Gives Birth to Spirit

When a person hears the gospel and is convicted of its truth, he or she often responds by **trying** to be a Christian in his or her own strength. This person will repent of the sinful way of life, place intellectual belief in Jesus as Lord and Savior, and try to live the Christian life. As the person proceeds along this road, he or she realizes the difficulty of being a Christian.[7] The pull of the world, the resistance of Satan, and the individual's moral weaknesses all are too much to allow a person to succeed at attempting Christianity. Moreover despite Christianity's claim to bring joy and peace, the individual only experiences conflict, struggle, and defeat. The person discovers spiritual truth which Paul described.

> *I know that nothing good lives in me, that is, in my sinful nature. For I have the desire to do what is good, but I cannot carry it out. For what I do is not the good I want to do; no, the evil that I do not want to do—this I keep on doing. Now if I do what I do not want to do, it is no longer I who do it, but it is sin living in me that does it* (Rom. 7:18-20).

At this point one of three things occurs. First the person may give up and discount Christianity altogether as a collection of human ideas and moral assumptions that don't work. They often leave the church, never to return. Or the person may remain in the church under the assumption that Christianity has some value. But the person continues living only with a marginal commitment to Christ. Our churches are filled with these kinds of people. They keep one hand on Christianity while the other extends as far into the world as possible. Out of the corner of one eye they look at the Bible, usually accumulating dust on a shelf, while they focus their attention on living a good life in the present world. Although considered Christians, as they often occupy leadership positions in the church, God knows whether they really have experienced new life resulting from faith in Jesus Christ. The third possibility is that the person truly realizes his or her lost condition and complete moral bankruptcy. People realize they are filled with sin through and through and are unable to do anything to be saved. At this point the person trusts totally and completely in Jesus. The person realizes He alone has the power to be saved. Paul writes, *the wages of sin is death*. All of us, left on our own, are required to pay sin its proper wages. But God, in His wonderful mercy and grace, provided us with a marvelous gift too indescribable for human words: *the gift of God is eternal life in Christ Jesus our Lord* (Rom. 6:23).

Through the work of the Holy Spirit Jesus brings about new life in the person who believes in Him.[8] As Gordon Fee writes, "The Holy Spirit is the one who effects salvation experientially, effectively appropriating the benefits of Christ's saving work to [believers'] lives."[9] The Holy Spirit takes the truth about Jesus, as proclaimed in the gospel, and applies it to our hearts so we can understand who Jesus is and what He has done for us. Then we place our trust in Him.[10]

Like Nicodemus we are unprepared to accept the truth of Jesus' testimony about *heavenly things* (John 3:11-12). We are incapable of accepting this truth on our own, because our understanding is *"darkened"* because of the *hardening of* [our] *hearts* (Eph. 4:18). So Jesus sends the *"Spirit of truth"* to *"guide* [us] *into all truth"* (John 16:13). Concerning the Holy Spirit Jesus says,

> *"He will not speak on his own; he will speak only what he hears, and will tell you what is yet to come. He will bring glory to me by taking from what is mine and making it known to you"* (John 16:13-14).

Jesus descended *from above* as God's self-revelation so we could know and have a relationship with Him. The Holy Spirit takes this revelation and confirms its truth in our hearts. When we respond to this truth with faith, God's Spirit breathes new life into our spiritually dead souls. Just as God's Spirit breathed physical life into Adam (Gen. 2:7), He now breathes spiritual life into us.[11] God's gift *from above* is the new birth and new life (John 3:3).[12]

When the Holy Spirit births spiritual life in us, we are liberated from the powers of Satan, sin, and death.[13]

In Romans 8:9-11 Paul talks about this freedom that characterizes our new life.

> *You, however, are controlled not by the sinful nature but by the Spirit, if the Spirit of God lives in you. And if anyone does not have the Spirit of Christ, he does not belong to Christ. But if Christ is in you, your body is dead because of sin, yet your spirit is alive because of righteousness. And if the Spirit of him who raised Jesus from the dead is living in you, he who raised Christ from the dead will also give life to your mortal bodies through his Spirit, who lives in you.*

These verses contain an amazing synthesis of ideas. Those who believe in Christ are under the Spirit's control—understood to be both the Spirit of God and of Christ. The Spirit frees them from the control of sin so they can be righteous. These spiritually controlled believers are alive spiritually and physically. They now enjoy life and can plan to live forever. This is because the Spirit, Who brought their spirit to life, is the very same Spirit Who physically raised Jesus from the dead. Someday this Spirit will raise their mortal bodies as well. We receive all of these wonderful blessings in a single package. They all are part of one gracious gift God provided for us through His Son, Jesus. Christians call this whole package deal ***salvation***. To receive this gift Jesus said, *"You must be born again."*

"You Must Be Born Again"

Nicodemus went to Jesus—not as an empty cup waiting to be filled, but with the sum of his life experiences: all of his "doubts, uncertainties, wishes, hopes, fears and habits—good and bad—built up through the years."[14] He probably thought, "Can a person leave all of these things behind and begin anew?"

> *"How can a man be born when he is old?" Nicodemus asked. "Surely he cannot enter a second time into his mother's womb to be born!"* (John 3:4).

Nicodemus was a prime example of someone who attempts to seek God on his own terms. Nicodemus did not oppose the spiritual. As I have said, he was a religious, spiritually-minded person. But he also wanted to maintain control. He wanted to understand the spiritual so he could manage its impact on his life. As Godet notes, this was a case in which the "flesh rules the spirit."[15] Nicodemus tried to use religion to make himself a better person. He wanted to discover what he could learn from Jesus to become a better person.

Nicodemus' approach to God, Christianity, and Jesus cannot work. One reason is because human nature, which controls the process, is flawed. This is not so much a knock against Nicodemus as it is a knock against all of us. As Paul writes, *All have sinned and fall short of the glory of God* (Rom. 3:23). This corruption of human nature not only affects our actions, it also affects what lies behind our actions—namely our thoughts, motives, and will. Our thoughts are blind to spiritual truths, so we are unable to understand the things of God without the aid of the Holy Spirit (1 Cor. 2:14). We are motivated by a desire to do what is pleasing to us, whether or not what we do pleases God.

> *For the sinful nature desires what is contrary to the Spirit, and the Spirit what is contrary to the sinful nature. They are in conflict with each other, so that you do not do what you want* (Gal. 5:17).

Finally our will rebels against God. We place a high value on human free will—on personal choice. We want to call the shots. When God wants us to do something that sounds good to us, we agree with His decision. But when He wants us to do something with which we don't agree, we believe we have the right to say no. But sin is the very essence of saying *yes* to self and *no* to God.[16] Sin is the result of a self-directed, self-pleasing, and self-centered life.

The approach also fails to acknowledge God's power. We fail to recognize that only God's Spirit working in us brings about new spiritual life.[17] The Holy Spirit is God's breath on weak and helpless humans as it brings about "re-creation, resurrection, and a great transformation." The product of this act of God is far beyond what any human psychologist, philosopher, or theologian can comprehend or explain.[18]

In Ezekiel the Spirit of the Lord led the prophet to the middle of a valley full of dry bones. Then the Lord asked him, *"Son of man, can these bones live?"* Wisely Ezekiel answered, *"O Sovereign Lord, you alone know"* (Ezek. 37:1-3). Ezekiel knew God determines life and death. God's Spirit breathes life into His creation. No life exists in which the Spirit is not present and at work. However what especially is significant is what the Lord told Ezekiel to do next.

> *"Prophesy to these bones and say to them, 'Dry bones, hear the word of the Lord! This is what the Sovereign Lord says to these bones: I will make breath enter you, and you will come to life. I will attach tendons to you and make flesh come upon you and cover you with skin.; I will put breath in you, and you will come to life. Then you will know that I am the Lord'"* (Ezek. 37:4-6).

God alone has the power to give life. By Himself God could have brought the dry bones to life anytime He chose. But He did not. Instead God involved Ezekiel in the process to bring life at a place in which previously only death, decay, and dust existed. God said to Ezekiel, "You speak, and I will bring life through the breath of my Spirit." God commanded Ezekiel to speak God's Word to the dry bones, because His method always is to partner His Word with His Spirit to create life.

That night in Jerusalem the person with whom Nicodemus found himself talking was none other than God's Word in human flesh—Jesus. He introduced Nicodemus to the work of God's Spirit. This is incredibly important. **God's Word and God's Spirit work**

together to bring about life. The Word introduces us to the Spirit. The Spirit makes the Word effective in our hearts. While God's Word is essential, no amount of contact with the Word will bring about new life unless the innerworking of God's Spirit accompanies it. Furthermore the Spirit never works independently from the Word. Rather the Holy Spirit's method always is to apply the Word to the human heart to bring about new life through faith in Christ.[19]

What results from new birth is not merely a reformed human being but a human being reborn as a new person—a **new creation**. I think Paul says with great rejoicing, *The old has gone, the new has come!* (2 Cor. 5:17). Paul knew from experience. He tried to live the religious life but failed miserably. He writes,

> *If anyone else thinks that he has reasons for confidence in the flesh, I have more: circumcised on the eighth day, of the people of Israel, of the tribe of Benjamin, a Hebrew of Hebrews; in regard to the law, a Pharisee; as for zeal, persecuting the church, as for legalistic righteousness, faultless* (Phil. 3:4-6).

Paul exceeded Nicodemus in living out human-controlled, self-centered religion. Paul met and exceeded the requirements of his Jewish faith. He was the kind of man Jewish parents would point out to their children and say, "Look at this great man. I hope someday you will be like him." Paul was a Jew of the Jews but to what effect? In the name of his religion he helped kill one man (Acts 8:1) and threw others in prison (Acts 9:1-2). Paul was religious but spiritually dead. And the spiritual death that filled Paul's heart resulted in hatred for others different from himself. This hatred led to a desire to bring about destruction and death wherever he went.

When Paul met Jesus, everything changed. Paul experienced a new birth, became a new person, and discarded his old life. Paul put away things that once were essential but now seemed like *"rubbish"* (Phil 3:8). In their place was one, all-consuming passion: *I want to know Christ* (Phil. 3:10). This desire became the driving force fueling everything Paul did for the rest of his life.

An old bumper sticker on a bedroom wall in my wife's parents' house read, "Religion is fine, but have you tried Jesus?" I agree with the sentiment, but the wording leaves something to be desired. The problem with this statement is that often we allow religion to stand between us and Christ. Nicodemus surfaced from the darkness of night to meet the One Who ascended as the light for a dark world. Nicodemus not only met the source of light but also of life.[20] Jesus seems to say to Nicodemus, to Paul, and to each of us, "You have tried religion long enough. Put your trust in me."

Following the Wind

Jesus compared the Holy Spirit with the wind. Like the wind we can hear the Spirit. That is, we are aware of its effects but have no control over from where it arrives or to where it goes (John 3:8).[21] This immediately brings to mind Pentecost, when the Holy Spirit entered the place where Jesus' disciples gathered like the *blowing of a violent wind . . . from heaven* (Acts 2:2). The first Christians had no control over the Holy Spirit. The Holy Spirit simply arrived and did His work as the One sent from heaven. God directs the Spirit's movement to bring about new life within us.[22]

We tend to try to understand how the Holy Spirit works. Often we try to develop techniques to manipulate or control the Spirit. Of course no one says this. People will say God is in control. They do not want to presume on divine authority. But then they don't follow what they say. Some think if people pray certain prayers, or pray in certain ways, or observe certain rituals in worship, or sing certain styles of music, or pray and sing praise songs long and loud enough, then God's Spirit will bless them. This simply is not true. We cannot do anything to manipulate or control the Holy Spirit, because the Holy Spirit is God. He is God as the Spirit at work in our everyday lives, just as Jesus is God in human form.

The Bible says, *As you do not know the path of the wind, or how the body is formed in a mother's womb, so you cannot understand the work of God, the Maker of all things* (Eccles. 11:5).

Despite scientific advancements, such as those that help us explain fetal development and how atmospheric pressure relates to wind direction, the main point of this verse is: the way God chooses to work is beyond our human capacity to understand or control. God's work is a mystery, except that we know He works in His own time and His own way in accordance with His purpose and His grace.[23]

Jesus says what is true of the Spirit also is true to those within whose lives the Spirit works, "*So it is with everyone born of the Spirit*" (John 3:8). When we are born again, the Holy Spirit becomes the driving force in our lives. When the Spirit enters us to produce new life, He also begins to take control.

The result is a Spirit-directed rather than a self-directed life. God's Spirit wants to involve us in **His** activity. He wants to include us in what **He** is doing.[24] Just as the Spirit spoke through Ezekiel in the valley of dry bones and called Paul to be an apostle to the Gentiles, so does He speak to us and draws us into His work in the present world.

A Spirit-directed person's life has a distinct impression of God's grace. Not only did this person receive God's grace, he or she also is a conduit through which His grace flows to impact the world. God is able to work through such a person to accomplish His will in His way at His time.

This is what Paul gets at when He says the Spirit produces fruit in our lives: *Love, joy, peace, patience, kindness, goodness, faithfulness, gentleness and self-control* (Gal. 5:22-25). We can assume spiritual fruit, like any fruit, also takes time to ripen—first as a bud, then a blossom, and finally as the fruit. In the same way spiritual fruit is the result of a long process involving God's Spirit working in the lives of people who yield to His control. Paul concludes, *"Since we live by the Spirit, let us keep in step with the Spirit."* In other words, **since God's Spirit has given us life, let Him direct every aspect of that life.**

God's Love and Our Faith

In response to everything Jesus said up to this point, Nicodemus questions, *"How can this be?"* (John 3:9). How can a person be born again? How can the Holy Spirit give birth to a person's spirit? How can the Spirit be set free to work so this spiritual birth can take place?

Mary's question to the angel, Gabriel, after he told her she would give birth to Jesus, parallels Nicodemus' question. Mary knew the new life produced in her would be no ordinary human child. He would be God's Son embodied as a human being. So His conception could not occur in the ordinary way. Divine action was necessary for divine life to be present. So Mary asked the angel, *"How will this be since I am a virgin?"* (Luke 1:34). Gabriel told her that what humanly was impossible only could be brought about by God's Spirit, *"for nothing is impossible with God"* (Luke 1:35-37).

In the same way the spiritual birth Nicodemus seeks only can be brought about by God. Not only can He bring about this spiritual birth, he desires spiritual birth for Nicodemus and everyone in the world. God's love desires for every person spiritually to be born. *"For God so loved the world"* (John 3:16). His love's power lurked in the shadows the entire evening. Jesus reveals His power so Nicodemus can be overwhelmed. This is the answer to all of Nicodemus' questions. How can a person be born again? Because of God's love's power. How can the Spirit give birth to a person's spirit? Because of God's love's power. How can the Spirit be set free to work so this spiritual birth can take place? Because of God's love's power.

This is not an overstatement. No power in the universe compares with the power of God's love. Indeed all of our most fierce adversaries—trouble, hardship, persecution, famine, danger, death, demons—literally any power we could face in God's universe, in the present or future, is nothing compared with the power of God's love. *Nothing will be able to separate us from the love of God that is in Christ Jesus our Lord* (Rom. 8:35-39).

God's love in Christ had a profound effect on the writer of John's Gospel—so much so that John repeatedly identified himself as the *one Jesus loved* (John 13:23; 20:2; 21:20). Acting in accordance with human nature, John probably was uncertain of many things, but of one thing he was certain—Jesus loved him. No matter what the situation or circumstance John knew Jesus loved him.

In his first letter John tells us God is the source of love and showed His love to us through His Son, Jesus Christ. God so identifies with love, one cannot know God and not know His love. Love is synonymous with God's love (1 John 4:7-8). Not only does love originate with God, God is love (1 John 4:8, 16). God displayed His love for us by sending *his one and only Son,* so we can have life and forgiveness of sins through Him (1 John 4:9-10).

The supreme expression of God's love in Christ is Jesus' death on the cross.[25] *This is how we know what love is: Jesus Christ laid down his life for us* (1 John 3:16). *He loved us and sent his Son as an atoning sacrifice for our sins* (1 John 4:10). As Jesus told Nicodemus, "*The Son of Man must be lifted up, that everyone who believes in him may have eternal life*" (John 3:14-15). That this is understood to refer to Jesus' crucifixion is made clear in John 12:32-33, where Jesus says, "*When I am lifted up from the earth, I will draw all men to myself*" (12:32). *He said this to show the kind of death that he was going to die* (12:33). Jesus will be "lifted on the cross" to bring spiritual life to everyone in the world who believes in Him.[26]

Every time I read about Jesus's conversation with Nicodemus, I am amazed when I get to John 3:16. Surely by this time Nicodemus realized the One with whom he spoke was no mere prophet. Jesus not only spoke God's Word, He was God's Word. Nicodemus probably was filled with a sense of awe as he realized he was in the presence of God's Son.

Nicodemus probably felt as Moses did when he, at the burning bush, removed his shoes in God's presence because he was *on holy ground* (Ex. 3:5). Or perhaps he felt as the prophet Isaiah did when he realized his spiritual uncleanliness as he stood before Holy God (Isa. 6:1-5). Nicodemus sat in the presence of God's glory embodied as a human being. I am sure Nicodemus was captivated by Jesus.

Trying not to miss a thing, he probably intently looked into His face.

And then, at that very moment, Jesus revealed the nature of His glory, *"For God so loved the world that he gave his one and only Son."* Jesus was saying, "I am the final, complete expression of God's love. I was sent because God loves every person in the world, including you. I was sent to give everyone eternal life."

No other verse in the Bible better explains the relationship between divine election and human responsibility than does John 3:16. The doctrine of election (sometimes referred to as *predestination*) teaches that salvation is based on God's choice to save humans from our fallen, sinful condition. John 3:16 confirms this. God chose to save us from sin and death. He based His choice on love. Because of God's love for us, He chose to provide us the way of salvation. Salvation is not possible without God's love, which brought forth His choice, initiative, and act of sending His Son. No forgiveness, new birth, or eternal life exists without God's love.

God's decision to save us through His Son is based on His love. God's love extends to the whole world. So does this mean salvation also extends to the whole world? This is what Christian **inclusivists** claim. They believe if God loves people, if His choice is to provide a way of salvation for all people, and if Jesus died for everyone's sins, everyone is saved. After all, God is all-knowing and all-powerful. He can do whatever He chooses.

But inclusivists skip over the second part of John 3:16, *"that **whoever believes in him** will not perish but have eternal life"* (emphasis added). This verse tells us that while God loves everyone and provided everyone a way of salvation, **only those who believe in Jesus will be saved.** This doesn't limit God's power and authority. God can save whoever He wants to save. And God provided a way of salvation both available and sufficient for all people. Another way to salvation is unnecessary. The gift of His Son was enough. However only those who believe in His Son receive the gift.

Some will say, "If God loves everyone, how can He be so narrow-minded? How can He restrict salvation to one way? Why does only one Savior exist? Why can't God grant eternal life to people who believe in other religions?" This is religious **pluralism,** which asserts that all religions carry some truth, respond in some way to the questions of human life, and provide some hope for an afterlife.

No meeting place exists between pluralism and genuine Christianity. Jesus stands in the way. Jesus was not a pluralist. Jesus said He was the only way to salvation. He said, *"No one comes to the Father except through me"* (John 14:6). Jesus also was not an inclusivist. While He was sent to bring salvation to everyone, He knew only those who believe Him can have eternal life.

How can a person claim to follow Jesus and also deny the truthfulness of His words? Some say, "Jesus did not really say these things. Jesus loved people, so He would not have said anything so harsh." Some put words into Jesus' mouth and speculate as to what He really may have said. However the final result is vague religiosity that may meet the needs of the modern mind but fails to solve the dilemma of the human soul. To compromise on Jesus' own words on these two points is to cease to be a follower of Jesus Christ.

The center of Christianity is this wonderful interaction between God's love and our faith. Jesus is the object of both. In love God has spoken to us through His Son. Jesus is God's Word to people trapped in a world made dark by sin and death. God sent His Word into the world to provide us with light and life (John 1:4). Only the *darkness of rebellious pride* prevents people from believing in Jesus and receiving new life through God's Spirit.[27] When we believe in Jesus, we make this God-given gift our own.[28]

John does not tell us whether Nicodemus believed in Jesus. That is not the point. The point is, **do you believe in Jesus?** And do the people in your circle—your family, friends, co-workers, church members, and community—believe in Jesus? Those who believe in Jesus receive a new birth and life through the power of God's Spirit. Jesus' words to Nicodemus also are His words to us, "*You must be born again.*"

Responding to His Voice

1. Have you really been born again?

2. What will you put aside in order to focus on Christ?

3. Reflect in Galatians 5:22-25 on the fruit of the Spirit. Are you *in step with the Spirit?* Or are you running behind?

4. How does God's love, as He has displayed to us through the gift of His Son, impact your everyday life?

Chapter 4

The Deep Well

Jesus answered her, "If you knew the gift of God and who it is that asks you for a drink, you would have asked him and he would have given you living water."

"Sir," the woman said, "You have nothing to draw with and the well is deep. Where can you get this living water? Are you greater than our father Jacob, who gave us the well and drank from it himself, as did also his sons and his flocks and herds?"

Jesus answered, "Everyone who drinks this water will be thirsty again, but whoever drinks the water that I give him will never thirst. Indeed, the water I give him will become in him a spring of water welling up to eternal life."

The woman said, "I know that the Messiah" (called Christ) is coming. When he comes, he will explain everything to us."

Then Jesus declared, "I who speak to you am he" (John 4:10-14, 25-26).

What Do You Have to Offer a Thirsty World?

In 1997 Tom and Dana Larson left business careers in Denver to live, for a year, in La Victoria, Dominican Republic. They found themselves in a "narrow-minded, legalistic, and judgmental" church in a country in which contaminated drinking water led to chronic dysentery. In 1998 after a hurricane contributed to bad water conditions, a friend in Denver approached Tom Larson about installing a water-purification system in the church in La Victoria. After they installed the water system, the church image changed. "Suddenly we were seen as a church that wanted to help, not withdraw and judge," Larson said. "The water became an agent of healing, both physically and socially." People who formerly would "drive by the church, honk their horns, and shout insults" now "flocked to the church for clean water." They created Healing Waters International, a non-profit organization aimed at placing water-purification systems in churches throughout the Dominican Republic.

Through this program people received clean, fresh water as an expression of Christ's love. An open relationship between the church and surrounding communities developed. "Life in the Dominican Republic is so hard," Larson said. "People struggle to live day to day. I like to think that now people can come to church to get a cool drink of water. They can come to church and be refreshed."[1]

In many places people seek clean, fresh water that is not readily available. Tokyo has safe drinking water. Many other cities in East Asia don't. When I traveled to Seoul, Manila, Taipei, and Chiang Mai, I was warned against drinking the tap water. When I brush my teeth in these places, I first use bottled water to moisten my toothbrush, rinse my mouth out, and finally wash the brush off. I often try to imagine what might happen if I used just tap water. Each time I decide to be safe rather than sorry and to use the bottled water. Thus far I have managed to return home from each of these expeditions without the least incidence of dysentery or indigestion.

In John 4 two thirsty people met at a well. One had a bucket with which to draw water from the well. Today this water would meet the Samaritan woman's physical thirst. Tomorrow and the next day and the day after that she would have to return, because physical satisfaction only is temporary. Everyone spends a lifetime quenching physical thirst. Souls remain dry, barren wastelands in which nothing can survive unless they meet someone who can provide **living water.**

The other person at the well had nothing with which to draw water. Jesus had no bucket, bowl, or ladle. He didn't even have a cup. But He did have water—life-giving water that could quench the woman's spiritual thirst and forever satisfy her soul.

This kind of water is a precious commodity worth a fortune. But the water cannot be purchased. The water is not for sale. **This living water is a gift—free to all who ask.**

When churches in the Dominican Republic installed water-purification systems, crowds began to gather. People gathered because they were thirsty for the water churches could provide. What would have happened if the church members had said to the crowds, "Go away. This water is for us"? Church members would have been satisfied, but those on the outside still would have thirsted. And as thirst increased, so would their desperation. Some may join the church just to get water to drink. Most would not. Who wants to be part of a group of selfish people unwilling to share what they have with those in need? To die in thirst would be better than to be a part of such a group. Such unresolved need, in full view of what is needed, leads to animosity and hatred.

Jesus does not give living water only to satisfy. Rather, this water overflows from us to quench a spiritually dry world. Become "*springs of water*" (John 4:14) or "*streams of living water*" (John 7:38). A stopped-up spring is not a spring. A river that does not flow is not a river. Water that is alive flows! In the same way our spiritual vitality is measured by how much God's life-giving water overflows through us to a world dying of thirst.

The Gift of God

Jesus' encounter with the Samaritan woman at the well in Sychar reminds us that human relationships always occur in context. When two people meet, both carry past baggage limiting what each presently can say and do. Jesus' request for a drink of water (John 4:8) seemed simple enough and might have been if not for previous bad dealings between Jews and Samaritans.

In 537 B.C. when the Jews returned from Babylonian exile, they refused to allow Samaritans to participate in rebuilding the temple in Jerusalem. The Jews considered the Samaritans an impure race, because intermarriage with surrounding people resulted in their being "tainted by pagan blood and pagan religion." The separation between Jews and Samaritans was confirmed "when the Samaritans built their own temple on Mount Gerazim about 315 B.C. in opposition to the temple in Jerusalem." When the Jewish king, John Hyrcanus, destroyed the temple on Mount Gerazim in 128 B.C., the act cemented "religious and national animosity between the two peoples."[2] Most likely every Samaritan child grew up knowing what the Jews had done to his or her people. Samaritan identity involved a strong sense of knowing what separated Samaritans from the Jews. As though she were speaking well-rehearsed lines learned during childhood and continually recited until the day she met Jesus at the well, the Samaritan woman pointed out this distinction: *"Our fathers worshiped on this mountain, but you Jews claim that the place where we must worship is in Jerusalem"* (John 4:20).

This woman fully knew of the wall of separation between the Jews and Samaritans. She said, *"You are a Jew and I am a Samaritan woman. How can you ask me for a drink?"* (John 4:9). Jewish laws permitted purchasing and using eggs, fruits, and vegetables from Samaritans. Using their cups and bowls strictly was forbidden. If Jesus drank from the Samaritan woman's water pot, He would expose Himself to ceremonial uncleanness. The woman knew this and was surprised Jesus would make such a request.[3]

An interesting contrast exists between Nicodemus and the Samaritan woman. Nicodemus was a man of high social, moral, and religious standing—"a Jew, a Pharisee, a member of the supreme court of Israel." The woman was a social, moral, and religious outcast—"a Samaritan, with an abortive form and concept of religion, five times married, and now living in adultery with a sixth man" (John 4:18). Despite these differences Nicodemus and the woman essentially were spiritually the same. Both needed God's provision of salvation available to them through faith in Jesus.[4]

In verse 9 the woman's statement seemed to mask a heart crying out for help. Behind words she actually said were words couched in the pain of a failed life—a life in which, many times over, she was used, abused, and discarded by men who claimed to love her. In her own town of Sychar this woman knew people thought she was nothing. So why would this Galilean Jew take the time to speak to her? What she really wanted to say to Jesus probably was something such as, “Why do you ask me for water when the people of my own town won’t have anything to do with me?”

Notice how the Samaritan woman’s and Jesus’ priorities differed. Jesus clearly was tired and thirsty (John 4:6). But the woman allowed their differences in ethnicity, religion, and gender to take priority over providing for His needs. On the other hand Jesus set aside His physical needs to provide for the woman’s spiritual needs. As R.A. Torrey writes, “Immediately a new thirst took possession of Him—not thirst for water for His body, but a thirst for the salvation of that outcast woman’s soul.”[5]

As the Lord of the universe, Jesus had the answer to this woman’s problems but did not relate to her in this way. He approached her not as God-to-person but as one person to another. Jesus began talking to this woman from the point of **His** own need. He asked her for a drink of water. By beginning with His own vulnerability Jesus opened her heart, so she would be ready to hear the gospel.

This illustrates how Jesus approaches people differently than we do. We allow human differences—such as ethnicity, language, culture, and gender—to divide people. So needs go unmet. We do this each time we refuse to deal with people because of skin color, language, or the way they speak or act. We cut people off because their value systems—their concept of right and wrong—differ from ours. By presenting our own superiority we hope those we put down will realize their need for our assistance. Instead they sense our callous, uncaring attitudes and walk away. They cannot see in us the source of the living water they need to quench eternal thirst.

In contrast Jesus approached the Samaritan woman as one needy human being to another. Jesus did not allow the gap between His divine perfection and the woman’s fallen human condition to divide them and prevent Him from meeting her needs. Jesus’ nationality, culture, and religion all differed from those of the Samaritan woman. Moreover I am certain He did not approve of her multi-marriage lifestyle. In spite of these differences Jesus reached out to her because He loved her. His love for people transcends human distinctiveness. He knows every person by name, face, and heart. Jesus knows everyone as someone He created in the image of God. In Christ, *there is neither Jew nor Greek, slave nor free, male nor female, for you are all one in Christ Jesus* (Gal. 3:28).

Often we focus on a person's physical, psychological, or social needs and don't address spiritual ones. But Jesus places priority on spiritual needs, not because He considers other needs unimportant. When we solely focus on needs, we can see the person's most profound need goes unsatisfied. Ultimately when we focus on spiritual needs, we provide for the needs of the whole person.

Let's return to the water-purification system story in the Dominican Republic. If the point only was to provide clean drinking water for the people, then the purification systems could have been installed anywhere: in parks, at stores, or even at service stations. So why were purification systems placed in churches? Because the desire to provide for physical thirst flowed out of a desire to quench spiritual thirst. God's Spirit flowing through us brings life to all who seek Him. When God works through us to transform physically broken, emotionally distraught, and spiritually dead people, we become new, complete people flowing with the energy and vitality of life.

Jesus answered the woman's question, *"If you knew the gift of God and who it is that asks you for a drink, you would have asked him and he would have given you living water"* (John 4:10). **God's gift** which Jesus offered the woman was **Living Water**—the source of eternal life. But she could not have the gift without receiving the Giver. "The Son whom God gave (John 3:16) and the salvation which he gives are, of course, inseparably united."[6]

Fredrikson expresses this connection so beautifully when he writes,

> Jesus seeks to penetrate the woman's spiritual darkness. Unless she comes to know and accept the One Who speaks to her, His gift can never be hers. For the Father shares this

living water through the Son. It springs forth from an unfailing Source and is not water that seeps into an earthen well.[7]

Living Water

Jesus told the woman at the well that He is the source of *"living water"* (John 4:10) which, when received, *"wells up to eternal life"* (John 4:14). The Old Testament uses *living water* as a metaphor for God's life-giving activity. According to Psalm 36:9 the Lord is the One Who has the *"fountain of life."* In Isaiah 55:1 God issues His invitation: *"Come, all who are thirsty, come to the waters."*[8] In Jeremiah 2:13 the Lord declares that the people have committed two sins. First, *"they have forsaken me, the spring of living water."* Second, they, *"have dug their own cisterns, broken cisterns that cannot hold water."*

In other words, the people abandoned God, the source of Life, to attempt to make a life by themselves—to live in accordance with their own will for their own pleasure. Sadly the cisterns they made could not hold water. As a result of abandoning the Lord, the people now had no life at all.

These words certainly would have connected with the experience when Jesus met the woman in Sychar. Each day she drew water from Jacob's well to maintain her existence. But what she daily experienced really was not life. She responded to Jesus, *"Sir, give me this water so that I won't get thirsty and have to keep coming here to draw water"* (John 4:15). This woman was tired of her present state of existence and wanted something better. She longed for something, as the song says, "that would fill her heart and satisfy her soul."[9]

Ezekiel 47:9 and Zechariah 14:8 look forward to the day when a river of living water will flow out from Jerusalem so everything the river touches will have life. When Jesus speaks of being the Source of living water, He claims to be the One Who fulfills the prediction of the Old Testament prophets.[10]

Chapter seven in John's Gospel references the living water. Jesus stood in the temple on the last day of the Feast of Tabernacles and, in a loud voice, said,

> *"If any man is thirsty, let him come to me and drink. Whoever believes in me, as the Scripture has said, streams of living water will flow from within him"* (John 7:37-38).

At that time the Feast of Tabernacles was an eight-day celebration held each year in Jerusalem. For the first seven days a priest led a profession of praise to the temple. He would carry a water-filled golden pitcher from the Pool of Siloam. When the priest carrying the pitcher approached the altar at which burnt offerings were made, the people shouted, *"Lift up your hands!"* As the priest lifted his hands, the people gathered in the temple shouted the words in Isaiah 12:3: *"With joy you will draw water from the wells of salvation!"* This ceremony memorialized God giving water to Israel from the rock when the Israelites wandered in the wilderness (Ex. 17:2-7).[11]

Jesus' statement referred not to the temple rite itself but to the historical event behind it. No one actually drank water from the golden pitcher but did drink water flowing from the rock.[12] Jesus was saying He, rather than the rock in the wilderness, "was the source for their real need." Jesus simply said, *"If any man is thirsty, let him come to me and drink"* (John 7:37). The water is available. But everyone drinks of his or her own will for personal salvation.[13]

John 7:39 tells us the **living water** to which Jesus refers is the *Spirit, whom those who believed in him were later to receive. Up to that time the Spirit had not yet been given, since Jesus had not yet been glorified.* John ties the gift of the Holy Spirit to the completion of Jesus' ministry.[14] A sequence of events takes place. Leon Morris notes that John,

> sees the atoning work of Christ as the necessary prelude to the work of the Spirit. Without trying to divide up the believer's experience too minutely it is yet plain to see that

> his sin must be dealt with before he can enter on the life of the Spirit . . . The Spirit could not come during the time of Christ's earthly ministry" (16:7). "But when the work was consummated the Spirit was given" (20:22; Acts 2).[15]

Once again we see here the indissoluble link between Christ and the Spirit. **The Holy Spirit brings life, but Jesus is the giver of the Spirit. We only can receive God's life-giving Spirit by acknowledging Jesus as the Spirit's source.** Anyone who thirsts for life can know Jesus and quench his or her thirst. We seek Christ by faith. Christ gives the Spirit to those who believe in Him (John 7:38).

No room for merit or good works exists. We cannot earn the life of the Spirit. Without Jesus' intervention, our condition is as hopeless as is that of the Samaritan woman. We thirst for life-giving water unattainable on our own. The life the Spirit brings purely is an act of God's grace. God, working through His Son, does everything; we can do nothing except believe in Him. Through and through Jesus' gift is life to those who believe. Truly, *from first to last, we live by faith* (Rom. 1:17).

He Never Will Thirst

Jesus said, *"everyone who drinks this water will be thirsty again, but whoever drinks the water I give him will never thirst"* (John 4:13-14). Jesus used "physical thirst as a metaphor for spiritual thirst." Jesus invited the woman to fulfill her spiritual yearning for life in relationship to God.[16]

Many people confuse spiritual and physical thirst. They try to satisfy their spirit by fulfilling fleshly cravings. They try to satisfy eternal needs with temporary things of the present world.

For example you can drink deeply from the fountain of wealth but will not be satisfied for long—you soon will thirst again. You can drink deeply from the fount of worldly fame, honor, or power, but you will have the same result—you soon will thirst again. The same goes for the fountain of human knowledge, science, philosophy, music, or art; you soon will thirst again. Yes, you even can deeply drink of the most nearly divine of all human fountains—the fountain of human love—but soon you will thirst again. "Not one of these things fully satisfies, neither do they satisfy for very long."[17]

The Samaritan woman often drank from the fountain of human love. She married five times and lived with a man who was not her husband (John 4:18). When Jesus told the woman, *"The man you now live with is not your husband,"* He indicated He knew the man with whom she lived actually was another woman's husband.[18] Through relations with men the Samaritan woman desperately tried to satisfy spiritual thirst in her heart. However, rather than bringing satisfaction, drinking from this well caused the woman only to thirst for more. No man could satisfy this woman's spiritual need for a relationship with the God Who created and loved her.

A young woman in my church asked me whether the Bible absolutely forbids sexual relations between men and women before marriage. Churches in Japan severely are deficient in moral teaching. So this was a moral question. But her question seemed to reveal an unmet need. She sought to satisfy her need for companionship by yielding to pressures men placed on her. I told her, "Relationships between men and women are important, but what you long for cannot be satisfied through a relationship with a man. Do not allow your desire for a boyfriend to take priority over your relationship with Jesus. Only Jesus can satisfy the longings in your heart."

I know people who try to use pornography, alcohol, drugs, entertainment, or the achievement of fame, power, or financial gain to fill the spiritual void in their hearts. None are successful. The person always thirsts for more. One porn video leads to another until the person is hooked. One beer leads to another and then to a glass of wine and then on to the stronger stuff until the person is a confirmed alcoholic. Drug addicts begin with only one joint or one pill. To relieve stress television couch-potatoes begin by watching one program. Music-video junkies are created from listening to one song. The ongoing quest for fame, power, and fortune continues. The more a person gets, the more he or she wants. The rich never seem rich enough. The powerful always seek to be more powerful. The famous always clamor for more fame. Where does all this end? Everything ends back at the well—the point at which the person returns to receive satisfaction. Or, should I say, **dissatisfaction**.

When Jesus gives us the Holy Spirit, He places within us the Source of our joy. If we depend on things around us to give joy, we only will be happy when things go well and miserable when they don't. We are happy when we have what we want but miserable when we long for more. If the Source of joy is in our hearts, we can be joyful no matter what goes on around us. In our darkest hour we may find ourselves overflowing with joy only God can give.[19] This is because, during those times, when we have only God's Spirit to which to turn for comfort and strength, we find He is our *strong tower* (Ps. 61:3), our source of *refuge and strength* (Ps. 46:1; 62:7; 71:7, etc.), and our *ever present help in trouble* (Ps. 46:1).

We, along with the apostle Paul, can say,

> *I have learned to be content whatever the circumstances. I know what it is to be in need, and I know what it is to have plenty. I have learned the secret of being content in any and every situation, whether well fed or hungry, whether living in plenty or in want. I can do everything through him who gives me strength* (Phil. 4:11-13).

The presence of the Holy Spirit is the basis of the Christian life. The arrival of the Spirit "marks the beginning of the Christian life" (Gal. 3:2-3). The teaching of the Spirit enables us to understand the things of God (1 Cor. 2:10-14). The leading of the Spirit makes us God's children (Rom. 8:14-17).[20] Only knowing God and having a relationship with Him satisfies the thirst of the human spirit.

The Eternal Spring

To describe those who believe in Him Jesus used two word pictures. First Jesus says the water He will give the believer *"will become in him a* ***spring of water*** *welling up to eternal life"* (John 4:14, emphasis added). Then He says, *"Whoever believes in me . . .* ***streams of living water*** *will flow from within him"* (John 7:38, emphasis added).

Jesus is the source of *"living water."* The person who receives this water cannot contain it. The believer cannot be a stagnant pool in which the blessings of life in Christ only accumulate. Rather he or she is a fountain from which this ***"living water"*** springs forth—a river through which the blessings of spiritual life flow to others.[21] As Christians live the *"abundant life"* (John 10:10) Christ gives, He has a way of *"begetting life"* in those they touch.[22]

Every Christian who has experienced a long, weary day can relate to what Jesus felt that day at the well in Sychar. He was tired and thirsty. A day on the hot, dusty roads made His feet dirty and sore. Jesus needed a good meal and a night's rest before He could continue on His journey. The disciples had gone into the village to rustle up a meal. Jesus just needed a cool drink of water.

This situation reflects the situation in which many of us find ourselves while we travel through the bustling highways of the 21st century. Whether we spend the day at the office, the shopping mall, or home with the children, by the end we can eat a good meal, drop into a comfortable chair, and veg away the remainder of the evening, as we watch some mindless television program. In this world, in the context of this hectic life, God has placed us to be channels through which **His living water** can flow. Using our neediness, God can reach out and meet the needs of others.[23]

Jesus is the source of life. If those we know are to see, touch, and experience this life Jesus brought, they do so through us. Although this may sound impossible, or at best improbable, it really can happen. Because God's Spirit lives and works in us and because the Spirit truly made us alive, our thoughts, words, and actions all are channels through which living water can flow.

In every sense God intended us as channels of life. Jesus is the world's Creator and Sustainer as well as its Lord and Savior. Jesus is the Giver of physical, moral, and spiritual life. Through us He means to give all forms of life. We are channels of life when we proclaim the gospel so spiritually dead people have the opportunity to believe in Christ. We also are channels of physical and moral life when we provide pure drinking water, feed the hungry, say *no* to abortion, and say *yes* to peace instead of war.

Jesus said, *"Whoever wants to save his life will lose it, but whoever loses his life for me will save it"* (Luke 9:24). Perhaps this verse best explains what is necessary to become a channel of life. As long as we hold on to life as a precious possession that belongs to us and for us to use as we see fit, we will be a blocked channel. Life flowing into us can be stopped by the dam of our possessiveness, where it stagnates and dies. Only when we give away the physical life Jesus gave us do we fully experience what salvation and eternal life mean. Jesus is the source of life; we are channels of the life He gives us. When we realize this, we will do all to nurture and sustain the life Jesus created. People then can experience life through us.

"I . . . Am He"

When the Samaritan woman heard all Jesus had to say, she responded, *"I know that the Messiah . . . is coming. When he comes, he will explain everything to us"* (John 4:25). Then Jesus spoke the words that transformed her life, *"**I** who speak to you **am he**"* (John 4:26, emphasis added). This was Jesus' first use in John's Gospel of an *"I am"* statement. The reference pointed toward His identity as God in human form. In Isaiah 52:6-7 the Lord speaks of a time in which people will know who He is because He clearly will speak to them. Then the good news of salvation and God's reign will reach the end of the earth. In John 4 Jesus tells us the long-awaited time when God will speak and grant salvation has arrived.[24] The woman sought the Messiah. Jesus meant not only the Messiah whom she sought but also God. This explains why, if the woman had asked, Jesus could have given her living water.[25] His identity as God gave Jesus the authority to be the Savior of the world (John 4:42).[26]

The woman at the well in Sychar remains anonymous to us. We are given no name for this misused, abused, and tossed-aside woman. This reminds me of the crowd's nameless faces that are tossed aside. In this world they are treated as unimportant—even non-existent. But the Creator and Lord of the universe sought the woman who considered herself worthless. Jesus was there to give her life.

When she realized Who Jesus was and that He wanted to help her, she forever was changed. When she realized that God loved her, she was transformed. Imagine what thoughts filled her heart: "I am loved by God!" She could not keep this life-giving water for herself. The woman left her water jar and went back into town. What brought her to the well no longer concerned her. What happened at the well superceded it. Because she had met Jesus, everything up to this point in her life paled by comparison. She had to tell those she knew that, because she met Christ, her life forever had been changed (John 4:28-29).

Millions of faces in the crowd remain anonymous. But Jesus knows the names that go with each face. He knows the pain in their hearts. He knows about every wrong word or deed—both those done by and to them. He loves them. He longs to meet them at the well and say to them, "I . . . am He. If you knew me, you would know I bring living water. I was sent to give you life through my Spirit."

This spiritual thirst will be with us until the end of the age. In every generation people will seek the One Who satisfies the longing in their hearts. You have tasted this life-giving water; now invite others to the rock in the wilderness to drink from the well that never runs dry and to meet the One Who said, *"I have come that they may have life, and have it to the full"* (John 10:10).

The Spirit and the bride say, "Come!" And let him who hears say, "Come!" Whoever is thirsty, let him come; and whoever wishes, let him take the free gift of the water of life (Rev. 22:17).

Responding to His Voice

1. Have you tasted the Water of Life?

2. Have you tried to quench your spiritual thirst with something other than Jesus?

3. Does the Water of Life flow freely through you? If not, what are you allowing to block the stream?

Chapter 5

The Cost of Doing God's Work

Then Jesus said to him, "Get up! Pick up your mat and walk." At once the man was cured; he picked up his mat and walked.

The day on which this took place was a Sabbath, and so the Jews said to the man who had been healed, "It is the Sabbath; the law forbids you to carry your mat." . . .

So, because Jesus was doing these things on the Sabbath, the Jews persecuted him. Jesus said to them, "My Father is always at his work to this very day, and I, too, am working." For this reason the Jews tried all the harder to kill him; not only was he breaking the Sabbath, but he was calling God his own Father, making himself equal with God (John 5:16-18).

Is the Result of Doing God's Work Worth the Price?

Obedience to God is risky work. Just ask Peter and John. One day on their way to the temple they stopped just long enough to help a man get to his feet and begin to walk. From the time of his birth the man had been crippled (Acts 3:2) and never had walked a day in his life. Worshipers that day in the temple knew this. The man was making quite an impression by *walking and praising God* (Acts 3:9). I imagine he even may have shouted, jumped, and danced a few steps. After all this was the first time in his life he could use his feet and would want to see what they could do. Soon a large crowd gathered to see what all of the commotion was about. *They were filled with wonder and amazement at what had happened to him* (Acts 3:10). Peter told those gathered in the temple this man was healed by the power of Jesus, whom they killed but whom God raised from the dead (Acts 3:12-16). In response several people became believers in Jesus Christ. When Jewish authorities heard about what happened, they brought forth Peter and John and commanded them *"not to speak or teach in the name of Jesus"* (Acts 4:5-18).

Peter and John replied, *"Judge for yourselves whether it is right in God's sight to obey you rather than God. For we cannot help speaking about what we have seen and heard"* (Acts 4:19-20).

From the first century until now Christian history has been filled with stories of men and women who chose to suffer and die rather than to give up speaking about what they experienced as a result of faith in Christ. In the early second century Ignatius, a leader of the church in Antioch, was thrown to the lions. He refused to renounce his faith in Christ. Soon before his death sentence was carried out, Ignatius wrote,

> Now I begin to be a disciple. I care for nothing, of visible or invisible things, so that I may but win Christ. Let fire and the cross, let the companies of wild beasts, let the breaking of bones and the tearing of limbs, let the grinding of the whole body, and all of the malice of the devil come upon me; be it so, only may I win Christ![1]

Polycarp, the bishop of Smyrna in the mid-second century, had to recant his faith in Christ or be burned at the stake. He answered, "Eighty-six years have I served him, and he never once wronged me; how then shall I blaspheme my King, who has saved me?"[2]

In the 1740s David Brainerd served as a missionary to the Native Americans in New York and Pennsylvania. In the summer of 1745 Brainerd began a five-year work that resulted in revival among Native Americans living near Crossweeksung, NJ. Before he finally died of tuberculosis on October 9, 1747, Brainerd repeatedly suffered from loneliness, hunger, sickness, and numerous other difficulties.[3] John Piper writes that Brainerd's *Life and Diary* portray the "life of the missionary as a life of constant warfare in the soul" in which the "suffering and struggle make us feel the supremacy of God."[4]

On January 8, 1956 five young, American missionaries—Peter Fleming, Roger Youderian, Ed McCully, Nate Saint, and Jim Elliot—were speared to death on the shore of the Curaray River in the Amazon jungle by Auca Indians they were trying to reach with the gospel.[5] Elisabeth Elliot later risked her own life to work among the Auca who had killed her husband. She writes,

> I found peace in the knowledge that I was in the hands of God. Not in the confidence that I was not going to be killed. Not in any false sense of security that God would protect me, any more than He protected my husband . . . from the wooden lances. Simply that He held my destiny in His two hands, and that what He did was right.[6]

Martin and Gracia Burnham realized God does not guarantee safety to those who give their lives to serve Him. The Burnhams served 15 years as missionaries in the Philippines. On May 27, 2001, they were taken hostage at gunpoint by members of the Abu Sayyaf, a militant Muslim group. Martin was killed; Gracia was rescued on June 7, 2002. Gracia writes of the experience,

> What happened to Martin and me was no one's fault except that of sinful human beings, the kind that we came to the Philippines to help. This ordeal went with the territory. I refuse to let this dampen my joy or detract from the love that God means to flourish in my heart.[7]

The day Martin was killed, he told his wife,

> I really don't know why this has happened to us. I've been thinking a lot lately about Psalm 100—what it says about serving the Lord with gladness. This may not seem much like serving the Lord, but that's what we're doing, you know? We may not leave this jungle alive, but we can leave

> this world serving the Lord *with gladness,* we can *come before his presence with singing* (Ps. 100:2).[8]

With the number of Christian martyrs worldwide exceeding 160,000 per year and expected to exceed 200,000 by 2025[9] we may find ourselves, like the Burnhams did, questioning why God allows so much suffering on the part of His people. In August 2003 why, for example, did God allow more than 170 worshippers at a house church to be arrested by Chinese government officials?[10] And why, in November of that same year, did God allow six Christians to be targeted and killed by an Al Qaeda bomb in Riyadh, Saudi Arabia?[11]

Jesus prayed to the Father for us: "*I have given them your word and the world has hated them, for they are not of the world any more than I am of the world*" (John 17:14). Although Jesus' prayer is encouraging, the reason He prayed for us is not. Jesus prayed for us because He knew those who choose to follow Him will suffer. Those who do God's work often suffer at the hands of the very people they try to help.

Jesus knew this because He experienced it firsthand. And for the last 2000 years many others—such as Ignatius and Polycarp, David Brainerd, Jim and Elisabeth Elliot, Martin and Gracia Burnham—also have known this suffering. Christians in China, Saudi Arabia, and many other places around the world continue to experience firsthand what it means to suffer for Christ. After Peter reflected on what he saw—Jesus' suffering, he wrote,

> *But how is it to your credit if you receive a beating for doing wrong and endure it? But if you suffer for doing good and you endure it, this is commendable before God. To this you were called, because Christ suffered for you, leaving you an example, that you should follow in his steps* (1 Pet. 2:20-21).

John 5 points toward the suffering we endure if we are to do God's work in the world. Jesus was to do His Father's work. Some people did not like Jesus. They did not like what He was here to do. So they persecuted Jesus. They plotted against Him and, in the end, killed Him. If we think only about the price Jesus paid to do God's work, we miss the point of the story. The point is, while Jesus paid a high price, what He accomplished was worth the cost. He gave people new life—both now and in eternity.

As we join Jesus in doing God's work in the present world, we also will pay a price. Some people will not like us because we are Christians. They will not like the work we do in the name of Jesus. Piper writes,

> Christ is calling his church to a radical, wartime engagement in world missions. He is making it plain that it will not happen without pain . . . Those who have suffered most speak in the most lavish terms of the supreme blessing and joy of giving their lives away for others.[12]

When we see people who have been transformed by God's power, we realize the result of what God does through us is worth every drop of sweat and blood we shed for Jesus.

"Get Up! Pick Up Your Mat and Walk"

When Jesus went to the Pool of Bethesda, He encountered a large number of *disabled people . . . the blind, the lame and the paralyzed,* who hoped to be healed when pool waters were stirred (John 5:3, 7).[13] No doubt Jesus had compassion for them all and could have healed them all. But He did not. Jesus chose one man out of the crowd—a man who had been lame for 38 years (John 5:5).[14] Although the man wanted to be healed, he did not believe such healing ever could take place. This is because the man could not heal himself and had no one to turn to for help. So Jesus inquired about the man's desire to be well. He replied, *"I have no one to help me into the pool when the water is stirred. While I am trying to get in, someone else goes down ahead of me"* (John 5:6-7).

This was a man who desired and believed but had no hope. The man desired to be well—for 38 years he desired to walk like any other. And the man believed the stirring waters of Bethesda could make him whole. But the man had no hope that the waters ever actually would heal him. Someone else always would be ahead of him in line to receive the blessing. Desire and belief without hope result in despair. And the weight of despair brings a sickness to the soul which spiritually, psychologically, and physically takes the life out of a person. That day this man, as much as anyone, needed the Lord's healing touch at Bethesda.

At first the man disregarded Jesus. He did not think of Him as a source of healing. Rather the man focused his attention on the pool. This is because the man believed in the pool and not in Jesus.[15]

This situation is instructive for us as we try to reach people with the news of Jesus Christ. Getting a hearing for our message sometimes is difficult, because people focus on something else. They believe in, desire, and view as a source of hope someone or something other than Jesus. As long as people believe that hope **someday may be realized**, they will not be ready to listen to what we have to say. As time drags on and the tragedy of a wasted life in want of unrealized hope dawns, despair enters. Ironically, along with despair, the opportunity for God's grace to work brings new life.

Sometimes we wish for a perfect world without problems. Because of the worldly pain, we are driven to cry out to God.

Even when we clearly do not comprehend our own despair, the God Who created and loves us knows our hearts. Even when we do not know what to say, God's Spirit speaks for us.

> *In the same way, the Spirit helps us in our weakness. We do not know what we ought to pray for, but the Spirit himself intercedes for us with groans that words cannot express* (Rom. 8:26).

God knows everything about us. Not a detail of our lives escapes His notice. Our every frailty brings God's compassion; our every problem brings His concern.

When Jesus saw the man lying on the pallet with an interminable illness and with no hope of any other kind of existence, He had compassion for him. He asked the man, "Do you want to be well?" Jesus was moved with concern for the man's well-being. Jesus wanted the man to be well. Jesus wanted the man to have a new life that qualitatively would be different than anything he before had experienced. Jesus wanted the man to experience a life of joy and happiness rather than merely continuing in suffering and despair.

So Jesus said to the man, *"Get up! Pick up your mat and walk"* (John 5:8). "The cure [was] instantaneous and complete."[16] For 38 years this man couldn't walk. His muscles would not have developed. His legs would have been small and shriveled, with thin skin barely covering the bones. Imagine how this man felt when he heard Jesus' words. Suddenly he felt muscle fill the space between bone and skin. He felt strength and power enter his legs where none had been before. For the very first time he could rise, stand on his feet, and walk!

In the mass, urbanized world in which we live, sometimes we see only the crowds. As we gaze at the sea of people passing before our eyes, we can be overwhelmed by all of their needs. But genuine, Christlike love demands that we learn to look, one face at a time, at the people in the crowd. Learn to look at one man, one woman, or one child to meet the needs of that one spirit, soul, and body, because each person's needs are as individualistic as is each person. No two people are alike.

Jesus could look into a person's eyes and see all the way to the heart. This is something you and I cannot do. As perceptive as we may be, we miss cues and clues to who a person is and what he or she needs. Learn to ask, "What do you need?" People do not want voluntarily to tell what they need. They are reluctant to let down their guard—to open up their true selves. So continue asking and continue loving. Only when Christ's love works through us to heal real needs will people experience the new life God intends.

One clue to the neediness of those around us is our own neediness. Our own suffering enables us to identify with the suffering of those we are called to love and serve. No one is better equipped to help someone who has lost a child in an accident than is someone who has endured the pain of the loss of his or her own child. A person who has grieved the loss of his or her spouse is best prepared to help another person enduring similar grief. One recovering alcoholic is uniquely equipped to help another not so far along on the road to recovery. A Christian who has endured suffering and persecution as a result of his or her faith is able to encourage a new believer who experiences resistance from his or her family and friends.

When we express hope in the midst of despair, we become a source of light in the midst of a dark world. This hope not only enables us to keep going when the powers of darkness array against us, but it enables us to lead other people through the valley of sin and death. Because of this they can experience the brightness of God's glory awaiting us on the other side. In many cases even those who inflict suffering become Christians when they see the power which our hope in Christ brings. Paul participated in Stephen's martyrdom but went on to become a dynamic apostle for Jesus Christ. The Auca Indians who killed Jim Elliot later turned to Christ through Elisabeth Elliot's witness. Those who try to humiliate and harm us because of our faith also can be changed.

Doing What the Law Forbids

On a Sabbath Jesus healed the lame man. When the Jewish leaders saw the healed man carrying his mat, they reminded him, *"It is the Sabbath; the law forbids you from carrying your mat"* (John 5:10). Later, when the Jewish leaders found out Jesus healed him, *because Jesus was doing these things on the Sabbath, the Jews persecuted him* (John 5:16).

The Jews regard the Sabbath as the culmination of the week. The whole "week is lived in anticipation of the [Sabbath]. Everything leads to it; everything points to it."[17] For this reason the days of the week are called in accordance to their relationship to the Sabbath. For example Sunday becomes *yom rishon beshabbat,* or the "first day toward Sabbath."[18] The Sabbath is the celebration of the completion of the week's creative activity. The Sabbath is a foretaste of the next world which will be an eternal Sabbath of continual rest in paradise—a return to the "ideal state in the Garden of Eden."[19]

The theological basis for the Sabbath in Jewish thought is God's rest from His creative work (Gen. 2:1-3). Since God stopped creating on the Sabbath, we also stop creating on the Sabbath.[20] Observance of the Sabbath reminds people of "God's creation of the world and covenant with man" (Ex. 31:17).[21] During this "island in time" human beings are pulled up out of the humdrumness of everyday life and allowed to "embrace eternity." People meet with the God Who both created them and, through His covenant relationship, incorporates them as co-workers in his own creative activity.[22]

On this theological basis Jewish law forbids doing "creative work" on the Sabbath.[23] Thirty-nine specific categories of "creative work" are prohibited, including kindling a fire (Ex. 35:3); plowing, harvesting, and reaping (Ex. 34:21); gathering wood (Num. 15:32-35); baking and cooking (Ex. 16:22); and buying and selling (Neh. 13:15-17). However the obligation to preserve human life supercedes observing the Sabbath law. This is because "God gave the Torah and its commandments to man so that 'He shall live by them' (Lev. 18:5) . . . 'and not die by them.'"[24]

Although preserving life on the Sabbath is allowed, deeds of healing are not.[25] So Jewish authorities censured both Jesus and the man He healed. Keeping the Sabbath was a holy duty given to the Jews by God. God commanded them, *"Remember the Sabbath day by keeping it holy"* (Ex. 20:8; Deut. 5:12). From their viewpoint if Jesus healed on the Sabbath day, He was doing evil and was violating God's law.

However Jesus said He was doing good, because He was doing God's work. Jesus said, *"The Son can do nothing by himself; he can only do what he sees his Father doing, because whatever the Father does the Son also does"* (John 5:19). At the end of this chapter I will call attention to the remaining significant theological points here. First let's think for a minute about how Jesus' words applied to the deed of healing. Jesus was saying that God was the ultimate

Source of the man's healing. Only God could have healed, in this way, a man who had been lame for so many years. God worked through Jesus to accomplish this deed of healing. Since God's works always are good, this certainly was a good deed. A deed cannot be both good and evil, so Jesus did good, not evil. Jesus had given this man rest from years of laboring under the burden of his disability. So, in reality, **Jesus' act of healing had fulfilled, rather than violated, the purpose of the Sabbath.**

Sometimes doing God's work necessitates violating laws and customs people make. When a nation's laws or a society's customs result in its people suffering, Christ's followers obey God rather than people. We may have to work to free people from oppression, even if this results in our own suffering.

What I am saying sounds, on the surface, much like the political theology some theologians now advocate. Political theology, sometimes referred to as liberation theory, advocates freedom from social and political oppression as a form of salvation in the present world. I agree with this to the extent that I believe Christians have a moral obligation to work so oppressed peoples of the world can have political and social freedom. Historical precedence exists for this in Christian support for the abolition of slavery, universal voting rights in democratic states, and the end of apartheid in South Africa. However don't confuse political liberation with the biblical concept of **salvation** (forgiveness of sin and new life through faith in Jesus Christ) or with what Jesus in John 5 is doing.

Much that enslaves human beings in the present world is not directly related to any political or economic system. For example in John 5, paralysis of his legs for almost 40 years had enslaved the man who Jesus healed. He needed to be healed to be freed from this bondage. In our day in many parts of the world, people also remain under physical bondage to dreaded diseases—cancer, heart disease, and AIDS—and other diseases that result from hunger and poor nutrition. Healing yields freedom.

Others are in bondage because of personal habits. Alcoholism, drug abuse, and pornography all result from inappropriate personal habits. Overwork, overeating, and overindulgence in television or the Internet, while often rationalized, can be destructive to mind and body. A need for caring Christian intercessors and counselors, willing to pay time, energy, and emotion, exists to help people free themselves from addictive behavior.

Others are in bondage because of psychological disorders. The number of people diagnosed with depression, bipolar disorder, attention-deficit disorder, and related conditions continues to rise. Not only do diagnosed people suffer, so do their immediate families and friends. Often an ongoing sense of crisis exists, with no possibility for relief in sight. This is because, while all these psychological conditions may be treated, none can be cured. To receive hope, individuals and families who suffer because of psychological issues need strength and encouragement from Christian counselors, psychotherapists, and support groups.

For all people the greatest source of oppression is a personal problem with sin. *We all have sinned* (Rom 3:23). All of us fail to do the good we want to do and continue doing evil things we do not want to do (Rom. 7:18-19). Without Jesus Christ, Who sends the Spirit to free us from sin and death, we cannot escape our bondage to sin (Rom. 7:25-8:2).

Whatever the source of human oppression, whether spiritual, psychological, physical, social, or political, God desires to give people freedom. In every case Jesus Christ is the ultimate source of freedom. Jesus provides freedom as He works through His people to bring new and abundant life to others. To accomplish this Jesus works through His people in various stations and callings in the world—missionaries and pastors, government officials, business people, doctors and nurses, and teachers and social workers. As people in each role live transformed lives, Jesus works through them to bring healing and freedom to the world.

Of course whatever Jesus accomplishes through His people during current times will remain incomplete. As long as we live in a fallen world, sin, suffering, sickness, and death will be present. Because of this continual state of darkness in the present, everything Jesus accomplishes through us becomes a beam of His glory shining through the clouds and pointing toward the eternal brightness of the following age. At the moment someone is healed, encouraged, fed, clothed, or when someone attains faith in Christ, everyone who witnesses the event gains hope for the new day only a trumpet call away.

The Jewish leaders wanted to kill Jesus because He was doing God's work (John 5:18). If we really are trying to do God's work, we can expect opposition. We always will have to pay a price to bring hope to someone else. It will cost time, money, and physical and emotional strength. It also may cost ostracism, ridicule, harassment, and, in extreme cases, imprisonment or death. But, whatever the cost, doing God's work is worth the price.

Doing His Father's Work

The Jews rejected Jesus for two reasons: He broke the Sabbath law and made Himself equal to God by calling God His Father (John 5:18). First-century Jews regarded Jesus' claim of divine incarnation as blasphemy and heresy. Moreover they expected the Messiah to bring "world peace and political harmony" under the leadership of re-established Davidic monarchy. Instead Jesus seemed to threaten "what little political and religious hegemony" the Jewish authorities managed to maintain for themselves thus far in the context of a brutal Roman occupation. "Jesus was regarded as having broken the law of Moses, an act that was viewed traditionally as a sign of a false prophet."[26] In Deuteronomy the Scriptures say,

> *If a prophet, or one who foretells by dreams, appears among you and announces to you a miraculous sign or wonder, and if the sign or wonder of which he has spoken takes place, and he says, "Let us follow other gods" (gods you have not known) "and let us worship them," you must not listen to the words of that prophet or dreamer. The Lord your God is testing you to find out whether you love him with all your heart and with all your soul. It is the Lord*

> *your God you must follow, and him you must revere. Keep his commands and obey him; serve him and hold fast to him. That prophet or dreamer must be put to death, because he has preached rebellion against the Lord your God* (Deut. 13:1-5a).

During an age in which tolerance and individual freedom of conscience are regarded as virtues, the Jewish authorities' response to Jesus is regarded as an example of religious fundamentalism of the worst sort. From a contemporary, postmodern perspective these political and religious leaders oppressed Jesus' freedom of expression. Ideally Jesus would have been free to believe and teach anything He wanted about Himself as long as it did not infringe on anyone else. But this is where postmodernists' insistence on personal freedom, tolerance, and the relative nature of truth fails to coalesce with the message of Jesus Christ. Jesus' saying He was doing His Father's work (John 5:17, 19) implied such a close relationship between Father and Son that the authority with which Jesus spoke and acted was nothing less than the authority of God.[27]

> The works of the Son and the Father are the same, for the Son and the Father are One! That eternal, intimate relationship is the source of His authority and mission. The initiative is God's, not man's.[28]

Since Jesus really is God, His divine authority supercedes everyone's rights. Jesus is none other than the God Who commanded us to love Him with all our hearts and souls, follow and revere Him, obey Him, and serve and hold fast to Him (Deut. 13:3, 4).

The Jews rightly understood that if Jesus was Who He said He was, then they were obligated to bow before Jesus in worship and to give their lives to Him in service. They merely could not leave Jesus alone and continue to live as they always had. Jesus did not allow for such a choice. Either they had to believe in Jesus and become His followers or reject and condemn Him. No room for the tolerance of religious pluralism existed. Oscar Cullmann so well explains how this dilemma with which Jesus presents us was just as difficult for people in the first century as for us today.

> It was just as difficult for the men of that time as it is for us today to believe in what was a *skandalon* to the Jews and "foolishness" to the educated Greeks. It must be stressed again and again that the difficulty in believing this does not lie in the Bible's outdated "mythological cosmology." The technical progress of our time with its electricity, radio, and atomic bomb has not made faith in Jesus Christ as the centre of the divine redemptive history one bit more difficult than for the ancients. Rather, the *skandalon,* the foolishness, lies in the fact that historically debatable events ("under Pontius Pilate") are supposed to represent the very centre of God's revelation and to be connected with all his revelations. That was just as hard for men of that time to accept as for us today.[29]

When we identify with the scandal of the cross and the foolishness of Christ (1 Cor. 1:18, 24), we are considered out of step with our times. People say the old message doesn't meet 21st-century needs. They say God is much bigger than what the Bible tells us about Him and that listening to worldly religions helps us see the whole picture. People will insist everyone who earnestly seeks God can find Him—whatever their source of revelation.

But we have a ready reply to those who claim we unnecessarily are intolerant and narrow. The message of Jesus Christ we teach, preach, and live by, is *not . . . words of human wisdom* (1 Cor. 1:17). If so our message would have no greater impact or importance than would any other religious or philosophical teaching in today's world. Rather Christ's message is the *power of God* (1 Cor. 1:18, 24). This is because the work God sent Jesus to do was not merely the work of an inspired person nor the work done on God's behalf but the work on God Himself. As a result those who see Jesus' work and respond in faith to Him experience new life through Him.

Equal with God

Jesus said He completely identified His own work with the work of God the Father; *"The Son can do nothing by himself; he can do only what he sees his Father doing, because whatever the Father does the Son also does"* (John 5:19b). This unity of work between the Father and Son is a result of a oneness of "essence" and "will." Jesus does the same divine work as the Father, because He is God, just as the Father is God.[30]

In response to persecution Jesus pointed to His own authority over the Sabbath based on His relationship with God the Father, *"My Father is always at his work to this very day, and I, too am working"* (John 5:17). In Mark 2:28 Jesus spoke more clearly of His divine authority, *"The Son of Man is Lord even of the Sabbath."*[31]

God's work in creation through His Word, the Son, is complete with the Sabbath. Only true rest in God's creation exists when we have a sense of fulfillment or completion of purpose. A temporary cessation of labor while work remains incomplete is not true rest. Delaying labor for a day may restore the body and mind but does not bring about spiritual renewal. So the Son brings healing to an invalid man so he can become whole and thus enjoy God's intended rest.

The Son's work is the complete and perfected expression of the Father's love for a suffering, sin-infested world. *"For the Father loves the Son and shows him all he does"* (John 5:20). *"This is how God showed his love among us: he sent his one and only Son into the world that we might live through him"* (1 John 4:9). R.V.G. Tasker writes,

> In the relationship between God the Father and God the Son, the Son can, and indeed must be true to the Father's purposes and do the Father's work, because the love of the Father and the obedience of the Son are perfect. Such a divine Son is so completely controlled by the Father's love that He displays it in all He does.[32]

The Son completes the Father's redemptive work. Through the Son the Father *"raises the dead and gives them life"* (John 5:21; 1 Cor. 15:22). Judgment takes place by the Son (John 5:22; Rom. 14:10). Here we see two results of Christ's work. He brings life to those who receive and believe in Him. He brings judgment to those who reject Him. In either case Jesus carries out the Father's will and acts on His authority as God's Son.[33]

Jesus has the Father's authority to complete His work. The result depends on our response to Christ. He allows us freedom to choose life or judgment. We all are challenged: "At his bidding I can either take up my bed and walk or linger in death among the lame and the blind."[34]

When we say *yes* to Jesus we *"take* [His] *yoke upon* [us]*"* (Matt. 11:29). We *deny self, take up* [His] *cross daily, and follow* [Him]*"* (Luke 9:23). Prepare to suffer the same abuse at the hands of the world in which Jesus suffered. The final result of choosing Jesus far outweighs any cost we ever pay, because Jesus holds both life and judgment in His hands. When He died on the cross for our sins, He endured God's judgment for us to give us life through Him.

Unfortunately our world is filled with physically lame, spiritually blind, and morally diseased people. They will continue suffering until they, too, experience the healing power of Jesus Christ. Jesus tells them, "Get up and walk!" **They will hear Jesus' voice when He speaks to them through us. The clearest announcement of the truth of the gospel is a life transformed by its power. Jesus works through us to bring about His good work in those whose lives we touch. No greater reward this side of heaven exists for serving Jesus!**

Responding to His Voice

1. What work does God want to do through me?

2. What does God's work cost?

3. How do these costs compare with the price Jesus paid to give me life?

4. Am I willing to pay any price so others can experience new life in Christ through me?

Chapter 6

Many Will Turn Away

Then Jesus declared, "I am the bread of life. He who comes to me will never go hungry, and he who believes in me will never be thirsty . . . I tell you the truth, unless you eat the flesh of the Son of man and drink of his blood, you have no life in you. Whoever eats my flesh and drinks my blood has eternal life, and I will raise him up on the last day." . . .

On hearing it, many of his disciples said, "This is a hard teaching. Who can accept it?"

Aware that his disciples were grumbling about this, Jesus said to them, "Does this offend you? What if you see the Son of Man ascend to where he was before! The Spirit gives life; the flesh counts for nothing. The words I have spoken to you are Spirit and they are life. Yet there are some of you who do not believe." For Jesus had known from the beginning which of them did not believe and who would betray him. He went on to say, "This is why I told you that no one can come to me unless the Father has enabled him."

From this time many of his disciples turned back and no longer followed him.

"You do not want to leave me too, do you?" Jesus asked the Twelve.

Simon Peter answered him, "Lord, to whom shall we go? You have the words of eternal life. We believe and know that you are the Holy One of God." (John 6:35, 53-54, 60-69).

When the Crowds Turn Away from Jesus

More than 20 years ago I went to Japan to serve for six months as a student missionary in Nagasaki. At the time I thought, "If I can just get people to understand the gospel, surely they will believe in Jesus. No one who really understands Who Jesus is and what He has done for them will reject Him." However I've learned this really is not the case. I have met many who are interested in Christianity and faithfully participate in weekly Bible studies, sometimes for several years, until they clearly understand Who Jesus is and what He expects of them. They then reject Jesus and walk away into eternity without Him.

When people heard Jesus' claim to be the *"bread of life"* (John 6:35) and require they *"must eat* [His] *flesh and drink* [His] *blood"* (6:53), they responded, *"This is a hard teaching"* (6:60). Jesus' words were not difficult to understand but were difficult to accept. Ray Summers astutely writes, "Their problem was that they did understand."[1] After they understood Jesus' words they realized they could not accept them. Many who pursue Jesus up to this point have *turned back and no longer followed him* (6:66).

People have many reasons for rejecting Jesus knowingly. Some do so because of **pride**. They have their own life agendas, including self-devised plans to relate to God and reach heaven. They are unwilling to surrender their personal plans for their lives and to follow Christ.

Other people reject Jesus because of the **price**. The cost, in terms of what they will have to give up to follow Jesus, seems too high. They are like the rich young man to whom Jesus said,

> *"If you want to be perfect, go, sell your possessions and give to the poor, and you will have treasure in heaven. Then come, follow me." When the young man heard this, he went away sad, because he had great wealth* (Matt. 19:21-22).

Some who turn away from Jesus because of the cost do so with sadness and regret. Others make this decision without much hesitation. Their desire for money, possessions, and pleasure they can gain in the present world has such a strong hold on them, they are unable to consider the blessings of the new world. So in seeking to *"gain the whole world",* they forfeit themselves (Luke 9:25).

Still other people reject Christ as a matter of **preference**. They choose their present identity over the new identity they would have as a result of a relationship with Jesus Christ. Sometimes this happens when people are forced to choose between their families and following Christ. In Japan I have seen many instances in which the choice to become a Christian meant instant and total rejection from a person's parents and siblings. Many say *no* to Jesus because they prefer to maintain good relationships with their family. They don't consider that becoming a follower of Jesus actually will make them a better family member. People are too concerned with remembering people after death through ancestral rituals to think about the need for quality family relationships in the present life. And so they say, "I would rather forever be with my family in hell than forever be separated from my family in heaven."

Another case in which preference prevents people from trusting in Christ is when nationalism closely ties to religion. Religious nationalism especially is strong in Muslim nations, among Hindus in India, and also, to an extent, among Buddhists in Thailand and Japan. In such instances to renounce traditional religion in order to follow Jesus is tantamount to renouncing national identity. In other words a person is not truly Saudi Arabian or Iranian if he or she is not a Muslim. To be Indian means to be Hindu. And to be Thai or Japanese means to be a Buddhist. This is as if someone were saying, "All Americans are Christians." I know some leaders in American society claim religious affiliation and others claim no religion. However in the Asian countries I mentioned, religion is an integral aspect of national identity. And so, to maintain their personal identity as a Thai, Indian, or Saudi, many reject Christ.

Finally people reject Jesus because of **preoccupation**. In their harried lives they get caught up in career commitments, the pleasure of pursuit, or devotion to a relationship. While Jesus and the promise of salvation He brings sound attractive, at best this only can be the sideline to the main show. As a result they immediately dismiss Jesus' demand that a person leave all to follow Him.

This reminds me of the young woman who wanted to become a Christian but wanted even more to be married to a certain young man who wanted nothing to do with Christianity. When he told her she had to make a choice between him and Jesus, the young woman denied Jesus and followed her heart. She since has lived to regret giving her life to a selfish man who acts as though the world revolves around him.

Whatever reason people have for turning away from Christ, the result can devastate those who opened their hearts to share faith with people and show them Christ's love. As believers our own identity in Christ is so strong, their rejection of Christ equates personal rejection. When this happens, remember we are not the first to be rejected in this way nor will we be the last. Jesus also was rejected.

John 6 helps us think through issues of why people who know Who Jesus is and who know His purpose choose to turn away from Him. This passage points to the aspect of the Christian message which turns so many off. This often is referred to as the "scandal of the cross", which acts as a *stumbling block to the Jews and foolishness to Gentiles, but to those whom God has called, both Jews and Greeks, Christ* [is] *the power of God and wisdom of God* (1 Cor. 1:23-24). We can't share the gospel without relying on the cross; we simply cannot avoid the body and blood of Jesus Christ. Bring everyone to the foot of the cross. We cannot control whether they will kneel before the crucified Savior or spit in His face and turn away. When people arrive at the cross, its message is a *double-edged sword* (Heb. 4:12) that divides its listeners into redeemed and unredeemed sinners.

When we proclaim the gospel to the masses, not all will choose to follow Christ. Many realize Who Jesus is but reject Him. Although some want us to continue pouring time and energy into those who **already** have rejected Christ, in John 6 Jesus provides a different pattern. Instead focus on those who commit their lives to the *"Holy One of God"* who has brought the *"words of eternal life"* (John 6:68, 69).

The Bread of Life

During the time for the Passover feast a crowd of more than 5,000 men gathered on the shores of Galilee to hear Jesus teach (John 6:4, 10). Resources were limited to five small loaves of bread and two fish to feed the multitude (6:9). Yet using these meager means, Jesus was able to feed all of these people to the point of contentment and had 12 basketfuls of food left over (6:12-13). So when mealtime rolled around the following day, the crowds looked for Jesus again. They knew a good thing when they saw it and definitely would not pass up a free meal. Word of mouth likely spread far back into the Galilean hills, "All you have to do is sit and listen to Jesus speak for a few hours. When he finishes talking, Jesus will pray. His disciples will pass around the food. Everyone will have plenty and enough to spare." When the people found Jesus, He knew why and did not hesitate to speak the truth:

> *"I tell you the truth, you are looking for me, not because you saw the miraculous signs but because you ate the loaves and had your fill. Do not work for food that spoils, but for food that endures to eternal life, which the Son of Man will give you. On him God the Father has placed his seal of approval"* (John 6:26-27).

Some tend to use the size of the crowd to evaluate whether God is working. If the crowd is large, people quickly say, "God is doing a mighty work in that place." Then pastors and missionaries from all over the world flock to whatever corner of the globe the crowd gathers to bask in the "divine glory", consult with the expert, and then go home to try to replicate the occurrence in their own place.

When people gather and leave with the sense that what they experienced has met some need, they will return and bring friends the next time. And so gathers the crowd. But people may be drawn together for many reasons—food, psychological reinforcement, or an emotional high. Honestly evaluate what is "dished out" before you conclude that the gathered crowd is a sign of God's blessing.

When I was in college, dormitory cafeterias were closed on Sunday evenings. Area churches quickly seized any opportunity to bring students into their fold and to offer free Sunday-evening meals for college students. Students, being excellent economists as well as connoisseurs of fine cuisine, freely shared information about which church, on any given Sunday, served the best food. Churches with great Sunday-evening meals developed a reputation they did their best to uphold. These churches could gather the biggest crowds. Some excellent eating and good fellowship took place during these gatherings. But this did not necessarily translate into discipleship and spiritual growth.

Missionaries from Western nations often are accused of using gifts of food, water, medical care, and education to buy conversions among the poor in the countries in which they work. Some complain that destitute people are willing to sell their eternities to Jesus in exchange for what they need to sustain life or even to prosper in the present world. Some find dismissing this criticism with an "end-justifies-the-means" argument to be easy. The argument goes, "Sure, we give them food to lure them in. But then we preach Jesus so they will be saved."

Western missionaries find making a distinction between product and method easier than for those they try to reach with the gospel. These people all too easily will confuse physical bread for this life and spiritual bread for the next life. So results cannot be measured by the size of the crowd that gathers or even by the number of "decisions" recorded. Wait to see the number and quality of **disciples** of Jesus Christ produced.

Jesus' words point to our need to be more circumspect in our crowd evaluation. Jesus was not impressed by the thousands gathered to hear Him preach, because He knew their motives. The people did not want to witness God's power at work through Jesus' ministry. They gathered because Jesus filled their stomachs with food. They wanted Him to do it again.

Jesus told the crowd, *"I am the bread of life. He who comes to me will never go hungry, and he who believes in me will never be thirsty"* (John 6:35). Jesus concluded a series of statements in which He contrasted the manna which God provided for the Hebrews in the wilderness with the *"true bread from heaven"* (6:30-32). Jesus pointed out that the source of heavenly bread is God rather than Moses (6:32). He went on to say that while manna was sent, the *"bread of God is he who comes down from heaven and gives life to the world"* (6:33). While the manna in the wilderness was able to nourish and sustain life, it could not produce life. Only the real bread from heaven actually had the power to give life.[2]

Moreover God personally was present within this life-giving bread. Jesus most clearly made this point with His words, "***I am*** *the bread of life.*" Jesus was the One Who was from God. He was the One Who could satisfy their hunger and quench their thirst.[3] This is another ***"I am"*** statement which reflects back on God's self-revelation to Moses in Exodus 3. It is the living God—the eternal One Who was, is, and will be—Who has entered the world in the person of Jesus Christ to give life. Jesus arrived "not just **offering** the life-giving bread from heaven; he **was** the life-giving bread."[4] Jesus has "*come down from heaven"* to do his Father's will (6:38)—to receive everyone who seeks Him (6:37). Jesus offers Himself as "*the living bread*"(6:51) inasmuch as the Father also gives that bread (6:31).[5] The *"Father's will is that everyone who looks to the Son and believes in him shall have eternal life"* (6:40). People who seek Jesus and believe in Him will receive the gift of eternal life. While their hunger and thirst for temporal, physical needs will continue, all of their spiritual needs forever will be satisfied in Christ.[6]

Jesus' words do not represent merely an abstract statement about Who He is. They are an "appeal"—an invitation—"to come to him and to believe in him."[7] Since Jesus is the divine ***Logos,*** He can provide direct access to God for those who believe in Him.[8] As such Jesus not always is "the bread" which people now seek but always ***is the only One Who can satisfy their hearts' spiritual longings.*** They may look for physical bread to fill their stomachs. They may seek psychological support or encouragement. They may want to be healed from emotional and physical scars resulting from life in a fallen world. Don't downplay as insignificant any of these needs, but also don't let them overshadow each person's ultimate, eternal need for a personal relationship with God. Jesus was sent so we could meet God and experience fulfillment resulting from a loving, personal relationship with Him. In this relationship with God and in other resulting blessings we experience the "bread of life." As Jesus says in prayer to the Father, *"Now this is eternal life: that they may know you, the only true God, and Jesus Christ, whom you have sent"* (John 17:3).

Jesus' Flesh and Blood

To fully understand John 6 place yourself in the shoes of Jesus' first-century Jewish listeners. They believed only one God—Jehovah, the God of Abraham, Isaac, and Jacob—existed Who revealed Himself most fully and decisively to His people, Israel, during the Exodus. During this time God sent His people "bread from heaven" in the form of manna. God's revelation through Moses to the Israelites during this period was the foundation of the Jewish faith.

Everything since then was placed on top of this foundation. In this theological milieu Jesus acceptably could have shed new light on the meaning of the heavenly bread which the Jews first experienced in the wilderness of Sinai. He might even have encouraged the people by saying, "God offers you the same kind of bread now that He gave to his people then." They did not accept Jesus' claim that He was God Who was sent to them as the bread of life. For them God was an almighty Spirit in heaven. How could this God now stand before them in the form of a man?

If Jesus' claim to be the bread of life was shocking, what He said next probably seemed horrendous, monstrous, or even diabolical: *"I tell you the truth, unless you eat the flesh of the Son of Man and drink his blood, you have no life in you. Whoever eats my flesh and drinks my blood has eternal life"* (6:53-54a). If His words were to be taken literally, His promise of eternal life would have been limited to the finite number of people on that day and in that place who would have been willing to ingest portions of His body and blood.[9] Since Jesus' Jewish listeners were forbidden to partake of blood (Gen. 9:4)[10] and never would have considered the possibility of consuming human flesh, indeed few people would have taken His offer.

The imagery here immediately brings to mind the Lord's Supper. When He instituted the Lord's Supper, Jesus referred to the bread and cup as His blood and body (Luke 22:19-20). Whether this connection between the elements of the Supper and the body and blood of Christ are thought of literally, spiritually, or symbolically depends on the theological position of the church or denomination.

While the wording in John 6:53-54 suggests some connection with the Lord's Supper, some pretty good reasons exist not to overemphasize this connection. The Greek verbs for *eat* and *drink* here both are in the aorist tense, which identifies definitive, completed action. In other words, everyone partakes of the body and blood of Jesus Christ at a specific point in time. Otherwise they do not have eternal life.[11] **This partaking of the body and blood of Christ is a one-time occurrence**—not an ongoing, repeated action, as would be the case in the Lord's Supper.

Second, in verse 63, Jesus warned about taking too literally the meaning of His words, *"The Spirit gives life; the flesh counts for nothing."* Eternal life is a spiritual reality brought about only by spiritual means. **While the physical acts of eating bread and drinking wine symbolize and bear witness to this process, in themselves, they do not produce eternal life**. James Dunn writes,

> Any reference to the sacrament itself reveals not an exaltation of the sacrament as a means of receiving the Spirit and life of Christ, but rather a fairly blunt warning against any such false literalism. The eucharistic flesh avails nothing; life comes through the Spirit and words of Jesus.[12]

The best position is to interpret this passage and the Lord's Supper as pointing us to the same truth: that **Jesus' body and blood were given for us to provide the means of eternal life**.[13] The symbolism used by Jesus here suggests the Passover lamb whose sacrifice secured for the Israelites both freedom from bondage and escape from death (Ex. 12:1-42). In this case the shed blood of Christ brings about our cleansing from sin and reconciliation with God. The body of Christ is the means by which the Spirit works to bring about our relatedness to Christ and other believers.[14]

A person partakes of the flesh and blood of Jesus Christ by entrusting himself or herself to the cross as the sole means of salvation from sin and to eternal life. In doing so this person gives up any notion of any possible value in another approach to spiritual life. Other gods are regarded as powerless. Moralism, social justice, and political liberation are regarded as dead ends. Religious rituals seem empty and void. Everything that once had great value now freely is discarded simply *for the sake of Christ* (Phil. 3:7). With Paul the believer exclaims,

> *I consider them rubbish, that I may gain Christ and be found in him, not having a righteousness of my own that comes from the law, but that which comes through faith in Christ—the righteousness that comes from God and is by faith. I want to know Christ and the power of his resurrection and the* ***fellowship of sharing in his sufferings, becoming like him in his death****, and so, somehow, to attain the resurrection of the dead* (Phil. 3:8b-11, emphasis added).

Eating Christ's flesh and drinking His blood refers to the spiritual unity which takes place between Jesus and those who trust in Him.[15] The one who eats and drinks "*remains in*" Christ and Christ "*in him*" (John 6:56). The closest possible fellowship exists between Christ and believers.[16] As a result Christ begins to live out His life among us in the context of our everyday lives, whether we are at church or home, work or play. In these situations the bruised and bloody marks of the crucified Savior transform us to be like Him.[17]

They No Longer Followed Him

John writes that when Jesus' disciples heard His words about the bread of life and His flesh and blood, they responded, *"This is a hard teaching. Who can accept it?"* (6:60); then many *turned back and no longer followed him* (6:66). The word ***disciple*** is used in the sense of a learner. These are people who "attached themselves" to Jesus "to listen and to learn."[18] In contemporary mission work we often refer to such people as "seekers." For a time they attach themselves to a church, Bible study, or Christian cell group. They don't do this because they have made a commitment to Jesus. They do this because they hope to discover some sort of spiritual truth which will transform their lives. In many cases these contemporary seekers, such as the disciples in John 6, eventually turn away.

Don't fall into the trap of thinking if people really understand Who Jesus is, they will decide to believe in Him. Often the failure to trust in Christ is not a matter of knowledge but a matter of will. The reason so many seekers turn away from Christ is that they begin to **understand Who Jesus really is** and **decide** He is not what they really want. They decide they do not want the new life Jesus offers if this means following Him through the way of the cross (Luke 9:23).[19] So they reject the way of life which Jesus offers to continue living their own way in a fallen world.[20]

People reject Jesus because they are unwilling to stake their eternity on the cross. To them, if the crucifixion happened at all, then the 2,000-year-old event was nothing more than Jewish and Roman authorities' unlawful killing of a Jewish carpenter. How can an isolated, long-ago event have anything to do with their own lives, with the difficulties and struggles they face, and with what will happen to them after they take their final breaths? They fail to see the shadow of the cross stretching across time from the first light of creation to the dawn of the following age. They do not recognize the power of Christ's flesh and blood to remove their sins and to give them new life. So they do not place their faith in Him.

A good example of what I'm discussing is the response to the Mel Gibson movie, *The Passion of the Christ*. For Christian believers who stake their eternity on the cross of Christ, the movie was a veritable spiritual feast providing the opportunity to contemplate afresh, and perhaps more deeply, what Jesus endured for us. Every agony was an amazing revelation of God's love and grace poured out on behalf of a lost world. But the unbeliever who either rejected the cross or who knows nothing of its power sees only political intrigue and brutality. Gibson's movie brought these people to the foot of the cross, but many left without experiencing the transforming power of God's love and grace in their lives.

The thing so disheartening about all of this is that although people decide Jesus is not Who or what they want, He still is what they really need. Dorothy Lee comments,

> In the decision against faith, in the refusal to move beyond the materialistic worldview, they belong to a realm of [flesh] which is unenlivened by the divine Spirit . . . They have closed themselves against the presence of the life-giving Spirit which manifests itself in [flesh].[21]

The Son works through the Spirit to give life. Those who reject the Son sentence themselves to an eternal, lifeless existence. They cut themselves off from the life-giving power of God's Spirit.

Too many times have I brought people to the foot of the cross only to have them say, "No, thanks. Now that I understand Who Jesus is and what following Him means, I think I would rather continue living my life, as I have to this point, without Jesus." I have had no greater discouragement than to see someone knowingly and willingly choose to turn away and walk into eternity without Jesus.

I am sure this is how Jesus felt when the crowds gathered around Him at the Sea of Galilee got up and left. Jesus knew they rejected Him and, in doing so, they also rejected God's provision of forgiveness and eternal life. Yet Jesus did not allow Himself to become distracted by the thousands who turned away. Instead He focused His attention on the few who remained. Jesus focused His time, energy, thoughts, and words on those who chose to follow Him. Those who remain are willing to forsake all else to follow

Him. Those who remain have open hearts and open ears to listen to His words and apply them to their lives. Those who remain experience new life through the power of God's Spirit.

The Word and the Spirit Bring Life

Rather than allowing His thoughts to be consumed by the thousands who rejected Him, Jesus turned His attention to the twelve who remained. Jesus asked them, *"You do not want to leave too, do you?"* (John 6:67). The phrasing of this question is that of a negative invitation. Rather than inviting the twelve to follow Him, Jesus gives them the opportunity to walk away. Jesus says to them, "I am not forcing you to be here. The door is open. You can hit the road anytime you choose. Are you going to stay or go?"

Social pressure creates a powerful suction. When almost everyone moves in one direction, the few who don't want to do so still tend to be drawn into the flow. While I have lived in Japan, I have seen this many times. When I taught Christianity at a college for women in southwestern Japan, every year 10 to 20 students showed interest in becoming Christians. One or two eventually did profess faith in Christ. As a result of social pressure from friends, the rest chose to leave school without deciding to follow Christ. During college even some of our Christian students hid their faith because they feared rejection by the non-Christian majority that engulfed them.

An easier approach would have been for the twelve to have said, "Jesus, thanks for the memories. We enjoyed this while it lasted, but obviously your day in the sun is past. You're past your prime. Time for us to move on. Best wishes. If we're ever in Nazareth and need a carpenter, we'll look you up." Every human instinct the twelve had probably told them to go with the tide now scattering into the Galilean hills. But they did not. When everyone else turned away from Jesus, the twelve chose to remain. When going would have been much easier, why did they choose to stay?

To the twelve something had happened which set them apart from the crowd. The *"Spirit* [Who] *gives life"* (6:63) had moved in their hearts and filled them with Jesus' words and God's truth so the twelve could believe and have life.[22] Aside from the work of God's Spirit people merely are flesh—earthbound, time-oriented creatures who neither can recognize nor receive the things which God will do for us in Christ.[23]

> *The man without the Spirit does not accept the things that come from the Spirit of God, for they are foolishness to him, and he cannot understand them because they are spiritually discerned* (1 Cor. 2:14).

God the Father *"enabled"* them to meet the *"Son"* (John 6:65). "Salvation is always God's first move. Apart from God's initial action in offering salvation, no one can be saved."[24] The Father both **sends** the Son and **draws** us to the Son, so we can have life through faith in Him.[25] As Morris writes,

> People do not come to Jesus because it seems to them a good idea. It never seems a good idea to natural man. Apart from the divine work in their soul (John 16:8) men remain contentedly in their sins. Before men can come to Christ the Father must give them to him.[26]

Simon Peter spoke for the twelve when he said, *"Lord, to whom shall we go? You have the words of eternal life"* (John 6:68). Jesus' words "are in themselves living, deal with the subject of eternal life, and convey eternal life to those who believe."[27] Peter went on to say, *"We believe and know that you are the Holy One of God"* (6:69). Jesus is God in human form. His words are the Word of God Who speaks through the Son.[28] When Jesus speaks, His words are *"Spirit and they are life"* (6:63). The Holy Spirit is at work in the hearts of those who hear these words to produce faith which results in eternal life.[29] So the twelve chose to remain with Jesus because they believed He could provide the spiritual life they sought.[30]

Resist the tendency to boil down merely to a human process what happens when the gospel is proclaimed. Often missionaries, pastors, and teachers focus on the issue of communication—the need to explain God's Word so listeners can understand. But as we have seen in this chapter, **understanding alone cannot produce faith.** People may turn away just at the point when they understand Who Jesus is.

To proclaim the gospel effectively in a way that brings forth new life, a divine human process has to be at work. **Only God can produce faith**. Faith is God's work, just as the whole process of salvation is God's work. God produces faith by working in every part of this gospel-communication process: preparing and sending the speaker; awakening spiritual hunger in the hearts of the hearers; helping the speaker convey the message effectively; opening the ears, minds, and hearts of the hearers so that they will be impacted by the message; and piercing hearts with the truth of God's Word to bring about faith that results in salvation.

When people choose to remain and believe rather than to go with the crowd, something supernatural occurs. No greater occurrence in this age exists than a person who partakes of the bread of life. This happens at the moment someone realizes Christ's body and blood were broken and shed on the cross for his or her salvation. He or she decides to entrust all of his or her hopes, desires, and aspirations, for now and eternity, in this one crucial event. The crowd may say *no*, the person's family and friends may say *no*, his or her culture and training may say *no*, but Someone within him or her says *yes*. In that moment, when he or she chooses to say *yes* to Jesus, something new that lasts for eternity is born in him or her.

Rather than continuing exclusively to focus on the **many** who are lost, at a certain point focus your attention on the **few** who already have said *yes* to Jesus. I am not telling you to give up on evangelism. But I am saying evangelism alone does not fulfill the Great Commission. Jesus sent us to make disciples of all nations—not only by *"baptizing"*, but also by *"teaching people to obey everything"* that Jesus has commanded (Matt. 28:19-20). Give significant time and effort to those who already have placed their faith in Jesus to accomplish our Lord's command, rather than continually focusing on the crowd of could-have-been and might-someday-be believers. These are the people who have been given to us by the Father. They are the ones who have yielded to the prompting of God's Spirit and said *yes* to the gospel. In their hearts they now have new life in embryonic form This new life needs to be cherished and nourished so it will grow to be spiritually mature.

Many will say *no* to Jesus. But for those who say *yes*, God's **goal is not merely conversion. God's goal is transformation into the image and likeness of His Son, Jesus Christ.** When the outside world looks at a mature Christian, it will see the character and attitude of Christ. The world will see the imprint of the loving God Who gives life through His Word and Spirit.

Responding to His Voice

1. Is Jesus Himself enough, or do you seek something more from Him?

2. Do you believe in the adequacy of Christ's body and blood to meet the spiritual needs of every person?

3. When the crowds turn away from Jesus, will you remain with the few who stay?

4. What does *making disciples* mean?

Chapter 7

The Truth That Frees Us

But he continued, "You are from below; I am from above. You are of this world; I am not of this world. I told you that you would die in your sins; if you do not believe that I am the one I claim to be, you will indeed die in your sins." . . .

"The one who has sent me is with me; he has not left me alone, for I always do what pleases him." Even as he spoke, many put their faith in him. To the Jews who had believed him, Jesus said, "If you hold to my teaching, you are really my disciples. Then you will know the truth, and the truth will set you free" (John 8:23-24, 29-32).

Do You Believe Jesus Is the Truth Setting People Free?

On August 28, 1963 Rev. Martin Luther King Jr. told a crowd of between 200,000 and 250,000 people gathered between the Washington Monument and the Lincoln Memorial in Washington, D.C., "I have a dream." King dreamed of an America where all citizens equally would share in freedom and justice guaranteed by the U.S. Constitution. He dreamed of a day in which Americans of every ethnicity and religion would "be able to join hands and sing the words of the old spiritual, 'Free at last! Free at last! Thank God Almighty, we are free at last!'"[1] Martin Luther King Jr. believed God's will was to achieve a "political and social community" in which all people had "basic human rights."[2] He thought this kind of free society would become a reality "when enough people open their lives to God and allow him to pour his triumphant, divine energy into their souls."[3]

The American civil rights movement in the 1960s, during which Martin Luther King Jr. played a major role, has been only one expression of the universal urge for freedom. All people desire freedom. What this freedom is or how it ought to be achieved is vague. Often what is viewed as freedom for one cannot be seen as freedom for all. Conflict ensues when two contrasting views of freedom clash. For example in Western nations many desire freedom from restraint in their actions, from fear, and to attain material prosperity to live what they regard as "the good life." But many in Islamic nations view these Western freedoms as enslavement to lust, greed, and desire for power. Many in the Middle East see a lack of restraint by the U.S. and Europe in enforcing their will on other nations as the source of their own economic hardship and personal suffering. They make such statements as, "We must watch our own children go hungry and die of disease for lack of medicine, while American children grow fat and lazy."

These Muslims do not say freedom itself is a bad thing. They also dream of freedom but of a different kind: freedom to believe and practice Islam; freedom from harm inflicted by the bombs and guns of Western armies; freedom from the threat of encroachment by materialism and immorality; and freedom to continue to live in accordance with the traditional values their cultures have practiced for more than a thousand years.

The situation in our contemporary world parallels with the first-century world. The armies of the Roman Empire fanned out across Europe, the Middle East, and North Africa to enforce Roman hegemony and bring about Roman prosperity at the expense of the people of other nations. The Jews, among others, resisted this imposition of Roman will. They resented paying taxes to the emissaries of Caesar. They regarded the worship of foreign gods as the greatest form of profanity—the pollution of all the Jews regarded as holy and sacred. These Jews longed for a Messiah to free them from Roman domination so they could worship their own God and live according to their own traditional values and customs.

Jesus entered this world to bring freedom. But Jesus lifted the meaning of freedom above the usual human definitions. We human beings often speak of freedom concretely in social, political, and economic terms: social justice, equal rights, and equal opportunity for economic advancement. We also may speak of freedom abstractly in moral, religious, and intellectual terms: freedom of conscience, freedom of religion, and freedom of thought. But Jesus spoke of freedom in **spiritual** terms: freedom from sin and death; freedom to know God and live in relationship to Him; and freedom to fulfill the purpose for which God created us.

The freedom Jesus brings cannot be limited by the circumstances in which people live. Jesus said through wealth and poverty, feast or famine, health, disease, or even death, **those who trust in Him truly are free.** His promise of freedom in the midst of harm and hopelessness has the power to re-create a world damaged by sin. God's truth revealed to us in Christ frees us from the bondage and destruction of Satan's lies.

As Christians our personal understanding of spiritual freedom defines how we use the terms *gospel, salvation,* and *missions.* When we see spiritual freedom primarily in terms of social justice and political equality, we define *salvation* as freedom from political oppression. *Missions* becomes involvement in social action and political processes to bring about a just world. And the *gospel* is hope for a just world in which all people have freedom from political, social, and economic oppression.[4]

This view fails to take into account the reason for all human suffering at the hands of other human beings whether the result of war, slavery, political and economic oppression, or even religion. The reason for all of this suffering, and what all humans really need to be free from, is **sin**. When we remember this truth, **gospel, salvation,** and **missions** take on proper spiritual dimensions. The **gospel** message is that people can be freed from sin and have eternal life through faith in Jesus Christ. **Salvation** is the condition of having the freedom and life God intended for us to have in Christ. Finally **missions** is sharing the gospel so every person can have the opportunity to experience true freedom through faith in Jesus.

Jesus charged us to carry His message of freedom and hope to a world locked in the chains of sin and trapped in the dungeon of despair. But we cannot give to others that which we do not first possess ourselves. First possess freedom in Christ. Jesus bought this freedom for us with His own precious blood shed on the cross for our sins.

Two Worlds

As I've mentioned, for six years I taught Christianity at a Baptist women's college in southwestern Japan. In Japan such schools are referred to as "mission schools", because they were founded by missionaries for the purpose of evangelizing a primarily non-Christian student body. Fewer than one percent of the students at the school at which I taught were Christians. Most who attended had no prior exposure to Christianity.

Students in my class had negative attitudes. The class was required; Christianity had nothing to do with their own personal lives. Probably they would not be able to understand what I taught them about it. However, as we moved through the school year, a certain number of students were drawn into what I said. They were interested in the spirit world. Also they were curious about how spiritual things impacted their everyday lives.

After class one day two of my students dropped by my office. In class I had talked about some eschatological issues: life after death and the need for faith in Christ in order to have eternal life. So they asked me, "Do you really believe in life after death?" Many young people in Japan, from first grade through high school, are taught scientific, evolutionary theory and a materialistic worldview. Many believe nothing exists beyond death. They believe personal existence ends with the grave. But one of these young women had a friend who recently died tragically. In search for some hope she felt compelled to reconsider a materialistic position. Students began asking whether this friend who died might, somehow and somewhere, still be alive. So these young women were curious about how I, with a university education and a Ph.D., could believe in life after death. I assured them that indeed I believed in eternal life for those with faith in Jesus Christ. I told them, “If I did not believe that these things are true, I would not be teaching them to you.”

They then asked what they really wanted to know: “How can you know about life after death? How can anyone know the truth about these things?” At this point I fell back on the only and best recourse I had. I appealed to divine revelation. I told them, “As a Christian, I believe the Bible is true. The Bible teaches us about heaven and eternal life, so I believe such a thing as eternal life really exists and that such a place as heaven exists.” By the expressions on their faces I could tell these two young women were not entirely satisfied with my answer. The reason for this lack of satisfaction was because of uncertainty that the Bible was true. As non-Christians they still were trying to make up their minds about the issue of life after death. And these students wondered how I could be so certain I knew the truth. As David Hesselgrave writes,

> Behind **what** we know—or think we know—always lurks the question of **how** we know what we know. Behind the **assertions** and **affirmations** of Christian doctrine are the **explanations** of **how** those teachings were believed in times past and **how** and **why** to believe today. Knowing Christ is an ontological state and is intimately related to the spiritual, psychological, and rational processes whereby we arrive at that state. Therefore Christian missionaries should not be afraid of, or unprepared for, questions that relate to the **whys** and **hows** of Christian faith any more than they should fear questions that relate to the **what** of the Christian faith.[5]

When people ask how we know about spiritual truth, this always shields the deeper question of how they can know what we say really is true. We tend to try to say that the distance between the speaker and the hearer is the reason why people are uncertain when we try to communicate the Christian message to them. Some think that if the speaker can enter into the hearer’s world and explain the Christian message in terms the hearer understands, then the hearer understands and perhaps believes. This turns sharing the gospel into a process between two people. If God is not at work, no matter how good our communications skills are, little can be accomplished. On the other hand God is powerful enough to make up for any shortcomings you and I may have in this area. Hesselgrave reminds us we,

> have to take with utter seriousness the biblical doctrine of illumination . . .. The Bible discloses that the Father reveals the truth concerning the Son (Matt 16:17); the Son reveals the Father (Matt. 11:27); the Holy Spirit has been given to lead us into truth (John 16:13); and the Spirit bears witness with our spirit that we are sons of God (Rom. 8:16). Are we guilty of taking our methods of presenting the Gospel and our arguments for Christian truth more seriously than we take the Spirit's power to teach and convict and assure?[6]

Take, as an example, Jesus' discussion in John 8 with the Jews. Jesus both was a Jew and a master communicator, so usual human barriers to communication do not factor in. Jesus knew how the Jews thought and the right words to communicate what He intended. But the Jews questioningly approached Jesus in the same way my two students approached me. The Jews heard Jesus talk about forgiveness of sins and eternal life. They heard Jesus tell them to believe in Him. *The Pharisees challenged him, "Here you are, appearing as your own witness; your testimony is not valid"* (John 8:13).

The reason the Jews did not understand Jesus and believe in Him had nothing to do with human factors such as language and culture. Rather it had everything to do with their **spiritual** condition. As Jesus explained, *"You are from below; I am from above. You are of this world; I am not of this world"* (John 8:23). The world **above** from which Jesus was sent is based on trusting the Father and carrying out His will. So Jesus said, *"The one who sent me is with me; he has not left me alone, for I always do what pleases him"* (John 8:29). However the world **below** is populated by people who live "independently of . . . and in opposition to" God's will.[7] This is a world "made evil" because its people refuse to believe in Christ.[8] The actual condition of these people is the opposite of what they consider it to be: "they think they are free (8:33), while they are slaves to sin (8:34); . . . they claim God as their only Father (8:41), but their father is in fact the devil (8:44)."[9]

Jesus realized the problem these Jews had with believing His word "was not intellectual, but spiritual." Jesus was very blunt.

> *"Why is my language not clear to you? Because you are unable to hear what I say. You belong to your father, the devil, and you want to carry out your father's desire. He was a murderer from the beginning, not holding to the truth, for there is no truth in him. When he lies, he speaks his native language, for he is a liar and the father of lies"* (John 8:43-44).

The Jews' acceptance of Satan's lies perverted their understanding, so they could not recognize the truth.[10] They followed Satan's evil desires. This prevented them from committing to do God's will.[11]

Take seriously the barrier between the world **above** from which Jesus was sent and the world **below** in which we live. Those who belong to this world suffer from spiritual blindness because *they exchanged the truth of God for a lie, and worshiped and served created things rather than the Creator* (Rom. 1:25).

In his book, *The Serpent of Paradise*, Erwin Lutzer writes at length about the threefold lie Satan uses to mislead people. First Satan "lies about who he is." Satan disguises himself so he can appear "to soothe, to encourage, [and] to instruct" while hiding his real intentions which mislead and destroy.

> Satan wants to keep us ignorant of the intriguing dynamics taking place in the spirit world. He wants our circumstances to appear ordinary and his traps unsuspicious. Yet behind the trap is the trapper, and behind the lie is the liar.[12]

Secondly Satan "lies about who God is." Satan wants people to doubt God's Word. He wants people to think God is untruthful and that serving God will harm them. Satan cons people with the "idea that God's way is not the best for us."[13] He is a "lying spirit" trying to convince people to blame God for their problems while they "attribute to Satan more sovereignty than he deserves."[14] If Satan can convince people the world in which they now live, which he controls, somehow is superior to God's world which Christ brings, he has them firmly in his grasp.

Thirdly Satan lies about the benefits of sin. Satan has failed in his bid to take God's place and now invites us to participate in his disaster. Satan tells people if they trust him, he will give them "special knowledge" which God tried to keep from them.[15] Satan's goal is to "persuade them to worship another god."[16]

This false religion has five major premises. These premises long have been found in traditional religions in the East but also have woven their way into the West in the guise of New Age thought. The first premise is that of **reincarnation**—a direct contradiction of Hebrews 9:27: *man is destined to die once, and after that to face judgment.* Satan uses this tactic to make his lie to Adam and Eve, *"You will not surely die,"* (Gen. 3:4) believable. In place of God's truth reincarnation promulgates the lie that human beings go through an endless round of existences which allow us all the time we need, by ourselves, to reach the goal of perfection.[17] According to reincarnation life is like having batting practice before a baseball game—we do it over and over again until we get it right. This eliminates the need we have for a personal God Who both holds us accountable and helps us.

The second premise of Satan's false religion is **esotericism**. This is working out of Satan's ancient promise to Eve that her *"eyes will be opened"* (Gen. 3:5). Most non-Christian world religions search for "enlightenment."[18] For example in the ancient Greco-Roman world Gnosticism taught the possibility of liberation from the darkness and evil of the present material world through the attainment of special knowledge.[19] The goal of Hinduism is *moksha*, or "release" from *karma*, the "law of cause and effect" which entraps people in the present world and only can be achieved by means of discovering one's "true self."[20] The adherents of Buddhism seek to escape from the suffering of personal existence through the realization of "non-existence" (*anatman*). This goal also is thought to be reached through achieving "enlightenment," or attaining spiritual truth.[21] In the materialistic West, since the **Enlightenment** in the 17th and 18th centuries, an insatiable quest for knowledge has emerged as the solution for all humanity's problems. Each case mentioned describes a search for **truth**. This desire for truth has no relationship to the God Who has revealed Himself to us in Jesus Christ. Without God humans can have knowledge but cannot know the Truth Who sets us free.

The third premise of false religion is **pantheism,** which teaches, "God is all and all is God." "Several years ago, on a TV series, Shirley MacLaine ran onto a beach shouting, 'I'm God! I'm God!'"[22] In Hinduism a person's "true self" (*atman*) is considered to be none other than god. But this is god in a depersonalized sense—god as an "it." All humans participate in this one divine nature which makes up the whole universe.[23] This sounds much like Satan's promise to Eve that she would *"be like God"* (Gen. 3:4). If this promise is true, man is god and needs no Savior other than himself.[24]

The fourth premise of Satan's false religion is **relativism**. Satan promised Adam and Eve they would *"know good and evil"* (Gen. 3:5). The basis of this knowledge was personal experience rather than God's revelation. The result is the present situation in which everyone does *"as he sees fit"* (Deut. 12:8). So what is regarded as good, right, and beautiful varies according to the language, culture, and individual.[25] When relativism is taken to its logical conclusion, the meaning of truth is lost. As Vinoth Ramachandra explains,

> There is no truth that is truth for all, no moral values that are binding for all, because universal values derive from a universal purpose and there is no purpose to human life or the universe.[26]

The final lie in Satanic religion is **hedonism**. Hedonism encourages people to seek pleasure above all else as the greatest good.[27] When people talk about their greatest desires, they usually use words such as *happiness, peace of mind,* or *personal fulfillment*, with no concern for God or eternal life. People want heaven and want it **now**! And, with Satan's enticement, they will do whatever they can to get it.

Most of the people with whom we have the opportunity to share the gospel are unprepared to hear what we have to say. This is because all they know is the present world. Their worldview has been so warped by Satan's lies that, left on their own, they are incapable of understanding God's truth. Living outside of the reality of God's mercy and grace they are convinced they have control over whatever peace and joy they will grasp. They are like the new missionary who told his seasoned colleague, "The local language is beautiful, but I have no earthly idea what it means." These are people of the world below who understand the "language" of Satan (John 8:44) but cannot comprehend the words of Zion. They cannot hear what God says because they *"do not belong to God"* (8:47). As a result they find themselves in the most desperate of all possible situations.

You Will Die in Your Sins

After His explanation of the two worlds, Jesus made His most direct statement in any of the four Gospels about the condition of people who do not believe in Him *"I told you that you would die in your sins; if you do not believe that I am the one I claim to be, you will indeed die in your sins"* (8:24). Jesus spoke from the perspective of One from above—one who both clearly saw the human condition and knew its eternal results. He left no doubt about what happens to those who fail to believe in Him: they will *"die in their sins."*

Jesus later explained, *"everyone who sins is a slave to sin"* (8:34). Sin does not consist of individual actions people can control by means of free will. Rather sin is “an alien power which takes possession of the will and makes use of the whole” person. Someone who commits sinful acts shows his or her personal enslavement to sin.[28] The grip of sin on the individual is so great that, no matter how much effort the person may expend, he or she cannot escape. This is what Paul describes when he writes on the basis of personal experience,

> *I know that nothing good lives in me, that is, in my sinful nature. For I have the desire to do what is good, but I cannot carry it out. For what I do is not the good I want to do; no, the evil I do not want to do—this I keep on doing. Now if I do what I do not want to do, it is no longer I who do it, but it is* ***sin living in me that does it*** (Rom. 7:18-20, emphasis added).

We often warn people about the perils of temptation. Satan does not have to concern himself with tempting most people. They are so caught up in the lies of the present world, they cannot easily escape the power of sin already within them. As James 1:14-15 tells us,

> *each one is tempted when, by* ***his own evil desire,*** *he is dragged away and enticed. Then, after desire has conceived, it gives birth to sin; and sin, when it is full-grown, gives birth to death* (emphasis added.)

When allowed to run its course sin inevitably leads to death (Rom. 6:23). Many people who are well on their way down this path toward destruction who have no idea of their eventual destination. *There is a way that seems right to a man, but in the end leads to death* (Prov. 14:12). Such people, who claim to be enlightened by the relativism and hedonism of the present world, are apt to say bad roads don’t exist. “All roads are good,” they say. “There are many paths to the summit of the mountain,” the Japanese explain. These hedonistic relativists insist that someone is wrong for telling people their actions are evil. They say, “Let people live a good life and enjoy themselves. You have no right to tell people they are going to hell."

Jesus' words in John 8:24 are as unpopular with the relativistic, live-and-let-live crowd of today as they were with the crowd to whom He spoke 2,000 years ago. But Jesus was not sent to earth to win a popularity contest. Jesus lived on earth to provide people with salvation. Jesus knew that to accomplish His mission He would have to tell people the truth, even when they did not want to hear it. Only people who understand the truth about Jesus and their need for Him will turn to Christ in faith. One necessary, albeit uncomfortable, part of this truth is that those who do not believe in Jesus will die in their sins. Turning to Jesus for forgiveness and life requires recognition of being a sinner.

While Jesus' statement in John 8:24 seems like condemning words, in reality, these words represent a call to salvation through faith in Him. The verse implies a twofold promise that, just as those who deny Jesus will die in their sins, those who believe in Him will be saved from death.[29] In the original Greek text the wording of John 8:24 was, *"If you do not believe that I am . . .."* The translators of the New International Version have added the words, *"the one I claim to be,"* to help us understand what Jesus meant. While this addition may give the typical reader a general sense of what Jesus was saying, it also may cause us to miss the fact that this is another *"I am"* statement, which Jesus used to identify Himself with God the Father. In this case Jesus referred to Himself.

> *"You are my witnesses," declares the Lord, "and my servant whom I have chosen, so that you may know and believe me and understand that I am he. Before me no god was formed, nor will there be one after me. I, even I, am the Lord, and apart from me there is no savior"* (Isa. 43:10-11).

Only one true God exists. He always has been God. No other god brought Him into existence. No other god will take His place. Jesus spoke from the eternal perspective of this God Who first spoke creation into existence[30] and Who now has the power to save us.[31] Jesus declared salvation from sin and death requires belief in Him.[32]

Christians sometimes hesitate to talk about sin and death. We're afraid we will drive people away. We're afraid they will see Christianity as harsh and God as unloving before they have the opportunity to hear the whole truth. But Jesus has provided us with an example of preaching the whole gospel: telling people about the results of sin as well as about the results of salvation.

Tell people what will happen if they reject Jesus, as well as what will happen if they believe in Him. Tell them the consequences of a sinful life beginning now and stretching into eternity. Saying this much will take courage. Carefully choose your timing and words. But until we have said to people, "If you do not believe in Jesus, you will die in your sins," we have not told them the whole truth.

Knowing the Truth

The crux of the issue with which we deal in this chapter is whether people believe what we are saying about Jesus is true. This is important because **this is the truth** has the power to set people free (John 8:32).

Many people have a tough time accepting the truth about Jesus. The Jewish leaders could not believe Jesus was God in the flesh sent to save them. So Jesus said they would *"die in their sins"* (8:21, 24). The two students that stopped by my office also had a difficult time accepting this truth. They left my office disappointed, because they thought Jesus' promise of eternal life was too good to be true. You probably have had similar situations—people who were interested in Christianity, who wanted to hear more about Jesus, but who just could not bring themselves to believe in Him.

If people are not willing to accept the truth about Jesus, we are left without a message to proclaim. Christianity stands or falls on this one issue: Is the gospel of Jesus Christ true or false? Nowhere is this clearer than in 1 Corinthians 15:13-19 where Paul writes,

If there is no resurrection of the dead, then not even Christ has been raised. And ***if Christ has not been raised, our preaching is useless and so is your faith****. More than that,* ***we are then found to be false witnesses about God****, for we have testified about God that he raised Christ from the dead. But he did not raise him if in fact the dead are not raised. For if the dead are not raised, then Christ has not been raised either.* ***And if Christ has not been raised, your faith is futile; you are still in your sins. Then those also who have fallen asleep in Christ are lost. If only for this life we have hope in Christ, we are to be pitied more than all men*** (emphasis added).

Notice how often in this one passage Paul writes that our faith is *useless*, *false*, *futile*, *without hope*, and *to be pitied* if this one, central tenant of the Christian faith—the resurrection of Jesus Christ—is not true. Paul basically says that if what we believe about Jesus is not true, then our commitment to Christ and the lives we have lived as Christians all have been a waste. What we believe about Jesus is that crucial.

This is why Satan has thrown everything into convincing people that what Christianity teaches about Jesus is **not true**. Satan is perfectly happy if people believe in Jesus as a good man, as a prophet, or even as one possible way of salvation. These kinds of beliefs about Jesus just help Satan confuse and prevent people from realizing the truth. What Satan does not want is for someone to take Jesus at His word. For example Satan does not want people to believe Jesus' words in John 8:24: *"if you do not believe that I am the one I claim to be, you will indeed die in your sins."* Satan does not want people to believe Jesus' words in John 14:6: *"I am the way and the truth and the life. No one comes to the Father except through me."* And Satan certainly does not want anyone to believe Jesus' words in John 3:16: *"For God loved the world so much that he gave his one and only Son, that whoever believes in him shall not perish but have eternal life."* Belief that any one of these statements Jesus made is true is enough for a person to begin moving away from sin and toward faith in Christ. The result of this road is salvation. Satan cannot bear the thought of any person receiving this gracious gift from God.

This also is why **Jesus is concerned for people to know the truth**. He said that those who really are His disciples will *"hold to"* his teaching (8:31). The word translated *hold* in the New International Version means more literally to **dwell, abide,** or **remain**. Jesus' true disciples are those who continually receive His words and dwell on them.[33] Once again this brings to mind John 6:66-68 which says the twelve decided to remain with Jesus when the rest of the crowd chose to leave. Peter explained the basis for their decision, *"You have the words of eternal life"* (6:68). The reception of the truth people seek does not result from a momentary decision to follow Christ. Many who claim to believe in Jesus quickly turn away "when they grasp the full meaning of Jesus' divinity and pre-existence."[34] Only those who remain with Jesus dwell on His words and allow them to indwell in them, so they may receive the truth that sets them free.

The truth that sets us free neither is entirely intellectual nor entirely void of intellectual content. This truth is a result not only of a subjective spiritual encounter or merely an intellectual pursuit for rational truth. The kind of truth that involves the head also changes the heart. This truth begins with **who we know** and **changes how we live**. As Morris writes,

> The kind of faith that John envisages is impossible without having a certain high view of Christ. Unless we believe that He is more than a man we can never trust Him with that faith that is saving faith.[35]

In this regard, when John repeatedly uses the expression *lift up*, he points out the significance of Jesus' death on the cross (3:14; 8:28; 12:32, 34).[36] Jesus' "greatest glory consists in His accepting the shame and humiliation of the cross in order that thereby He might bring salvation to sinful men." It only is through Jesus' "exaltation" on the cross that He draw[s] all men to [himself]*"* (12:32).[37]

The Holy Spirit uses the message of the cross to confirm the truth about Who Jesus is and what He has accomplished for us. This brings about salvation for those who believe and judgment for those who reject the message of the cross.[38] We see here the *double-edged* nature of the Word of God (Heb. 4:12). When the message of the cross cuts to the heart, it has the power either to free people from sin or to produce in them a wounded spirit that wants nothing to do with Christ.

This will depend on their response to the cross. Either they will blaspheme the Crucified One and turn away or cry out to Him, "Lord, save me, a sinner!"

On the Day of Pentecost Peter had the opportunity to explain to an amazed crowd the *"wonders of God"* (Acts. 2:11) they had seen and heard. Peter used this wonder-filled opportunity to preach to the people about the cross and resurrection of Jesus Christ:

> *"This man was handed over to you by God's set purpose and foreknowledge; and you, with the help of wicked men, put him to death by nailing him to the cross. But God raised him from the dead, freeing him from the agony of death, because it was impossible for death to keep its hold on him . . . God has made this Jesus, whom you crucified, both Lord and Christ"* (Acts 2:23-24, 36b).

When the people heard this message, *they were cut to the heart* (2:37) and cried out because of their conviction of sin. More than 3,000 people turned from their sin, confessed faith in Christ, and were baptized (2:41).

We know the faith of those who committed themselves to Christ on Pentecost was authentic not only because of their repentance, their confession, and their baptism but because of what happened afterward: *They devoted themselves to the apostles' teaching and to fellowship, to the breaking of bread and to prayer* (2:42). They continued to hear and study God's Word, they dwelt in it, and God's Word transformed their lives. God's Word, centered in the cross and resurrection of Jesus Christ, has the power to set them free.

In your desire to contextualize the gospel so our hearers understand, resist the urge to make the cross **palatable** to their hearts. When the message of the cross is understood, it may be difficult to digest. This is because the message of the cross confronts the hearer with God's love and grace in response to the hearer's own sinfulness. The message of 1 Peter 3:18 is understood and made personal within the hearer's heart: *"Christ died for your sins once for all, the righteous for the unrighteous, to bring* ***you*** *to God"* (emphasis added). Through the cross the hearer realizes he or she actually is a spiritually dead human being enslaved by sin and without hope outside of God's gift of salvation through Jesus Christ.

In this sense **contextualizing the message of the cross means sharpening the gospel sword to make certain it cuts right to the heart**. Genuine contextualization will result in the hearer understanding clearly Who Jesus is and what He has accomplished. Moreover the person who hears the contextualized gospel clearly will understand his or her own need to be set free from sin and death through faith in Jesus Christ.

Don't be satisfied with mere understanding on the part of your audience. Rather strive to proclaim the cross in a way that cuts to the heart. Only when the gospel is preached with this kind of power can genuine transformation occur. Certainly many people who hear the message will choose to reject Christ and turn away. As we have seen from our study of John chapters 6 and 8, this always has been the case. He has the power to set free those who choose to receive the message of the cross and to believe in Christ.

"Free at Last!"

On August 28, 1963, Martin Luther King Jr. spoke of his dream for moral and political freedom for all U.S. citizens. Yet King knew this dream would remain unrealized unless people also experienced a corresponding spiritual freedom from sin. So Martin Luther King Jr. told his audience,

> In the process of gaining our rightful place we must not be guilty of wrongful deeds. Let us not seek to satisfy our thirst for freedom by drinking from the cup of bitterness and hatred. We must forever conduct our struggle on the high plane of dignity and discipline. We must not allow our protest to degenerate into physical violence. Again and again we must rise to the majestic heights of meeting physical force with soul force.[39]

When people commit to follow Christ and live in accordance with His Word, true freedom results. This is the freedom that results not only from knowing about Christ but **personally knowing Christ**. Jesus did not say He was sent only to teach the truth. Rather Jesus said, *"**I am . . . the truth**"* (John 14:6, emphasis added). The freedom received from knowing Christ is a synonym for the Christian experience of salvation.[40] As Jesus says in prayer to the Father, *"Now this is eternal life: that they may **know you**, the only true God, and Jesus Christ, whom you have sent"* (John 17:3, emphasis added). This personal knowledge of God from a relationship with Jesus Christ is the "truth which saves [people] from the darkness of sin."[41] When a person's heart is freed from bondage to sin, that person's also becomes free to carry out God's purpose and plan for his or her life.[42]

Unfortunately many people do not realize they are in spiritual bondage. This is because they tend to see themselves from the vantage point of one or more other conditions—political, social, economic, or even physical.[43] People view themselves either as politically free or not, socially advantaged or disadvantaged, economically prosperous or poor, or physically healthy or ill. So they fail to ascertain the reality of their spiritual condition: **they are slaves to sin in Satan's evil empire**.[44] This spiritual slavery does not result from ethnicity, language, culture, or social class. Rather they are in spiritual bondage because of choosing to live in accordance with Satan's lies.[45]

This condition of spiritual slavery will continue to be their experience unless people hear God's Word and abide in Him. Only when the power of God's truth is revealed can the power of Satan's lie be broken.[46] Purposely, carefully, and forcefully continue to proclaim the cross and resurrection of Jesus Christ. Unless beforehand we have made the decision **purposefully** to focus on Christ, we all too easily will find ourselves talking about other things. **Carefully** proclaim Christ in a contextualized manner to insure what you say is understood clearly and cuts to our hearers' hearts. Also **forcefully** proclaim Christ and urge people to turn from their sin now and to believe in Jesus as Savior and Lord.

Don't forget that only the truth about Christ we proclaim has the power to free people from Satan, sin, and death. In Revelation John writes of his vision of the redeemed of all nations who will join their hearts and voices together in praise: *"Salvation belongs to our God, who sits on the throne, and to the Lamb"* (7:10). The crucified and risen Lamb is the object of their praise because of what He has accomplished: "*You were slain, and with your blood you purchased men for God from every tribe and people and language and nation*" (5:9). A loud voice from heaven explains those who have been saved *"overcame* [Satan] *by the blood of the Lamb and by the word of their testimony"* (12:11). I can imagine one day this great throng might break into the refrain of that old spiritual: "Free at last! Free at last! Thank God Almighty, we are free at last!"

Responding to His Voice

1. How much has the "world below" prevented you from knowing God's truth?

2. Each day do you take time to dwell in the truth of God's Word?

3. To what extent have you allowed God's truth into your heart to free you from bondage to Satan's lies?

4. When preaching or teaching do you ever compromise the truth about Jesus in order to be accepted by hearers?

Chapter 8

The Shepherd's Love

"I am the good shepherd; I know my sheep and my sheep know me—just as the Father knows me and I know the Father—and I lay down my life for the sheep. I have other sheep that are not of this sheep pen. I must bring them also. They too will listen to my voice, and there will be one flock and one shepherd. The reason my Father loves me is that I lay down my life—only to take it up again. No one takes it from me, but I lay it down of my own accord. I have authority to lay it down and authority to take it up again. This command I received from my Father" (John 10:14-18).

Is Your Life Entrusted Life to the Shepherd's Care?

A few years ago my family and I were in Richmond, VA, as we took care of some business related to our work as missionaries. After being in Richmond for about one month, we packed for our return to Japan. Tuesday morning was laundry day. I had to take our clothes down to the hotel laundry room to wash, dry, and fold them so we could pack them away. We were planning to leave on Thursday and did not want to procrastinate until the last minute.

Carrying a load of clothes I passed through the hotel lobby. On the way back to our room a member of the hotel staff, whom we got to know during our stay, suddenly pulled me aside and said, "I think that you need to see this!" She took me into the hotel lounge, where I found 30 pairs of eyes glued to the picture unfolding before us on the large-screen television. Minutes before a jet had crashed into the North Tower of the World Trade Center in New York City. Then, as we looked on in horror, a second airplane crashed into the World Trade Center's South Tower. Reportedly, a few minutes later, a third plane crashed into the Pentagon in northern Virginia, only about 90 miles from Richmond. The hotel employee turned to me and said, "Kelly, please go back to your room and pray." On September 11, 2001, all air travel in the U.S. air space indefinitely was canceled.

The next week, when we finally got a flight out of Richmond, Molly and I sensed the world dramatically would change. A sense of darkness and fear, before absent, pervaded everything. As we boarded our plane, Molly and I wondered whether we were doing the right thing as we subjected ourselves and our children to the possibility of being the next victims of a terrorist attack on our way to Tokyo. Airport security officials repeatedly and meticulously searched our luggage to insure we were not terrorists.

The whole world now is caught up in a culture of death. People live apprehensively. They think they may be injured or killed in the ongoing violence filling our globe. Several missionary colleagues have been killed by terrorist attacks in East Asia and the Middle East. Hundreds of people were killed in Spain when railroad stations in Madrid were bombed. Both military personnel and civilians are killed each day by ongoing fighting in Israel, Palestine, Iraq, and Afghanistan. All of us live under tightened security as civil authorities brace for possible future attacks.

People want to blame someone for the current cycle of destruction and death, whether it be Al Qaeda terrorists, militant Islamic extremists, or the U.S. and its Western allies, who dominate the world with their economic and military power. However such finger-pointing only leads to greater divisiveness which, in turn, leads to more violence, destruction, and death.

We have only ourselves to blame for the havoc and slaughter now going on. All of us are at fault. All of us share the blame for the pattern of violence which now engulfs us. We have been unable to leave behind the hatred and prejudice, which separates us. As James aptly reminds us,

> *What causes fights and quarrels among you? Don't they come from your desires that battle within you? You want something but don't get it. You kill and covet, but you cannot have what you want. You quarrel and fight. You do not have, because you do not ask God. When you ask, you do not receive, because you ask with wrong motives, that you may spend what you get on pleasures* (4:1-3).

No amount of human ingenuity and activity can resolve this dilemma. When people refuse to listen to one another, diplomacy is ineffective. Warfare determines who is stronger and not who is right. Humanitarian action may address physical and psychological needs. But it does not deal with the underlying heart issues between us.

We are like two boys who fought every day after school. These boys were not bullies. They were both very likable. Each one had many friends. They did not like to fight. Their problem was they had some issue between them they simply could not resolve by themselves. And so, not knowing what else to do, they fought day after day. They hoped, somehow, the issue about which they fought would work out. But fighting could not solve their problems. This continued until one day a caring teacher happened by the vacant lot where the two boys slugged it out. The teacher got the two boys to stop fighting and talked with them about why they were fighting, about the disagreements they had with each other, and how these could be resolved. The teacher's intervention brought peace between these boys that they could not find themselves.

Like these two boys we need outside intervention from Someone Who cares. We need Someone Who will take us by the hand and lead us to a place in which we can experience peace and rest. We need Someone Who will overpower our hatred with His love—Someone Who will overshadow our distrust for one another with His utter trustworthiness—Someone Who will show us how to live at peace in the midst of death and destruction. The only One Who can do these things is Jesus. He is the Good Shepherd (John 10:14). Through Him we can experience the Shepherd's love.

One Shepherd, One Flock

Many voices in the world cry out to men and women and offer them hope for life in a better world. Tasker writes,

> They bid . . . people rely upon political alliances with foreign powers rather than upon God Himself. They give 'religious' support to the policies of reigning monarchs for the sake of personal gain in a manner contrary to the divine will. They encourage men to trust in themselves, as though, forsooth, sinful men could ever justify themselves in the eyes of the holy God.[1]

Jesus said those Who mislead people into believing such false hope are like *"thieves and robbers"* (John 10:8, 10). They are "spiritual charlatans" whose grandiose promises rob people of the "salvation that might otherwise be theirs."[2] All of these people, whether politicians, priests, or prognosticators, claim they can open doors that lead to a better life. But, in reality, these false promises only confuse people, enslave them to false hopes, divide them from one another, and rob them of joy.[3]

World leaders who make false promises are part of the system controlled by the *"prince of this world"* (John 12:31; 14:30; 16:11). When they mislead people into believing false hope rather than trusting in Jesus, these leaders are being duped—often unwittingly—into being used as tools for Satan's lying schemes. When he speaks through their eloquent voices, Satan exercises his authority over a domain which rightfully belongs to God. Satan is ***the thief*** who *comes only to steal and kill and destroy* (John 10:10, emphasis added). Everything Satan touches turns to rubble in his hands.

In contrast Jesus said He is the only way for people to have the life which they seek. *"I am the gate for the sheep"* (10:7), Jesus said, *"I am the gate; whoever enters through me will be saved"* (10:9). As *the gate*, Jesus is the "entrance into salvation." Simultaneously, as the Good Shepherd, He also is the "One who cares for the sheep and provides for their salvation at the cost of his life."[4] Jesus has entered this dark world from the heavenly kingdom of light. He broke down the dominion of satanic lies with God's trust and provided a way of life totally unavailable without Him. Jesus said, *"I have come that they may have life and have it to the full"* (10:10).

Although the imagery is inverted, in Luke 11:21-22 Jesus conveys the same idea :

> *"When a strong man, fully armed, guards his own house, his possessions are safe. But when someone stronger attacks and overpowers him, he takes away the armor in which the man trusted and divides up the spoils."*

In this parable Satan, armed with the power of his lies, is the *"strong man"* who guards the present world. When Jesus, Who is stronger, breaks in, He takes away the power of Satan's lies and frees those under his control.

Jesus said, *"I tell you the truth, the man who does not enter the sheep pen by the gate, but climbs in by some other way, is a thief and a robber"* (John 10:1). All who seek to lead people to life or introduce them to God do so by bringing them through Christ. To do so those who guide others first enter through the *gate* themselves. Otherwise their words about Jesus would be a mockery of God's truth.[5] Living a lie while they pretend to proclaim God's truth is extremely dangerous. Eventually the lie will be exposed; the *thief* will be shut out.

This brings to mind Simon the Samaritan, a sorcerer who sought the power to impart the Holy Spirit to others by laying on hands. Peter rebuked Simon, *"You have no part or share in this ministry, because your heart is not right with God"* (Acts 8:21). Simon could not share what he did not have. Simon never had experienced in his own life the transforming power of the Holy Spirit, so he could not pass the Spirit on to anyone else.

Another example is the story of the seven sons of Sceva who drove out evil spirits *"in the name of Jesus, whom Paul preaches."* One day an evil spirit answered them, *"Jesus I know, and Paul I know, but who are you?"* The evil spirit *overpowered them*, beat them up, and sent them away running and screaming into the night (Acts 19:13-16). As long as these sons of Sceva still were locked in Satan's prison, they did not have the key to unlock anyone else's door. While these men still were under domination of evil spirits themselves, they were not in a position to free others.

Jesus said all of those who hear His voice seek Him. So *"there shall be one flock and one shepherd"* (John 10:16). God's will is not that His people remain divided amongst one another by such human barriers as language, culture, and ethnicity. Even doctrinal disparity and denominationalism are no excuse for the division which now exist in the Body of Christ. God's people are to "become united in one flock . . . under the leadership of one shepherd."[6] Believers in Christ join together as a result of their "common faith in him."[7] If I may clarify Paul's words, *"one body"* exists precisely because only *"one Spirit . . . one Lord, one faith, one baptism; one God and Father of all, who is over all and through all and in all"* exists (Eph. 4:4, 5-6). We are to be one flock—one people of God, because Christ has chosen to make us one.

The greatest potential expression of Christ's power before the world is Christian unity. I am talking about genuine unity brought about by God's Spirit working among those who trust Jesus and follow Him as Lord. *"For we were all baptized by one Spirit into one body—whether Jews or Greeks, slave or free—and we were all given one Spirit to drink"* (1 Cor. 12:13). Only God's Spirit has the power to bring unity out of disparity, which now exists between men and women; people of diverse ages and life experiences; people of all nations, cultures, and languages. Only among those who trust in Christ can the promise of God's Word be realized: *"Once you were not a people, but now you are the people of God; once you had not received mercy, but now you have received mercy"* (1 Pet. 2:10). As Tom Wright has written, "God is calling for himself a people who are both the objects of his special love and the instruments through whom he will extend that love to the world."[8]

Unfortunately, at this juncture in history, this powerful potential for witness through Christian unity has been muted. Jesus plans to bring us together. Satan plans to tear us apart. One of Satan's primary strategies *vis-a-vis* the church is to divide and conquer. What he planned seems to be going all too well. Christ's body has been fractured by dispute over theology, church, and mission. If a limb of a body does not seem to be working properly, we seem content to amputate now and ask questions later. Imagine how filled with joy Satan is when denominations, churches, and families argue, fight, and go their separate ways. Christ never wills for His people to do such things. God never is glorified when we do. Often we forget that not we, but Jesus Christ, is the head of His body. Jesus' will is that all who hear His voice seek Him in faith, so Christians can be unified as one body, one people, and one flock.

I am not talking about the quest for denominational unity that has fueled the ecumenical movement since the early 20th century. What I mean is **spiritual unity** based on a common commitment to Jesus Christ. Those who trust Jesus for salvation covenant together to love each other and allow that love to become the basis for their actions. God's love that He has made known to us through Christ (1 John 4:10) can reverberate throughout the church and overflow into the world. His love can be *"made complete in us"* (4:12). The church can become one body united in love for one another. When Christ's voice bids us toward Him, we have all said *yes*. These two inseparable aspects of Christian unity are woven together beautifully in the words of 1 John 3:23, *This is his command: to believe in the name of his Son, Jesus Christ, and to love one another as he commanded us.* Only when those who hear Christ's voice join together in love for each other will the world clearly hear and powerfully experience the unadulterated Word of God.

His Sheep Hear His Voice

People in today's society daily are inundated by a multitude of voices crying out for their attention. This message may be as simple as what we eat (will it be a burger and fries or low-carb/low fat?) or as complicated as the meaning of truth—is it absolute, relative, or non-existent? With building waves of disconnected and contradictory messages continually pouring in from all sides, people find themselves crying out for help, while they drown in a sea of noise. Wolfgang Simpson refers to this condition when he writes,

> We have many radicals today, in both generations, most of them growing up into rebels. A rebel is a radical without the father's—or the son's—heart. He is left with one of the deepest traumas anyone can have: he is lost in the generation stream without a secure anchor and has become a spiritual orphan . . .. Spiritual fathering is one of the greatest needs of today's Generation X, many of them unable to believe in the consistent and unfailing love of the Father in heaven because of their fathers on earth. They are over entertained and underfathered. They are spiritual orphans.[9]

The New Testament tells us that spiritually lost orphans, unable to find the truth, in today's world wander around aimlessly and are inundated by an endless barrage of messages. Those who are lost in the present world end up stumbling into eternity without God.

God is deeply distressed by this condition of human **lostness**. He did not intend for humans, the pinnacle of His creation, to wander through life without direction and hope. So God sent His Son into the world to save people from **lostness**. Jesus responded to human **lostness** when He explained the purpose of His entire ministry on earth, "*The Son of Man came to seek and to save what was lost*" (Luke 19:10). When Jesus *saw the crowds, he had compassion on them, because they were harassed and helpless, like a sheep without a shepherd* (Matt. 9:36).

Jesus responded to the **lostness** of the crowds by sending out His disciples. He commissioned them with these words, *"The harvest is plentiful but the workers are few. Ask the Lord of the harvest, therefore, to send out workers into his harvest field"* (9:37-38). Jesus sent out His disciples as *"sheep among wolves"* (10:16). He sent them out to preach and teach, to heal the sick, and to cast out evil spirits (Matt. 10:1-42). But they were not to do any of these things in their own strength. They were to be guarded in their actions but bold in their witness, because the Holy Spirit would speak through them (10:17-20). David Bosch comments on this point,

> Mission never takes place in self-confidence, but in the knowledge of our own weakness, at a point of crisis where danger and opportunity come together.[10]

The **lostness of the world** continues to be the reason for missions and evangelism in our own day. Today the crowds on the streets of Shanghai, New York, and Cairo are just as lost as the crowds Jesus met on the streets of Jerusalem 2,000 years ago were. In spite of their veneer of self-sufficiency and independence, these modern-day sheep, knowing neither where they are going nor the way to get there, equally are harassed and helpless.

Perhaps one reason we are reluctant to make too much of this shepherd-sheep motif in missions and evangelism is that it too strongly suggests our own inadequacy. We cannot think about the helplessness of those who do not know Jesus without admitting our own complete dependence on Him as well. Remove all pretension of self-sufficiency and admit all of the missiological theory, strategy, and planning in which you engage are useless **unless** the Good Shepherd guides you. When all is said and done, we still only are sheep serving God in a world of wolves. We utterly are defenseless and without hope of accomplishing anything unless God's Spirit works in us.

The lost sheep in Jesus' story was unable to find its way home. Someone had to go out and find the sheep (Luke 15:3-6). John Ortberg writes,

> Sheep are notorious creatures of habit. Left to themselves they will follow a trail until it becomes a rut, graze hills until they turn into desert wastelands, pollute the ground from which they feed until corrupted with disease and parasites . . . Sheep are followers. If one sheep goes over the

> cliff a whole flock could follow. You'd think somewhere along the lines one sheep would notice, would stop and think . . . This never happens.[11]

This is the condition in which people without a personal relationship with Jesus Christ find themselves. *We all, like sheep, have gone astray, each of us has turned to his own way . . .* (Isa. 53:6). While every religion claims to have arisen out of the human search for God, in reality, religion is the expression of "foolish, darkened hearts" of humans who have *exchanged the truth of God for a lie, and worshiped and served created things rather than the Creator* (Rom. 1:21, 25). Ortberg compares this spiritual condition to a game of hide-and-seek in which God is It—therefore God seeks us. We hide behind our "rationalizations and denials" for fear of finding out the truth about God and the truth about ourselves. In this spiritual game of hide-and-seek,

> The irony is that I hide because I'm afraid that if the full truth about me is known I won't be loved. But whatever is **hidden** cannot be **loved**. I can only be loved to the extent that I am known. I can only be **fully** loved if I am **fully** known.[12]

Only when people hear the Good Shepherd and respond to His voice do they discover the truth about themselves and the purpose for which God created them. Jesus said, *"his sheep follow him because they know his voice"* (John 10:4). *"I know my sheep and my sheep know me,"* Jesus said, *"just as the Father knows me and I know the Father"* (John 10:14, 15). *"He calls his own sheep by name and leads them out"* (John 10:3). The sheep respond to the Shepherd because they know His voice, "but they do not know and do not respond to that of a stranger."[13] Like the knowledge between Father and Son, Jesus has an "intimate", personal knowledge with His followers.[14]

Although the word never appears in John 10, underlying this relationship between the Good Shepherd and His sheep is a deep sense of **trust**. On the one hand the Shepherd has proven to His sheep **He is worthy of their trust**. He has guided them for a long time and never led them astray. Many times the Shepherd has led them safely from the sheep pen to the green pastures and then home again.

On the other hand, when they hear His voice, the sheep are willing to obey the Shepherd because **they trust Him.** They have no reason to yield to a stranger's voice when this Shepherd, whom they know so well, always has provided everything they need. **This kind of personal trust is meant when Christians talk about faith in Christ or faith in God**. As Andy Stanley writes,

> Faith is confidence that God is who he says he is and that he will do what he has promised to do. Faith is not a power, force, or vehicle by which we can coerce God into something against His will. Faith simply is an expression of confidence in the person and character of God.[15]

When people hear the Good Shepherd's voice and trust in Him, their lostness and fear are transformed into a life lived in the light of Christ's love. The bewilderment of hearing many voices but not knowing to which to turn is replaced by the security of hearing the One whose voice of truth clearly says, "*Follow me*." Rick Ferguson delineates four aspects of this new security. First, in following the voice of Christ, people find **security in their relationship with God the Father**. They experience the joy of being called *God's children* (John 1:12) and of calling God *Father* (Rom. 8:15). They develop a relationship with God Who created them and Who, based on His love, unconditionally accepts them.[16]

Second, through following Jesus, they find **a secure purpose in life**. Their lives and schedules no longer are driven by meeting societal expectations or by gaining the approval from those around them. As a result they are free from the destructive bondage to sin, which controls the lives of most people in the present world. Instead they are driven by the desire to know God's will and to fulfill His purpose for their lives.[17]

Third they have a **secure future**. Since they trust God for their future, they no longer have to manipulate the present to make sure things go their way.[18] This is because the Lord Who guides the next step knows the way that leads home. He can be trusted to *make* [their] *paths straight* (Prov. 3:6). They have put their trust in the One Who has promised, *The path of the righteous is like the first gleam of dawn, shining ever brighter till the full light of day* (Prov. 4:18).

Finally those who follow the Good Shepherd are **secure in their individual identity**. They no longer have to prove to themselves or anyone else who they are. Rather their identity is "totally wrapped up in Christ."[19] Ferguson beautifully states the new identity of a believer in Christ when he writes,

> His power has become your power. His authority has become your authority. His glory has become your glory. His righteousness has become your righteousness. His wisdom has become your wisdom. His acceptance before the Father has become your acceptance before the Father. His possessions are now your possessions.[20]

The Shepherd's Sacrifice

Jesus said, *"I am the good shepherd . . . and I lay down my life for the sheep"* (John 10:14, 15). Because of our unfamiliarity with pastoral life in the first-century Palestine, the significance of Jesus' words largely is lost. We can appreciate the Shepherd's willingness to give up His own life for His sheep. But we tend to **miss the uniqueness of the Shepherd's sacrifice**. At that time, unless accidental, a shepherd dying in defense of his sheep was rare. The general idea was that the shepherd would **live** for his sheep. If the shepherd died, no one would lead the sheep. If he died, the sheep would scatter.[21]

Jesus contrasted His own work with that of all other shepherds—both good and bad. While even a **good shepherd** did not voluntarily give up his own life for his sheep, the **Good Shepherd** did. His death for His sheep was not an accident. Rather the Good Shepherd died for His sheep according to a set plan, so they could have life through Him.[22] In this final act of self-sacrifice, the Good Shepherd overcame His sheep's "greatest danger . . . the mightiest thief, the evil one."[23]

Fredrikson tells us, the Good Shepherd laid down His life because of "knowing love."[24] The Shepherd knows each of His sheep intimately enough to call them by name and willingly gives His life for them. Consider Romans. Not only because *Christ died for the ungodly* (5:6) or even that *while we were still sinners, Christ died for us* (5:8) are we to be amazed. But Christ, knowing the most intimate details of our every sin, still loved us enough to die for us. Through this "knowing love" Jesus provided us with forgiveness of sin. He freed us from the leverage Satan uses to control us.

Jesus was willing to die for us when no one else would. He is "for us." John Ortberg writes,

> If I love someone, it means that I have certain hopes and intentions and wishes for them. I'm in their corner. I long for them to flourish and blossom. I want them to realize all their potential. I want them to be filled with virtue and moral beauty . . . Love longs for the other to enter into the splendor God intended—no spots, no wrinkles, no blemishes. Removal of spots and blemishes is almost never pain free.[25]

God made him who had no sin to be sin for us, so that in him we might become the righteousness of God (2 Cor. 5:21). Because of Jesus' love for us He willingly took the pain of our sin, with all of its associated spots, wrinkles, and blemishes, on Himself. Jesus did this because He wants us to realize our full potential; He wants us to flourish and blossom—to experience all of the virtue and moral beauty God intends for us. In this way Jesus enables us to reach for the *glory of God* which we were unable to attain by ourselves because of our sin (Rom. 3:23). Certainly we will not attain this glory in the present life. At least, through Christ, we are able to take baby steps in that direction. The Good Shepherd has set us on the *path of righteousness . . . shining ever brighter till the full light of day* (Prov. 4:18).

This is why, while the world cringes at the cross, those who have committed their lives to Christ glory in it. On the cross Jesus took the full force of the evil power of this present world on Himself and defeated it. Tom Wright talks about how Jesus' death on the cross brought victory over evil.

> To say that the evil of the whole world was heaped onto Jesus on the cross is not simply to deal with theological abstractions. It is to speak of historical events . . . The victory of the cross is a victory that was won at the moment of Jesus' death. It was the victory of weakness over strength, the victory of love over hatred . . . In Jesus, God and the world meet, and on the cross God takes onto himself the full force of the evil that his creatures have devised. The astonishing truth of the cross is that, faced with his creation in ruins, God does not reject it. He redeems it . . . The cross shows precisely the radical nature of evil and the even more radical measures that God had to take to deal with it.[26]

The greatest gift a person gives for a cause is his or her life. Because this person is willing to sacrifice for something, he or she has "moral authority." Andy Stanley writes,

> Untested devotion does little to move the hearts of others. But once you demonstrate your commitment by personal sacrifice for the sake of the cause, your potential escalates considerably.[27]

When we theologically speak of the work of Christ, we tend to make big-picture, universal statements such as, "God sent His Son to free the world from sin," or "God sent His Son to defeat evil powers." While true, these statements do not capture the full weight of what Jesus accomplished. The **personal aspect** has been left out. To use Stanley's words, we cannot comprehend the "moral authority" of Christ by thinking of His sacrifice in terms of a "cause." Jesus did not just die because of sin but, rather, **for our sins**. **The Good Shepherd laid down His life**, not only because He was concerned about evil, but because He loved His sheep. As Jesus said,

> *"Greater love has no one than this, that one lay down his life for his friends.* ***You are my friends*** *if you do what I command"* (John 15:13-14, emphasis added.)

Jesus' willingness to lay down His life for us strengthens His voice and empowers His words, *"Follow me."* Indeed the word of the cross beckons men and women from all nations to disentangle themselves from their corner of the world and to follow Christ. The call to follow Jesus most clearly is understood when people understand the message of the cross. Here, on the summit of Golgotha, they see the weight of their own sins laid on the Savior's back. Here they experience the purifying power of His love. Here they clearly are confronted with the cost of discipleship. Jesus said, *"If anyone would come after me, he must deny himself and take up his cross daily and follow me"* (Luke 9:23). How can anyone consider the agony Jesus endured for us and miss the truth that those who follow Him also pay a price?

Center clear proclamation of the gospel on the love of the Good Shepherd, Who willingly laid down His life for us. When the Shepherd's sacrifice is emphasized, His voice speaks clearly above the din of the present world. He calls each of His sheep by name and tells them, "*Follow me*."

Laying Life Down to Take it Up Again

As I write this chapter, a friend of our family lies in a hospice ward suffering through the final stages of colon cancer. She has known missionaries for more than 20 years and has heard the gospel many times. She says she loves Jesus but so far has failed to give clear affirmation of faith in Him. Now she says she has difficulty believing in a God Who would allow her life to end with such suffering, and cause her to leave a husband and two daughters in great despair. Our friend's problem is not believing that God exists, but believing that she can trust Him. As this dear friend travels through her final days of life on earth, we continue to pray for her. We hope, somehow, she will trust in Jesus and find peace and rest in Him.

Trusting in Christ brings new hope unavailable from any other source. Belief in Jesus is linked with His promise to *"prepare a place"* for us (John 14:1-4). This hope is based on Jesus' authority not only to *"lay down his life"* but also to *"take it up again"* (John 10:17-18). In contrast to people who agonize at the point of death because they believe in nothing beyond the grave, Jesus continued to hope, even while He endured brutal scourging and death on the cross. Jesus did not give up hope, because He knew His death, rather than an end in itself, was related to a higher, more glorious purpose. Jesus died "**in order that** he may rise again"[28] Here, in the "cross and the resurrection, are two sides of one redemptive act" which Jesus accomplishes for the salvation of all who trust in Him.[29] As John Stott reminds us,

> The hope of glory makes suffering bearable. The essential perspective to develop is that of the eternal purpose of God, which is to make us holy and Christlike . . . The future prospect which makes suffering endurable, then, is not a reward in the form of a 'prize,' which might lead us to say 'no pain, no palm' or 'no cross, no crown,' but the only reward of priceless value, namely the glory of Christ, his own image perfectly recreated within us. 'We shall be like him, for we shall see him as he is' (1 John 3:2).[30]

God Himself experienced catastrophe and tragedy as only one chapter in the unfolding story of His glory.[31] Through the One Who "laid down his life" and "took it up again", we can see every moment in life from an **eternal perspective**. This eternal perspective helps us understand the **suffering we now endure only is a temporary, fleeting moment on the way to eternal joy in the presence of God**.

So, as strange as this may seem to those who do not believe in Christ, Christians can find a purpose for the suffering which we endure in this present world. Our present suffering points us to our need for Christ, causes us to trust in Him, and re-shapes our character to make us more like Jesus. Like Paul we are able to rejoice *in weaknesses, in insult, in hardships, in persecutions, in difficulties,* because during those times we have the greatest sense of *Christ's power* at work in our lives (2 Cor. 12:9-10). In the midst of pain, suffering, and death we are struck with the awesome truth that life is not our possession by right but, rather, a gift endowed to us by God's grace.

> *We have this treasure in jars of clay to show that this all-surpassing power is from God and now from us. We are hard pressed on every side, but not crushed; perplexed, but not in despair; persecuted, but not abandoned; struck down, but not destroyed. We always carry around in our body the death of Jesus, so that the life of Jesus may also be revealed in our body. For we who are alive are always being given over to death for Jesus' sake, so that his life may be revealed in our mortal body. So then, death is at work in us, but life is at work in you* (2 Cor. 4:7-12).

This is one reason the gospel is good news for an embattled world. The only way to really live in the midst of a world of death is to lay down our lives at the foot of the cross. The psalmist tells us to place our lives in the hands of the Shepherd Who is able to guide us *through the valley of the shadow of death* (Ps. 23:4).

Whether distressed by terrorism or death's darkness knocking on our door, we may be comforted by the Good Shepherd Who feels all our pain and understands all our fears. The Good Shepherd goes into the world. He calls each one of His sheep by name and says, *"Come to me, all you who are weary and burdened, and I will give you rest"* (Matt. 11:28).

Responding to His Voice

1. Do you hear the voice of the Good Shepherd speaking to you above the din of the world's noise?

2. Do your relationships with other Christians bear witness to the power of the unity that results when all of Jesus' sheep listen to his voice?

3. How do you respond to the truth that Jesus knows in detail about all of your sins but still loved you enough to die for you?

4. Have you laid every aspect of your life at the foot of the cross, so Jesus can enable you to take them up again?

Chapter 9

Through Death to Life

Now a man named Lazarus was sick . . . So the sisters sent word to Jesus, "Lord, the one you love is sick." When he heard this, Jesus said, "This sickness will not end in death. No, it is for God's glory so that God's Son may be glorified through it." . . .

Jesus said to [Martha], *"I am the resurrection and the life. He who believes in me will live, even though he dies; and whoever lives and believes in me will never die. Do you believe this?"*

"Yes, Lord," she told him, "I believe that you are the Christ, the Son of God, who has come into the world" (John 11:1a, 3-4, 25-27).

Does Faith in the Resurrected Jesus Impact Your Life?

An old gospel song speaks of the Christian hope that someday we eternally will dwell in the "land of cloudless day." We look forward to that eternal day because, in this life, our day always is under a dark cloud as we pass through the *valley of the shadow of death* (Ps. 23:4). Each day confronts us with the momentary nature of our present existence. Our lives on earth are like a breath of wind which passes suddenly and does not return. We are like flickering candles soon snuffed out with the onset of darkness. The psalmist, intensely aware of this mortality, says to the Lord,

You sweep men away in the sleep of death;
they are like the new grass of the morning—
though in the morning it springs up new,
by evening it is dry and withered (Ps. 90:5-6).

Recently I was in America celebrating, with family and friends, my father's 70th birthday. This gave me the opportunity to see some old photographs taken of my dad when he was a young boy. I noticed the freshness and innocence of his new face in the spring of life and then thought about the force of 70 winters now past. Aging does something to people. Years of working in the cotton field and carrying mail caused the young boy's fair face to become rough and darkly tanned. Over time nagging health concerns brought on the regular use of prescription drugs. Like most Americans these days my dad talks about the need to get more exercise and take off some weight. As we celebrated his special day together, I did my best to take in the moment. I knew that special moments such as these are rare. We never know when the grass, now withering, will pass away—when the dark cloud will pass over our pleasant corner of the world and blot out the light of day.

One day I received an email asking me to pray for a former missionary in Japan who taught me while I was a university student. Our paths crossed at an important juncture of life. I had experienced a call to missions in Japan and decided to begin studying the Japanese language. This former missionary took me under his wing. He not only introduced me to the Japanese language and culture, he also taught me what loving Japanese people means. Through the years since then he often reminds me of the price to be paid, so that the Japanese people would turn to faith in Christ. He continually prayed for me, encouraged me when I was discouraged, asked probing questions to correct my thinking when I was off-course, and provided words of wisdom from his own missionary experience. In short he has been a perfect mentor. According to the email he was fighting for his life. I lifted him up in prayer. I knew that, without a work of God, the light of his present life soon would be snuffed out.

One of the problems with death is that it usually is not instantaneous. Unlike the candle, the snuffing-out process for us can be slow and painful. The dark valley we pass through can be long and treacherous, with many ups and downs. The aging process takes its toll. Small children with birth defects and people diagnosed with terminal diseases may linger for weeks, months, or even years.

Those wounded in battle lie in hospital beds for what seems like an eternity before they finally pass into eternity. Sometimes we say to God, "We understand the need for death. But why do people suffer so much in the process of passing from this life? Lord, if you are going to take them, can't you do it quickly?"

The classic formulation of this issue is, "If God is all-powerful and all-good, why do good, innocent people suffer so much?" This poses one of the great problems evangelization faces today. Many people, such as our friend dying of colon cancer, ask, "If God loves me, why would He allow me to experience suffering before I die and leave a husband and two daughters behind to struggle without me?"[1] Why do thousands of innocent children die every year as a result of hunger and disease? And why do many non-combatant civilians die as the armies of the world wage war? For that matter why do soldiers die needlessly simply because their nations' leaders tell them to fight? If God allows people to endure such great suffering as they pass from this life, why entrust the next life into His care?

The Word of God provides us with a response to these different and important questions. Know that the God Who created and loves us is **not** the author of evil. Evil is a result of Satan's work. Stephen Noll writes that we often "minimize the hostility of Satan."[2] He is the *"prince of this world"* (John 12:31; 14:30) who is bent on destroying everything in his temporary domain, because he cannot have it permanently. This is why creation is *subjected to frustration*—waiting to be *liberated from its bondage to decay* (Rom. 8:20, 21). This also is why so much evil seems to occur without fulfilling any good purpose. **Evil, in itself, has no good purpose**. Evil is the result of bad choices made by Satan, evil spirits, and fallen human beings whose resulting actions bring about the destructive and chaotic world in which we now live.[3]

But the gospel tells us the suffering we endure during this life does not **have to be** a purposeless movement into oblivion. Somehow God and His Son, Jesus, can be glorified through it. God's will was not that Lazarus' sickness *end in death* (John 11:4). His will for the suffering is not that they endure either. God's hope is that He may redeem these evil events and use them for His glory! John Ortberg writes,

> The pain and suffering and sin of this world leads on to the cross. Always the cross. And somehow it is in the cross that the glory of God is finally revealed.[4]

This is because, as the old hymn says, "The way of the cross leads home." For Jesus the road to the resurrection went by the way of the cross. Only He could reach the garden tomb by crossing the steps of Calvary. So, for us also, the way to eternal life passes through suffering and the grave. But the suffering we endure can accomplish a higher purpose. The gospel tells us of hope for an "unclouded day" when we will behold the glorious face of the One Who said, *"I am the resurrection and the life"* (John 11:25).

This Sickness . . . is for God's Glory

Jesus did not rush to the aid of his friend when He heard of Lazarus' sickness. Rather, before He set out for Bethany, Jesus remained where He was for two more days (John 11:6). From a human perspective this decision is difficult to understand. Martha certainly was correct in saying to Jesus, when she met Him, *"Lord, if you had been here my brother would not have died"* (John 11:21). Repeatedly Jesus had displayed His power to heal the sick, the leprous, the lame, the deaf, and the blind. Doubtless Jesus could have healed Lazarus as well.

While, from a human perspective, preventing Lazarus' death would have been the most loving course of action Jesus could have followed, John 11:4 lifts the veil on the **divine perspective**, so we can see suffering and death from God's point of view. In this verse Jesus told His disciples, *"This sickness will not end in death. No, it is* ***for God's glory*** *so that* **God's Son may be glorified** *through it"* (emphasis added). Jesus was not "callous" about Lazarus' condition. He did not want to show He had the power to overcome death as well as illness and disease. Rather Jesus wanted to show how God's glory can extend beyond our physical life on earth and through death to the resurrection life which awaits us beyond the grave. "In other words, Jesus operates from a point of view in which the death of a friend can be for the glory of God."[5] Then from the divine perspective the most loving thing Jesus could do was not to heal Lazarus and prevent his death. The most loving thing Jesus could do was use this situation in Lazarus' life for God's glory.[6]

Sometimes we endure hardship, pain, and death. All of these things, as I have said, are the result of satanic influence over a corrupted race in a fallen world. The suffering we endure in this life is a great tragedy. From God's perspective the greatest tragedy is when people, who have been created in His divine image (Gen. 1:27), fail to reflect His glory.

While so much suffering that occurs in our lives seems meaningless, God's will is to lift our suffering beyond this fallen status and use it for His glory. This is the glory of the One Who has the power to overcome every sickness and disease, calm every storm, and even defeat death. Yet often God chooses to walk with us through these dark valleys of suffering to bring us into the land of unclouded day. God does this so we will draw closer to Him, trust in Him more deeply, and depend on Him more fully. God's will is that we walk with Christ and that His glory be made known through us.

In Thomas' words, *"let us also go, that we may die with him"* (John 11:16), we catch an inkling of what this means. Although Thomas did not understand the full meaning of what He was saying, first-century Christian readers would have understood these words as an invitation to take up their cross and follow Jesus to death (Luke 9:23).[7] This is because when we choose to give up our lives for the sake of the cross, we find true life (Luke 9:24) and God's glory revealed in us.

James and Charma Covell were American Baptist missionaries serving at Kanto Gakuin University in Yokohama in the 1930s. James was a committed pacifist who overtly resisted Japanese militarism. So as Japanese military activity in the Asia/Pacific region escalated, his position at Kanto Gakuin increasingly became precarious. Finally, in 1939, the American Baptist Mission Board reassigned the Covells to the Philippines rather than risk their internment by Japanese authorities. In 1940, after the Covells' eldest daughter, Margaret, completed high school in Manila, they decided that, because of the deteriorating political situation in the Philippines, they would send their three children back to the U.S. They planned to reunite the family during a furlough in 1942. Unfortunately these plans were disrupted by the Japanese invasion of the Philippines in 1941.

In April 1942, when the Japanese invaded the island of Panay on which the Covells were living, the family, along with nine other missionaries and one child, fled to a narrow ravine in the mountains. This mountain hideaway, only accessible by one winding, narrow trail, became known as "Hopevale." It remained a place of refuge and safety for American missionary and mining families until December 1943. On December 19 Japanese soldiers captured all of the missionaries along with some miners and three children. The adults were ordered to death by beheading and the children stabbed to death. The order was carried out the next day. Then the bodies were placed in a bamboo house and burned.

The Covell children were shocked by the news of their parents' deaths. However the eldest daughter, Margaret, began to believe that her best possible response to what happened was to love and forgive the Japanese people. As a result she made the decision to become a Japanese-speaking social worker in a Japanese relocation camp in Colorado. One Japanese prisoner-of-war who heard about this was so impressed by Margaret's care for Japanese people in response to her parents' deaths that he related the story to an old friend, Captain Mitsuyo Fuchida. Captain Fuchida was the naval pilot who led the Japanese assault on Pearl Harbor in December 1941. When Fuchida heard about what had happened to James and Charma Covell and how Margaret worked to care for Japanese people during the war, he was confronted by the power of love and forgiveness. As a result he bought a Bible and for himself searched out the basis of these Christian principles. Finally Fuchida committed his life to Christ and became an evangelist. He began publicly proclaiming the truth of the gospel on the streets of Osaka.[8]

The story of the martyrdom of James and Charma Covell and their companions at the hands of Japanese soldiers in December 1943 seems to have been a needless tragedy. From a purely human standpoint the Covells' lives would have been spared if, in 1940, they had returned to the U.S. with their children. Also God miraculously could have intervened to prevent the Covells and the other families from being captured and killed by the Japanese. Although God sometimes intervenes in this way, more often than not God allows the results of the tragic choices humans make to play out to their bitter end. Even so God is able to take these tragedies of life and death and redeem them using them for His glory. This is what we see when the murder of James and Charma Covell became the occasion for Margaret's ministry of love and forgiveness among Japanese relocated to Colorado during the war. In turn this led to Mitsuyo Fuchida's conversion. After the war he became an effective evangelist in Osaka.

God's desire to use our suffering for His glory does not mean He remains otherwise unaffected by tragedy we endure in our own lives. When Jesus saw Mary and the Jews who were with her weeping, *he was deeply moved in spirit and troubled* (John 11:33). Later, when they arrived at the place where Lazarus' body had been laid to rest, *Jesus wept* (John 11:35). His grief was triggered not only by the death of a close friend but also by the sense of hopelessness and despair He saw on the part of Mary and the Jews.[9] They needlessly suffered psychological anguish because they had before them the One Who had the power to bring life out of death but did not recognize who He was.[10] Finally Jesus knew this miracle would trigger a negative reaction on the part of the Jews and that this reaction would lead to His own death (John 11:45-53). That reality weighed heavily on Him.[11]

Jesus grieves with those who suffer, because He loves those who believe in Him. Jesus really loved Lazarus (John 11:36)! Because of Jesus' love He grieved that His friend had suffered. In the same way Jesus grieves for the suffering we endure, because we live in a fallen world. He weeps, not only because we endure suffering, but because sometimes we endure suffering to bring Him glory. When Jesus is glorified through His people's suffering, whether by Lazarus' death or the martyrdom of James and Charma Covell, He grieves because they suffered for His glory.

The realization that Jesus can take our otherwise senseless suffering and redeem and use it to bring glory to Himself enables us to find meaning in the most hopeless life circumstances. No situation exists in which God's redemptive hand cannot work. So whenever we, or those with whom we work, walk through the valley of the shadows of death, God still gives hope and assurance. Moreover the Lord works to accomplish His purpose, if only we will trust in Him.

"I Am the Resurrection and the Life"

When Jesus went to Martha, she spoke to Him of life and death as **events**. Martha regretted the **past**, because she believed that if Jesus was **present**, Lazarus' death could have been avoided (John 11:21).[12] She also expressed hope for the **future** resurrection of the dead (John 11:24). Like most pious Jews of her time Martha believed the resurrection would happen as the "opening act of the [future] Messianic kingdom" (Dan. 12:2).[13] Although Martha believed in both Jesus and the resurrection, she did not yet realize the relationship between them. As Lee points out, "Martha's struggle is to understand the meaning of Jesus' advent existentially, as it relates to the fundamental question of life and death."[14]

In response to Martha, Jesus explained the nature of death, resurrection, and life in terms of **His person and His relationship with us**. Life, death, and resurrection merely are not events to be experienced as stages of human existence. Rather they are linked together with the personal identity of Jesus Christ. Furthermore how we experience life, death, and the future resurrection completely depends on the quality of our relationship with Him.

Jesus' statement, *"I am the resurrection and the life"* (John 11:25), draws the future resurrection into the present and makes it personally present in Him.[15] Resurrection and life completely are tied up with Who Jesus is and what He has done for us. This is another one of those ***"I am"*** statements through which Jesus affirmed that He was none other than God, Himself, Who arrived to dwell among us as a person. Since Jesus is God, He is the sole source and creator of life. *Through him all things were made; without him nothing was made that has been made* (John 1:3). Jesus Christ is the only One Who can resurrect. Through His own "experience of dying and living, living and not dying" Jesus conveyed the "resurrection and the life" to us.[16] Since He was made alive, all *"in Christ . . . will be made alive"* as well through Him (1 Cor. 15:22). He is the *"heavenly man",* and those who are *"in him . . . shall bear his likeness"* (1 Cor. 15:49). Where Jesus is, resurrection and life exist. Where Jesus is not present and at work, "no resurrection and no life" exists.[17]

This means a person's participation in this resurrection and life is based on the status of his or her relationship to Christ. Eternal life depends on personal response to Jesus (John 5:21).[18] Jesus said, *"Whoever hears my word and believes in him who sent me has eternal life and will not be condemned; he has crossed over from death to life"* (John 5:24). Resurrection and life are reserved for those related to Jesus by faith (John 11:25).

As we often have seen before, the gospel continually points to the uniqueness of Christ as the only means to have eternal life. Jesus is the only One Who holds the power of life and death in His hands. He is the only One Who has overcome the power of death through His resurrection from the dead. He is the "resurrection and the life." Those who have resurrection and life have Him.

Faith in God Who became a person, lived among us, died, and rose again gives Christianity power and distinctiveness. Although many in our postmodern period encourage us to sacrifice these absolute truths on the altar of religious relativism, without them our faith sinks into a nebulous void of what-ifs. Paul writes, *If Christ has not been raised, our preaching is useless and so is your faith* (1 Cor. 15:14). Heed Timothy C. Tennent's warning words,

> we must not succumb to the forces of religious pluralism that seek to bring to the table of dialogue a version of Christianity that has been robbed of its distinctiveness. For too long interreligious dialogue has been advanced and identified with a pluralist agenda that openly seeks to accommodate other world religions by discarding distinctive Christian doctrines such as the incarnation and the resurrection of Christ.[19]

Instead of only sitting down and talking with adherents of other religions to build mutual understanding and goodwill, in the final analysis, we do them the greatest injustice possible if we neglect to tell them why we have based our own hope in Jesus Christ. Be unapologetic in maintaining that because of resurrection and life, only faith in Him brings life. Jesus' otherwise senseless suffering can be redeemed and given meaning and purpose. The Word of God shared in a forthright manner will burn within their hearts. Of course we cannot control the response of those with whom we speak. Some will hear our words with gladness and place their trust in Jesus, while others will turn and walk into eternity without Him. Whatever the response at least we can be confident we have been true to God's Word and faithful to the One Who called us to be His witnesses.

Never Too Late

Martha responded with dismay when Jesus told mourners gathering at Lazarus' tomb to roll away the stone. *"But Lord," she said, "by this time there is a bad odor, for he has been there for four days"* (John 11:39). The Jews at the time believed a person's spirit lingered with the body for three days after death. On the fourth day when "corruption made recognition of the person impossible," the spirit departed. The departure of the spirit on the fourth day led to the belief that death was considered final.[20] This is the reason for the dispirited tone in Martha's voice. Summers sees the implication of Martha's words, "Lord, you could have healed Lazarus while he was sick. You could have even raised him during the first three days after he died. But now it is the fourth day. It is too late for you to do anything to help him now."[21] He continues,

> Jesus' answer, "Did I not tell you that if you believe you would see the glory of God?" meant correspondingly, "Martha, where I, the resurrection and the life, am present, it is never too late!" Where the Lord of life is present, the powers of life over death are already at work.[22]

The restoration of Lazarus' physical life by Jesus is symbolic of the journey from death to life experienced by all who trust in Christ. For the believer the grave never is the end. The "material reality" of "natural life" is transformed into eternal spiritual life through the gift of Christ.[23] The Spirit of Christ Who dwells in us has given unending life to our spirits (Rom. 8:10-11).

One day the *perishable* will be clothed in *imperishable,* and the *mortal* will put on *immortality* (1 Cor. 15:53, 54). Already, even now, *though outwardly we are wasting away, yet inwardly we are being renewed day by day* (2 Cor. 4:16). So those who believe in Christ **never** reach a point too late for life. Even when they have been dead and buried for 1,000 years so that all that remains of their bodies is dust and bone fragments, they remain alive in Christ.

This is Jesus' promise to us, *"He who believes in me will live, even though he dies"* (John 11:25). The moment a person trusts in Jesus for salvation, he or she receives eternal spiritual life.

The person physically may die, but his or her spirit, now living as a result of faith, will not find final rest in the grave. Physical death cannot break the bond between the believer and his Lord (Rom. 8:38).[24]

Like Martha many are robbed of hope by their false perception of the finality of death. Recently a fellow missionary was talking with a Japanese woman. As the topic of conversation turned from life to death, my friend stated that, because of her faith in Christ, she was not afraid of death. The Japanese woman replied, "If you do not fear death, you have a message that people need to hear. Everyone that I know is afraid of death."

For the Japanese the Buddhist understanding of death stands behind this fear. The Buddha taught that the goal of his religion is *moksha*, translated "enlightenment." However the literal meaning is to be "blown out."[25] The Buddha said that personal experience is like the flame of a candle. As long as it continues, it will burn with the passions and desires that lead to suffering. Suffering ends when personal existence does—the candle is blown out.

I really felt the impact of this teaching when I learned that the usual Japanese translation from the term *moksha* is *mu*, which literally means "nothing." So, from the Buddhist perspective, the best hope that this woman had was that she would cease to exist. The thought of passing through this world of suffering into an eternal void really is no hope at all. It results in thinking, "If all I have is this life and I do not live this life well, then I have nothing at all." As life speeds by, filled with unrealized hopes and unfulfilled dreams, gloom sets in. The shadows of death crowd out the light of life.

This way of thinking is not distinctly Japanese. In these post-modern times the belief in *nihilism* is widespread. *Nihilism* maintains that life, the universe, and reality all are temporary phenomena. All of us, life itself, and even the universe in which we live ultimately will cease to exist. From this perspective death ends everything. This results in a morbid fear of death which casts a shadow over life. People do everything they can to **prevent death** through good health and medicine, to **flee from death** through lives of pleasure, and to **appease death** through participation in the occult and ancestral rituals. They even try to **hide from death** through funeral customs that shield us from the startling reality of death as a stage of life.

When my daughter, Maggie, approached her grandfather's casket at his funeral, someone asked her, "Doesn't your granddaddy look like he's asleep?" Maggie's reply, filled with the wisdom of an

8-year-old, reminded us of the necessarily sharp contrast between perception and reality. "No. People do not sleep on their backs in their nice clothes. Granddaddy is dead." Physical death is a part of life. But, through faith in Christ, we can face death with hope and assurance rather than with morbidity and fear.

Let's return to the candle flame as a symbol of life. If the goal of Buddhism is for the candle to be blown out, the goal of Christianity is for the flame forever to burn. Indeed not only does the candle burn, but it is like a *gleam . . . shining ever brighter till the full light of day* (Prov. 4:18). This only is possible because the Source of light is not the believer but, rather, God. The psalmist writes, *You, O Lord, keep my lamp burning; my God turns my darkness into light* (Ps. 18:28). John 1:4 also reminds us that the Word of God is the Source of light and life: *In him was life, and that life was the light of men.* For those who believe in Christ, death cannot be the end of life and personal existence. The candle has an eternal flame which cannot be blown out. Death, then, is reduced only to a momentary flickering in the wind as the flame continues to burn even brighter into the land of eternal day.

"He Who Lives . . . Will Never Die"

Jesus completed His promise: *"Whoever lives and believes in me will never die"* (John 11:26). This means that whoever believes in Jesus already has begun a spiritual life which will not end in spiritual death.[26] The spiritual life begins the moment a person trusts in Christ for salvation and continues forever. The believer, as we have said, physically may die. But this physical death only is a doorway which leads to complete and perfected life lived forever in the presence of the Lord.[27]

The New Testament greatly emphasizes the promise that one day **those who believe in Christ will be with Him**. For example Jesus promised His disciples *"If I go and prepare a place for you, I* *will come back and take you to be* ***with me*** *that you also may be where I am* (John 14:3, emphasis added). John comforted the thief on the cross with these words, *"Today you will be* ***with me*** *in paradise"* (Luke 23:43, emphasis added). Paul writes that when Jesus returns *we will be* ***with the Lord forever*** (1 Thess. 4:17, emphasis added). Finally in Revelation God promises a beautiful *"new heaven and a new earth"* where the *"dwelling of* ***God is with men****, and* ***he will live with them****. They will be his people, and* ***God himself will be with them****, and will be their God"* (21:1, 3, emphasis added). While those who study eschatology continue to wrestle with how to put all of these passages together into one consistent system, at the very best, we acknowledge that the Christian hope is **eternal life with God**. Indeed, as Boyd Hunt reminds us, the central teaching of Scripture regarding heaven is "where God's throne is, and where his will is perfectly and gladly done."[28]

True life always is lived in the presence of and in relationship with the Lord. Jesus said, *"This is eternal life: that they may know you, the only true God, and Jesus Christ, whom you have sent"* (John 17:3). Through knowing Christ and living in relationship to Him the power of the Holy Spirit, which produces eternal life, works within us (John 8:11). C.K. Barrett writes, "Wherever he is, the divine power . . . to give life is at work."[29] In union with Christ, Who is the Source of Life, the "dead lives, and the living does not die."[30]

I was talking with two missionary colleagues about the challenges involved in fulfilling the Great Commission (Matt. 28:18-20). One of them said, "Making disciples isn't only about winning the lost and baptizing them or even about teaching people to obey the commands of Christ. **We cannot make disciples until we are willing to give our lives to them**. Spend time with people so they can experience Christ's love through you. They won't become disciples until our actions show them how much Jesus cares for them."

I immediately was impacted by the truth of this brother's words but was even more carried away after realizing sacrificial living for others, necessary to make disciples, only is possible when we realize the life we now enjoy as believers in Christ has been given to us in unending supply.

As long as the possibility of death remains, life is a limited commodity to use carefully and sparingly lest we run out. So we ration it and try to make it last as long as possible. But, once the threat of death has been removed, we can give of our lives freely because we know that we never will run out.

Knowing Jesus has defeated death and that, through the presence of the Holy Spirit, the power of the One Who defeated death now lives in us, enables us to lay our lives down for God and other people. We are able to *"take up our cross daily"* (Luke 9:23) and to be *"crucified with Christ*" (Gal. 2:20) when we have confidence that the Spirit of Christ, Who now lives in us, (Rom. 8:11; Gal. 2:20) really is God's *deposit guaranteeing our inheritance until the redemption of those who are God's possession* (Eph. 1:14). When we realize that death only is a flicker of light in the course of eternity and is not to be feared, we sacrificially can pour out ourselves so others can experience God's love through us.

This is the kind of faith that enables Christian martyrs throughout the centuries, men and women like Justin Martyr, David Brainer, Jim Elliot, and James and Charma Covell—to give up their lives without hesitation for the sake of Christ. They knew death, however painful and difficult to endure it might be, was but a fleeting moment in the course of eternal life. If they had to die so others might seek faith in Christ, they considered it a small sacrifice well worth paying so others might have eternal life.

Of course multiple ways exist to lay one's life down for the sake of Christ. Laying one's life down does not always mean dying for Christ—it also means living for Him. **Christ lives His own life through us**. This means that Jesus uses all of the time, talents, energy, and abilities He allotted for us for His own purposes, so others can know and experience His love through us. As we offer ourselves as *living sacrifices, holy and pleasing to God* (Rom. 12:1),

He uses these sacrifices to glorify Himself. God does this by bringing other people to Himself through us.

If we effectively are going to live and proclaim the gospel, believe Jesus truly is *"the resurrection and the life"* (John 11:25). We can be so secure in our hope of God's gift of eternal life that we fear neither physical death in this age nor spiritual death in the following. This kind of faith in Christ and hope for eternal life enables us freely to give of ourselves so others can experience God's love through us. Surely this is what Paul means when he writes that the *only thing that counts is faith expressing itself through love* (Gal. 5:6).

I Believe in You

Jesus spoke with Martha both about who He is and **what He would accomplish**. Jesus is the "*resurrection and the life*." What Jesus **accomplished** is to give eternal life to those who believe in Him. We cannot overemphasize the significance of Jesus' words for Martha's understanding of the gospel. We tend to glance over Jesus' final four words and move on to other meatier morsels of Scripture. Resist this temptation. While everything that Jesus said to this point was about Himself, His final four words let Martha know what He said also was about her.

Jesus asked Martha, *"Do **you** believe this?"* (John 11:26, emphasis added). Everything Jesus has said about Himself was true. Unless Martha believed in His words, they would not impact her personal life. Unless Martha believed that Jesus is the resurrection and the life, she could not enjoy His free gift of eternal life.

We share the gospel with people. God saves them. While we forcefully try to share the gospel and convince people of the truth of our message, unless the Holy Spirit convicts people of sin and draws them to faith in Christ, they will not be saved.

On the other hand, avoid using God's power to save as an excuse for not calling people to faith. Don't just live and speak the gospel before people. Ask them, "Do you believe this?" "Do you believe that what I have been telling you about Jesus is true?" "Do you believe that Jesus is the Son of God who lived on earth to provide you with forgiveness of sins and eternal life?" "Will you entrust both your present life and your eternity into Jesus' care and make Him your Lord and Savior?" Unless you reach the point of asking people if **they believe in Him**, your telling them about Him does little good.

Martha responded to Jesus, *"Yes, Lord. I believe that you are the Christ, the Son of God, who was to come into the world"* (John 11:27). Martha did not fully comprehend all that Jesus had just said to her. She did not understand all of the fine points of Christian doctrine. I find faulting her for this to be difficult. Who of us honestly can say that we fully comprehend every detail that the Scriptures teach about resurrection and eternal life? This side of Jesus' resurrection we have the opportunity to understand more than Martha did. Martha's own brother, Lazarus, would be raised in a few days. Jesus' death and resurrection also was a few weeks away. And Paul's reflections on the significance of the resurrection (1 Cor. 15; 2 Cor. 5; 1 Thess. 4), on which we rely so heavily would not be written down for several years. All Martha had to go on were the words that Jesus had just said to her. She could not fully absorb them.

Martha expressed profound faith in Christ. She did not say that she understood and believed in the resurrection. Rather Martha said that **she believed in Jesus**. Although she did not understand everything that Jesus had said to her, **Martha trusted Jesus**. Martha affirmed that Jesus, alone in all of His greatness, was the One Who could provide all that she needed and even more.[31] She clung to Him as God's Son, Who had lived on earth, to stand with her and help her overcome death.[32]

The content of Martha's confession of faith differs very little from that of Peter, *"You are the Christ, the Son of the living God."* Jesus responded, *"Blessed are you, Simon son of Jonah, for this was not revealed to you by man, but by my Father in heaven"* (Matt. 16:16-17). If Peter's expression of faith was the result of divine disclosure, Martha's words also probably were influenced by God's Spirit working within her heart. First Martha said that Jesus was the *"Christ,"* the anointed One, who had arrived in fulfillment of Jewish prophecy. Second she denoted His deity and close relationship to God the Father when she called Jesus the *"Son of God."* Finally Martha said that He *"was to come into the world"* (John 11:27). This indicated her belief that Jesus was the "long awaited Deliverer, the One sent by God to accomplish his will perfectly." These words, profoundly doctrinal in content, were an expression of Martha's "saving faith."[33]

Sometimes we become concerned when average, ordinary people do not understand all of the fine points of Christian doctrine. I don't want to minimize the importance of theological orthodoxy and doctrinal teaching. However, when you deal with lost people, resist the urge to major on the minor points. Remember that if the atonement was easy for any of us to explain, including theologians, the world would not be full of so many theories. **Trusting in Jesus** for salvation is more important than is understanding all of the theories of the atonement, which seek to explain how Jesus' work on the cross provided us with salvation from sin. In my study I have several books noted scholars wrote on eschatology. No two books agree on every facet of the meaning of eternal life. Rather than explaining in detail every facet of the meaning of eternal life, focus on helping people get to the point at which they place their hope in **Jesus as the source of eternal life**.

My wife and I received news that our friend, who had suffered for so long with colon cancer, passed away. In accordance with Japanese custom a wake was held on the night before her funeral. At the wake her husband informed an astonished crowd of mostly Buddhist family members that, just before her death, our friend had decided to become a Christian. He went on to say that he also had decided to become a Christian.

This friend, who suffered for so long, failed to understand the reason for her suffering. She did not understand everything the Bible teaches about heaven and eternal life. But what she did finally realize was that **Jesus cared for her**. Based on that thread of knowledge she decided to place her faith in **Jesus**. Now she is enjoying eternity with the One who loves her, Who carried her through the valley of the shadow of death, and Who brought her, finally, into the land of cloudless day.

While death is the greatest enemy we face (1 Cor. 15:26), the gospel teaches us that death is no more than a momentary flicker of a light that burns forever. Death only is a bump in the road that leads to eternal life. Since Jesus is the *"resurrection and the life"* (John 11:25), those who believe in Him have no reason to fear death.

Responding to His Voice

1. Does the shadow of suffering and death prevent you from freely giving your life for the sake of Christ and others?

2. How can God use your suffering for His glory?

3. Do you believe that Jesus is the *"resurrection and the life"*? If so, how has this faith in Christ transformed your life?

4. When you share the gospel, do you encourage faith by asking people if they believe in Jesus?

Chapter 10

Knowing the Way

"Do not let your hearts be troubled. Trust in God; trust also in me. In my Father's house are many rooms; if it were not so, I would have told you. I am going there to prepare a place for you. And if I go and prepare a place for you, I will come back and take you to be with me that you also may be where I am. You know the place where I am going."

Thomas said to him, "Lord, we don't know where you are going, so how can we know the way?"

Jesus answered, "I am the way and the truth and the life. No one comes to the Father except through me. If you really knew me, you would know my Father as well. From now on, you do know him and have seen him" (John 14:1-7).

Pointing People the Way to the Father

I am intrigued by the interesting parallels that sometimes exist between languages which, from the standpoints of geography, history, and culture, seem totally to be unrelated. For example the Greek word *hodos* which, in John 14:6, is used for the word *way*, also may also be translated as *road*. So, literally, Jesus is saying that He is the "road to God." Similarly, in the Far East, the same Chinese character—pronounced *tao* in Chinese and *tow*, *dow,* or *meechee* in Japanese—also has the same two meanings: road and way.

The use of this Chinese character figures rather prominently in Eastern religions. For example the *tao* used in **Taoism**, one of the traditional religions of China. The **Taoist** "way" is that of trying to live in a state of perfect harmony with nature and one's environment. According to **Taoism**,

> Since ultimate reality is beyond categories, opposing values are not truly real; they are expressions of human conventions . . . Opposing categories such as beauty and ugliness, virtue and wickedness, difficult and easy, long and short, high and low and even the supposedly fundamental categories of being and nonbeing are merely relative. The only escape is to escape from making moral judgments all together.[1]

Taoists say that a person can have internal peace when he or she achieves an equilibrium between these contradictory poles that cause tension in life.

This same Chinese character for the words *road*, or *way*, also appears as the final syllable in the name of the traditional Japanese religion, **Shinto**—literally translated as "way of the gods." Japanese religions have no overarching creator. Rather they have a multitude of gods who are considered to co-inhabit, with the people, the islands of Japan.[2] As a result the Japanese traditionally have seen themselves as living perpetually in the presence of their deities, who manifest themselves as natural phenomena (such as waterfalls, mountains, and storms), the emperor, ancestral spirits, and both good and evil spirits. Since these gods are everywhere and influence everything, the people must live in harmony with the gods.[3] While many modern Japanese say they no longer believe in these ancient myths, the gods continue to influence the way they conduct their lives. Many don't consider buying property, building a house, or conducting a major business transaction without first praying to the gods for safety and success.[4] At the **Shinto** Shrine parents dedicate their babies and small children to the gods. They want to insure their children's protection and happiness.[5] In their cars, briefcases, and children's schoolbags people carry safety charms that **Shinto** priests have blessed, so the gods will protect them in their everyday lives.[6]

Everyone is looking for a way that will lead to peace, happiness, and spiritual fulfillment. But, if what Jesus said in John 14:6 is true, both **Taoism** and **Shintoism** and other world religions are dead-ends. Jesus was not talking about the way to happiness and success as the world defines these. He was not talking about the road to salvation and eternal life. He referred to something else much more basic and important. The destination to which Jesus in John 14:6 referred was none other than God.

This, above all else, is the language of divine-human **relationship**. In other words any connection between a person and God, the Father, takes place through Jesus Christ. Only when this **relationship with God**, which He intended for us from the beginning, is restored do people find the spiritual blessings they seek.

The **way** which men and women must walk to get to the Father is Jesus Himself. In this case ***way*** refers not only to the route but also to **how** to follow the route. In other words, human beings do not get to God merely by taking the right path. They also must walk the path **in the same manner that Jesus walked**. This is why Peter wrote, *To this you were called, because Christ suffered for you, leaving you an example, that you* ***should follow in his steps*** (1 Pet. 2:21, emphasis added).

My family and I were riding horses in Palo Duro Canyon, TX. Before we went on the ride someone told us, "You'll do better if you have your own horse. The horses that you rent in the canyon go only on the marked trails, where the guides want them to go." I guess my family and I were not very adventurous. Riding unknown horses on unmarked trails was not our idea of fun. So we played things safe—we rented horses. While riding through the canyon I thought to myself, "All of these trails crisscross through the cactus and sage brush. They all look the same. If we did not have a guide, I would have no idea where I was going or how to get there."

For many life is a lot like riding an unfamiliar horse on an unmarked trail. We live in a world of wayward people who, like Thomas, say, *"We don't know where we are going, so how can we know* ***the way****?"* (John 14:5, emphasis added). The world is full of crisscrossing roads that lead nowhere in particular. Most people travel through life in a continual state of confusion. They do not know where they are going. They have no goal in mind; they have no road to follow. So they either stand in place and mark time or wander around in circles. Some "experts" try to be helpful but actually add to life's complexity. They suggest *pluralism*—many ways to heaven; *individualism*—or that each person must find his or her own way; or *relativism*—any way a person chooses will work out in the end.

However, in contrast to all of this complexity and confusion, the answer which the Bible gives is really quite simple. One answer applies to all people everywhere. What could be more simple than that? **The Way** that people seek—the One Who can take them where they were intended to go—is Jesus. When we live and proclaim the gospel, we point people to the way that will lead them to God.

Someone in Whom to Believe

Jesus began His message, *"Do not let your hearts be troubled"* (John 14:1), because He was speaking to men with troubled hearts. As Jesus gathered with His disciples for the Passover, normally a time of great joy, He informed them that, during the time leading to His approaching death, one of their own would betray Him (John 13:21). Then, Peter said he was willing to follow Jesus even to the point of death. Jesus replied, *"I tell you the truth, before the rooster crows, you will disown me three times!"* (John 13:38).

The original version did not have a chapter and verse division between His words to Peter in 13:38 and His comments in 14:1.

Jesus was speaking to men who gave up everything to follow Him. For three years they had eaten together, talked together, and lived together. The disciples had seen Jesus' glorious miracles and heard His marvelous words. Now, within a few hours, Jesus would be taken away from them. The disciples would see the One they loved—more important to them than their own lives—beaten, mutilated, and put to death on a Roman cross. They would be left confused, distraught, and shattered.[7] Jesus knew what His disciples were up against, even if they did not. He told them, *"Do not let your hearts be troubled."*

Those of us who follow Jesus in the 21st century can identify with the 12 original disciples. We love Jesus. Many of us have given up everything to follow Him. Some follow Him at great sacrifice. Some missionaries, who live half a world away from family and friends, give their lives to share the gospel with people who, quite frankly, are not interested. Others remain in their own countries but pay an even heavier price. Many are disowned by their families, tortured, imprisoned, and sometimes even killed by their own governments. And all of this is for a Lord that we never have seen with our eyes, heard with our ears, or touched with our hands. Certainly we have experienced the truth of Jesus' promise, *"Blessed are those who have not seen and yet have believed"* (John 20:29). On the other hand we are nagged by doubts and fears that arise because Jesus is not with us in a physical sense. This is the trouble, Linders writes, of "serving an apparently absent Lord."[8]

Jesus' remedy for a troubled heart, struggling with the doubts and fears of life, is, *"Trust in God; trust also in me"* (John 14:1). When we trust in God, we sense His love for us. And since God's love for us is perfect, it *drives out fear* (1 John 4:18). When we live day by day and continually experience God's love, we sometimes may be nervous, upset, or afraid. But we never will become so consumed with fear that it controls our lives. *The man who fears is not made perfect in love* (1 John 4:18). All-consuming fear and God's perfected love mutually are exclusive.

This is because fear and love are aspects of two different worlds. **Fear** is related to **this world**—separated from God and under Satan's control. Satan manipulates and controls through fear. In Japan I see this every day. When people pray to their ancestors, buy and wear lucky charms, or dedicate their children to the gods, they largely are motivated by fear. They want peace of mind and protection. They are afraid that something in this life may destroy them. This is why a woman told my missionary friend, "If you are not afraid of death, people will listen to you. Everyone I know is afraid of death." For this woman escape from fear was a wonderful thought. She could not image how she, or anyone else, ever could achieve freedom from fear.

Japan is not the only country in which people are consumed with fear. In America worry, uncertainty, and trauma are synonyms people use to describe their fear. They are afraid because of relationships, business, and finances. People are afraid both of their futures and their pasts, so they are not willing to look around the corner or in the closet. Anything that helps people deal with fear—prescription drugs, psychiatry, alcohol, and the occult—is big business. They live in a world driven by fear.

Love, on the other hand, is a part of **God's world**—the world that people enter when they **trust** in Jesus Christ. According to John's Gospel, Jesus repeatedly told people to **trust** in Him. Jesus told Nicodemus, *"Whoever **believes** in me will not perish but have eternal life"* (John 3:16, emphasis added). He told the woman at the well that if she only would ask Jesus, He would give her *"living water"* (John 4:10). When Jewish leaders confronted Him about healing on the Sabbath, Jesus said to them, *"Whoever hears my word and **believes** him who sent me has eternal life and will not be condemned; he has crossed over from death to life"* (John 5:24, emphasis added). He told the crowd that gathered to see whether Jesus would give them bread, *"I am the bread of life. He who comes to me will never go hungry, and he who believes in me will never go thirsty"* (John 6:35). Jesus said to Martha, *"He who*

believes *in me will live, even though he dies; and whoever lives and* ***believes*** *in me will never die"* (John 11:25-26, emphasis added). Even Jesus' firmest words of warning are, in reality, a call to His listeners to trust in Him: *"If you do not* ***believe*** *that I am the one I claim to be, you will indeed die in your sins"* (John 8:24, emphasis added).

Sometimes in ministry we treat fear and faith as two different issues. Before we call them to faith, we want to counsel people to help them deal with their fears. But this approach is inconsistent with Jesus, Who taught us that the only real remedy for fear is to trust in Him. I think Neill Anderson is right on target when he writes,

> The essence of the victorious Christian life is believing what is already true about you. Do you have a choice? Of course! Satan will try to convince you that you are an unworthy, unacceptable, sin-sick person who will never amount to anything in God's eyes. Is that who you are? No, you are not! You are a saint whom God has declared righteous. Believing Satan's lie will lock you into a defeated, fruitless life. But believing God's truth about your identity will set you free.[9]

Faith in Jesus draws people into the presence of God. Here they experience what being a child who is loved by the heavenly Father is like. God's perfect loves drives away every fear.

"In My Father's House"

Jesus' disciples must have felt as if He were about to abandon them. With a promise Jesus responded to these feelings by saying: *"In my Father's house are many rooms; if it were not so, I would have told you. I am going there to prepare a place for you"* (John

14:2). Notice that Jesus' words were all **you**-focused. Everything He was going to do was for His followers. Nothing was for Himself. From first to last Jesus was motivated by love.

Here was Jesus, the Word of God through Whom the universe was fashioned, during His life on earth a carpenter, now promising to make an eternal dwelling place for His people.[10] "The primary emphasis here is on many rooms."[11] The word picture is similar to that of a hotel. One person goes ahead to secure accommodations for all of the guests in his party. The only difference is that in this case the reservations are permanent. Jesus has gone ahead to secure for His people "dwelling places" with God that will last forever.[12] Because He has "many dwelling places," we are assured that the Father's house has **enough room** for all of the redeemed.[13]

The promise of many dwelling places is incomplete without Jesus' words, *"I will come back and take you to be with me that you also may be where I am"* (John 14:3). We can understand in three ways Jesus' return for His people. First it can refer to Jesus returning for His people at the end of the age (1 Thess. 4:13-18).[14] In this case the heavenly dwelling places mentioned in John 14:2 may be seen as parallel to our *building from God, an eternal house in heaven, not built by human hands,* to which Paul in 2 Cor. 5:1 refers. According to this view Jesus really is not referring to a place or location. He is referring to the resurrection body, which Christ now is preparing for those who trust in Him. Paul tells us these heavenly dwellings *bear the likeness of the man from heaven* (1 Cor. 15:49). They are immortal, imperishable, spiritual bodies that will be *raised in power* (1 Cor. 15:42-54). Once we have *been clothed with our heavenly dwelling* (2 Cor. 5:4), we forever will be *at home with the Lord* (2 Cor. 5:8).

While John 14:3 primarily references the return of Christ, it also depicts Jesus returning for His people at the time of their death.[15] One example of this is the death of Stephen, when he *saw the glory of God, and Jesus standing at the right hand of God.* While being stoned to death Stephen prayed, *"Lord Jesus, receive my spirit"*

(Acts 7:55, 59).[16] The implication is that Jesus welcomes home those who die with faith in Him. Summers notes that this "would have been particularly meaningful for the apostles who themselves faced death at the hand of Jesus' opponents."[17]

Finally, in Acts 2, Jesus' return points to the bestowal of the Holy Spirit on the church. The Holy Spirit is referred to both as the *Spirit of Christ* (Rom. 8:9) and *Spirit of Jesus Christ* (Phil. 1:19). The context in Romans 8 makes clear that the Spirit must be present in all who truly are related to Christ. Jesus promised, *"Surely I am with you always"* (Matt. 28:20). No doubt He referred to the presence of His Spirit among believers. Since Christ's Spirit is present in us, He can transform us directly, so that we can have the *righteousness* and *life* of Christ (Rom. 8:10, 11).[18] We who believe in Christ are drawn up into His eternal communion with God, the Father, and thus have a "mutual indwelling."[19] No doubt this third meaning was part of what Jesus had in mind. Jesus highlights this,

> *"And I will ask the Father, and he will give you another Counselor to be with you forever—the* ***Spirit*** *of truth. The world cannot accept him, because it neither sees him nor knows him. But you know him, for he lives with you and will be in you. I will not leave you as orphans;* ***I will come to you****. Before long, the world will not see me anymore, but* ***you will see me****. Because I live, you also will live. On that day you will realize that* ***I am in the Father, and you are in me, and I am in you"*** (John 14:16-20, emphases added).

Because of the wonderful depth of John's Gospel, we don't have to choose from among these three meanings. All are true. For those who trust in Jesus, **He always is with us**—in life, at the point of death, and forever in the age ahead.[20]

This is the source of the gospel's power. The presence of Christ among His people changes us. He makes us new creations (2 Cor. 5:17). In doing so He energizes us to transform the world. Jesus said, *"Anyone who has faith in me will do what I have been doing. He will do even greater things than these, because I am going to the Father"* (John 14:12). Later I will return to this. As we move through this chapter, keep in mind how essential Christ's presence among us is. He is with us to give life and hope to a dark and dying world.

"I Am the Way"

Athletic superstars usually are considered to be strong individualists. Once every four years the world's best athletes express a remarkable unity of purpose—to participate in the Olympic Games. Reaching the Olympics takes long hours and many years of practice. The athletes are willing to walk this way because the reward is so great.

Christianity, also, has been compared to a great race. Paul employs this imagery when he writes, *"I press on toward the goal to win the prize for which God has called me heavenward in Christ Jesus"* (Phil. 3:14). The writer of Hebrews also urges us:

> *Let us run with perseverance the race marked out for us. Let us fix our eyes on Jesus, the author and perfecter of our faith, who for the joy set before him endured the cross, scorning its shame, and sat down at the right hand of the throne of God* (12:1, 2).

The goal of the Christian race is the Father. Jesus repeatedly emphasized this to His disciples. Jesus said He was the **way to the Father** (John 14:6). He then said that to **know Him was to know the Father** (John 14:7).[21] If reaching the Father and knowing Him are the goals of the race, then, as Christians, let our primary focus be not on heaven, eternal life, or even holiness. Avoid building our lives around ministry and service. As significant as all of these are, if any becomes the center of our Christian lives, we will miss out on the *surpassing greatness of knowing Christ Jesus* (Phil. 3:8).

In John 14:6 Jesus referred to Himself as **the way, the truth**, and **the life**. However since He was responding to Thomas' question about *the way*, Jesus' first statement is the primary emphasis and the second and third explain the sense in which Jesus' first statement is true. In other words **Jesus is the way to the Father, because He is the truth and the life.**[22]

The Truth "reminds us of the complete reliability of Jesus in all He does and is."[23] In John's gospel, Jesus repeatedly declared that He is the means by which **truth** is known (4:24; 6:32-33; 8:14, 32).[24] **As the Truth**, Jesus is the standard "by which all other truth is tested." Since Jesus is the "image of God's person" in human form (Col. 1:15; Heb. 1:3),[25] He enables us to see God clearly (John 1:18; 14:7) and to know God as He really is.

The life stresses that real life is more than "mere physical existence" but is a spiritual gift brought about through Christ's work in the human heart.[26] John's prologue tells us that both life and light are found in Christ (1:4). Jesus supported this with His own explicit claims to be the source of life (John 6:35, 41, 48, 51; 8:12; 11:25).[27] This is related to Christ's unique position as the One through Whom God created and maintains the universe (Col. 1:16-17).[28] *Through him all things were made; without him nothing was made that has been made* (John 1:3).

John 14:6 pulls together two of the main themes of John's Gospel. He then tells us why they are so important. If we read John's Gospel and only pick up that Jesus is the source of truth and life, we still miss the main point. The point is, **since Jesus is the Truth and Life, He is the way to the Father**. The inverse also is true, **since Jesus is the way to the Father, He is the source of truth and life**.

Real truth and life only are found through the relationship with God the Father that Jesus makes possible. John tells us that this is what his gospel is all about: *These are written that you may believe that Jesus is the Christ, the Son of God, and that by believing you may have life in his name* (20:31).

Jesus said, *"Enter through the narrow gate . . . Small is the gate and narrow is the road that leads to life, and only a few find it"* (Matt. 7:13, 14). Jesus' words reflect the Old Testament teaching that only those who listen to the Lord's instruction and do His will find life (Prov. 8:32-35).[29] This narrow way that goes to the Father passes through the *Via Dolorosa*. If you go to the Father, be willing to follow Jesus along the way of the cross (Luke 9:23-24; 1 Pet. 2:21).[30] This is not a moral imperative, which calls us to follow Jesus' example of doing good works. Rather these words call us to relinquish all reliance on self—to turn away from depending on our own abilities and strength—and to trust in the power of the cross.

The **way** of the cross "bridges" the chasm between heaven and earth[31] and provides "access" for human beings to the Father.[32] This profound truth is beautifully presented in the "bridge illustration" which the Navigators developed and the Campus Crusade for Christ tract, *Four Spiritual Laws*, popularized. According to this tract God loves us and created us for a loving relationship with Him. However our sin has separated us from God. Furthermore people cannot do anything to cross the chasm between themselves and God—not good works, not religious devotion—nothing. Only Jesus, God's Son, has provided **the way** to the Father. Jesus accomplished this by dying on the cross for our sins. To go to the Father people must believe in **the way** Jesus has provided. They must trust in Jesus for forgiveness of sins and eternal life.[33] No other way exists.

Since all of this can be explained in a few pages in a gospel tract, or even in one paragraph, some say the way to the Father is much too simplistic. They refer to this as "easy believism" and say that something more than the gospel must exist. However what easily is explained is not necessarily easily done. Jesus said,

> *"Not everyone who says to me, 'Lord, Lord,' will enter the kingdom of heaven, but only he who does the will of my*

> *Father who is in heaven. Many will say to me on that day, 'Lord, Lord, did we not prophecy in your name, and in your name drive out demons and perform many miracles?' Then I will tell them plainly, 'I never knew you. Away from me you evildoers!'"* (Matt. 7:21-23).

You simply cannot say, "I believe in Jesus as Lord." As James writes, *Even the demons believe that—and shudder!* (2:19). You also cannot just serve Jesus by preaching, combating evil, or doing good deeds. If we don't **know** Jesus, serving Him counts for nothing. A personal relationship with Jesus is based on **trust** in Him. The only possible means of salvation is to give up all pretense of goodness and to throw ourselves completely on the mercy and grace of God made available to us through the cross.

A few years ago I taught a class on Jesus as the only way of salvation. One person said, "I just can't believe this. I thought God loves people. If God loves people, why would He be so unfair that He provides only one way and lets all of the other people go to Hell? If God did this, He is a God of hate, not a God of love."

This statement implies two fallacies. One is that somehow people have done something good that is worthy of salvation. The truth is, nothing we do is good enough to get to the Father. If God operated on the basis of fairness, **all** people would go to Hell. God's mercy and grace allow us to seek Him. God has been extremely impartial in making His grace available. He doesn't limit His grace based on nationality, age, wealth, gender, or social standing. This is what Paul means when he writes, *There is neither Jew nor Greek, slave nor free, male nor female, for you are all one in Christ Jesus* (Gal. 3:28).

The same Lord is Lord of all, Jew and Gentile, and richly blesses all who call on Him. *"Everyone who calls on the name of the Lord will be saved"* (Rom. 10:12-13).

The second false implication of the statement by the Bible-class participant is that Jesus' work of salvation is inadequate to provide for the salvation of all people. Many versions of this argument exist. One is that Jesus is the Savior for Europeans and Americans but not for Asians and Africans. Another version reasons that since Jesus only saves those who believe in Him, other ways of salvation must exist for those who don't believe in Him. Whatever way this argument turns, it leads to *pluralistic universalism*—the idea that every religion provides a way of salvation and that everyone ultimately will be saved through his or her own religion.

The Bible clearly refutes *pluralistic universalism.* This begins with Jesus' own words in John 14:6: *"No one comes to the Father except through me."* Peter amplifies this same theme in Acts 4:12, *"Salvation is found in no one else, for there is no other name under heaven given to men by which we must be saved."* That God has provided only one way of salvation does not, in any way, indicate that God is unloving. God provided only one way of salvation for all people. He knew that one way was enough. As the writer of Hebrews tells us,

> *Christ was sacrificed once to take away the sins of many people; and he will appear a second time, not to bear sin, but to bring salvation to those who are waiting for him . . . We have been made holy through the sacrifice of the body of Jesus Christ once for all (Heb. 9:28; 10:10).*

As we move through the first years of the 21st century, we find striking confirmation of these truths. Note the growth of Christianity in two-thirds of the world. The majority of the world's Christians now live in Africa and Asia rather than in Europe and the Americas. The hues of their skin are much closer to red, yellow, brown, and black than they are to white. They speak a wide variety of languages. Most Americans would regard as quaint or even strange some of their social customs. A few are rich or middle class. Most are poor and live in abject poverty. But all have found **the way** to the Father. Since they know **the way**, they are bringing many other people to faith in Christ. Many have been disowned by family and friends. Some live as persecuted minorities in societies dominated by other religions and worldviews.

In spite of such opposition many have turned to faith in Christ. In Him they have found the power of life. Only those who forsake all and trust in Christ alone receive this power. These transformed people are living proof that the gospel provides the *power of God for the salvation of everyone who believes* (Rom. 1:16).

Knowing the Father

Jesus explains why He is the only way to the Father. In John 14:7, He says, "*If you really knew me, you would know my Father as well. From now on, you do know him and have seen him.*" Through Jesus we can go to God, because He has provided us with a "direct view of the Father."[34] To claim to know either God the Father or God the Son without knowing the other is to fail really to know either one. This is why Jesus answered, with some degree of disappointment, Philip's statement. He said, *"Don't you* ***know me,*** *Philip, even after I have been among you such a long time?"* (John 14:9, emphasis mine).

Jesus' own words rebuke a Hindu argument which reasons,

> If anyone who lives in the midst of Christendom goes up to the house of God, the house of the true God, with a true conception of God in his knowledge, and prays, but prays in a false spirit; and one who lives in an idolatrous community prays with the entire passion of the infinite, although his eyes rest upon the image of an idol: where is the most truth? The one who prays in truth to God, though he worships an idol.[35]

The problem with this statement is that it attempts to refute the uniqueness of Christ without taking into account **Who** He is. The only reason Christians have a "true conception of God" is that Jesus enables us to know God firsthand. Faith in Jesus allows us to know God as Father and ourselves as His children (John 1:12; Gal. 3:26). Only the Spirit of Christ working within us enables us to cry out to God, *"Abba! Father!"* (Rom. 8:14-16; Gal. 4:6). So a person who really approaches the true God cannot do so with a "false spirit."

The Trinity—the Father, the Son, and the Holy Spirit—**always** work together in divine harmony and **never** are at odds. Jesus refers to this when He says,

> *"Don't you believe that I am in the Father, and that the Father is in me? The words that I say to you are not just my own. Rather, it is the Father, living in me, who is doing his work. Believe me when I say that I am in the Father and the Father is in me"* (John 14:10-11).

Here Jesus further expresses His earlier statement, *"I and the Father are one"* (John 10:30).

I once was asked, "Do you think the Father and the Son are same or different from each other?" I gave the only answer I could: "Yes." While belief in one God but also three persons seems self-contradictory, that's what the Bible teaches. The Father, Son, and Spirit are unified in a way that allows them also to differentiate from each other. A "mutual interpenetration" exists between them so they all are together—that "each is in the other."[36] One example of this is Jesus' explanation that He is the "self-expression" of the Father Who allows us to see and know God as He really is (John 1:14, 18; Heb. 1:2; 1 John 1:1-2).[37] This is the "glory of the incarnation." Summers writes,

> Do we want to know what God is like? Let us look at what God incarnate is like. Do we want to know what God thinks

> about sin, salvation, and the redeemed life of love? Let us look at what God incarnate taught about them. That is the vision splendid, and it is the only way that we can "see" God in the days of our flesh . . . He has shown us the Father just by being what he is, the Son of the Father. Christ the God-like shows us God the Christ-like.[38]

In effect Jesus is saying, "When you have seen Me, you have seen all of God that there is to see." Through the revelation of Christ, we become "beholders of God." What more could we desire than this?[39]

Seeing God and basking in His glory is, in the final analysis, what Christianity is all about. Jesus was sent to earth so that we could *see his glory, the glory of the One and Only, who came from the Father, full of grace and truth* (John 1:14). We worship Him in response to what God, in Christ, has revealed of Himself. In John's Gospel, Thomas, confounded by the glory of the risen Christ, cries out, *"My Lord and my God!"* (20:17). Worship is attributing to God the "supreme worth and value" that are due Him. "When we worship God, **we celebrate Him**: We extol Him, we sound His praises, we boast in Him."[40]

This heartfelt desire to glorify and worship God fuels the Christian life. We experience its amazement when we bask in His glory, which drives us to offer ourselves as *living sacrifices, holy and pleasing to God* (Rom. 12:1). This desire to exalt God, not only on Sunday but in all of our thoughts, words, and actions, compels us *not to be conformed any longer to the pattern of this world, but to be transformed by the renewing of our minds* (Rom. 12:2). Finally the zeal to honor God ignites the flame of evangelism and missions. John Piper states this so well when he writes,

> In missions we simply aim to bring the nations into the white-hot enjoyment of God's glory. The goal of missions is the gladness of the peoples in the greatness of God . . .

When the flame of worship burns with the heat of God's true worth, the light of missions will shine to the most remote peoples on earth.[41]

We only will keep straight what living and proclaiming the gospel in a fallen world means if we remember that Jesus sought to reveal His Father to us. This revelation of God is, above all else, **personal**. In sending His Son, God intended for us to **know** God and to have a **relationship** with Him. Certainly things Jesus revealed are best explained in terms of Christian doctrine and ethics. But avoid becoming so caught up in the doctrinal and ethical implications of God's revelation in Christ that you miss out on this loving relationship with God. This relationship with God fires the soul, washes away the tarnish of sin, and produces new life in Christ which will last forever. This relationship through Christ with God is the one we most need to pass on to others.

Doing the Son's Work

Recently the leader of a local church told me, "People become so burdened trying to serve God." While this is true, it is the inevitable result of seeing Christian service as something we do **for** God rather than something we do **with** God. Jesus never intended this. Rather than using our own strength and abilities to do God's work, Jesus' plan was to equip us with His gifts. He wanted to invigorate us with His power so that He could do His work through us. Jesus said, *"Anyone who has faith in me will do what I have been doing. He will do even greater things than these, because I am going to the Father"* (John 14:12).

Notice the people who do Christ's work are not those who know about Jesus, respect Jesus, or even desire to follow His example. While knowledge, admiration, and obedience all are good things, only **faith** in Jesus enables people to carry out His work.[42]

Every aspect of the Christian life begins and ends with this simple matter of **trust** in Christ. Paul says it best when he writes, *For in the gospel a righteousness from God is revealed, that is by* ***faith from first to last****, just as it is written: "The righteous will live by faith"* (Rom. 1:17, emphases added).

While evangelical Christians agree that faith is necessary for salvation and spiritual growth, faith seems to be lightly regarded as a factor for ministry, evangelism, and missions. Much more talk is devoted to planning and strategizing than to faith. Evangelism training often deals with technique—namely what to say and when to say it. And, while we talk about how the person who hears the gospel needs to respond with faith in Christ, little, if anything, is said about the importance of faith on the part of the **witness**.

Increasing emphasis is placed on the importance of prayer. This emphasis is wonderful and contributes much to results in evangelism and missions around the world. But even prayer tends to be discussed as a **strategy**. For example spiritual-warfare specialists emphasize the need for prayer to combat evil spirits and to prepare areas for future spiritual harvest.[43] Many mission boards now have offices of strategic prayer. David Garrison outlines the strategic role prayer has played in the rapid multiplication of churches that has occurred in various parts of the world.[44]

However not much is said about the vital role **faith** plays in prayer. This is ironic when Jesus Himself said, *"If you* ***believe****, you will receive whatever you ask for in prayer"* (Matt. 21:22, emphasis mine). Jesus' promise to do whatever we ask for in His name (John 14:13, 14) is said in the context of his statement on faith. Prayer in Christ's name is

> . . . prayer proceeding from faith in Christ, prayer that gives expression to the unity of all that Christ stands for, prayer that seeks to set forth Christ Himself.[45]

Praying in Jesus' name takes for granted that we **trust** in Jesus and that we **believe** He will work in response to our prayers. And the work that Jesus does in response to these prayers brings glory to the Father.[46]

The truth is that **faith** is essential if we are to do Christ's work in today's world. This is because **faith** in Christ brings us into relationship with God. When we **believe** in Christ, we become interconnected with Him and what He is doing through his Spirit which He sends to dwell in us. The Holy Spirit encourages, equips, and empowers us to do what we would not and could not do by ourselves.

I'm amazed to see how Jesus works to accomplish His will through people who trust in Him. Jesus chooses people from small towns in the American South and Midwest and sends them to work in the large, bustling cities of East Asia and isolated villages in the jungles of sub-Sarahan Africa. Then He takes people from small villages in Southeast Asia, Africa, and South America and uses them to reach the lost of Europe and the Middle East. This is not how we would do it. We would send people to reach people with a language and culture that are most similar to their own. Why does God send people halfway around the world to reach people who are completely different than they are?

As I prepared to leave for Japan, many people said, "Plenty of lost people around here need Jesus. Why don't you let someone else share the gospel with the Japanese?" People are prone to this kind of common-sense reasoning. But thinking in this way fails to take into account the world seen through the eyes of faith in Christ.

This is a question that missionaries, in times of doubt and despair, often ask themselves, but the answer really is quite simple. By sending people into situations with which they cannot cope to do tasks which they never could do by themselves, God reveals His strength. Missionaries who accept God's call and step out on faith find out, with Paul, that God's power is perfected in their weakness (2 Cor. 12:9). ***When God's power is revealed, His glory shines!***

Jesus calls us to do His work His way through His power at work in us. Sometimes we look at the task to which God has called us; it seems insurmountable. At those times we are prone to look up to heaven, shake our fist at God, and cry out, "Why did **You** get me into this?! **I** never will be able to get this done!" When we do that, however, we only tell God what He already knows. Jesus did not call us to do it alone. Jesus called us to **trust** in Him, for when we trust in Him, **He** works through us. For times like these Jesus promised us, "*If you have faith as small as a mustard seed, you can say to this mountain, 'Move from here to there' and it will move. Nothing will be impossible for you*" (Matt. 17:20).

Responding to His Voice

1. What role does faith in Christ play in your salvation? Your everyday life? Your life's work?

2. Is the goal of your Christian life knowing God? Or have you settled for something else?

3. If other people watch the way that you are going, will it point them to God the Father?

4. What roadblocks do you need to remove from your life so that you can travel the way of Jesus?

Chapter 11

The Witness of the Truth

"But I tell you the truth: It is for your good that I am going away. Unless I go away, the Counselor will not come to you; but if I go, I will send him to you. When he comes, he will convict the world of guilt in regard to sin and righteousness and judgment: in regard to sin, because men do not believe in me; in regard to righteousness, because I am going to the Father, where you can see me no longer; and in regard to judgment, because the prince of this world now stands condemned.

"I have more to say to you, more than you can now bear. But when he, the Spirit of truth, comes, he will guide you into all truth. He will not speak on his own; he will speak only what he hears, and he will tell you what is yet to come. He will bring glory to me by taking from what is mine and making it known to you. All that belongs to the Father is mine. That is why I said the Spirit will take from what is mine and make it known to you" (John 16:7-15).

How Does the Holy Spirit Affect Your Witness?

A few years ago I heard about a conversation that took place between a Baptist missionary and a Charismatic Christian in Japan. This dear sister told my missionary colleague, "I can't work with you Baptists. You don't even believe in the Holy Spirit," to which the missionary retorted, "We can't do anything without the Holy Spirit." This interchange illustrates well the current situation among evangelical Christians with regard to the Holy Spirit. Those on the

Charismatic side often say that other Christians do not believe in the power and work of the Holy Spirit. The reality, however, is that other Evangelicals not only believe in the Holy Spirit, they have a growing awareness of the pivotal position that the Spirit occupies in Christianity. Many Evangelical Christians now realize that salvation, spiritual growth, the Christian life, church growth, evangelism, and missions all hinge on the work of the Holy Spirit. Donald Bloesch reminds us that Irenaeus once said, "Where the Spirit of God is, there is the church." Bloesch goes on to elaborate,

> There can be no vital Christian fellowship unless the Spirit is animating this fellowship and directing its members to trust in Jesus Christ. The Spirit is the agent of Christ as well as the partner with Christ in the revival of the church and the renewal of the world. It is not only Christ but also the Spirit who bids us drink of the water of life and thereby be empowered for service under the cross (Rev. 22:17).[1]

This growing awareness of the Spirit's importance and power has taken place within the context of increasing spiritual conflict. We see daily manifestations of our warfare against the *rulers, authorities, powers of this dark world, and spiritual forces of evil in the heavenly realms* (Eph. 6:12). We suffer direct attack in the form of temptation, discouragement, and distress. Our families are assaulted through the distortions of relationships and value systems now taking place in most societies. The spiritual beings who oppose God also incite the adherents of other religions and ideologies to persecute Christians in the name of cultural purity. The news of Christians being martyred for their faith has become so common in some countries that many cases go unreported. These increasingly violent acts done in the name of religion have caused us to become desensitized to the agony suffered by brothers and sisters in Christ for the sake of the gospel. We live in a day and time not unlike the one Jesus referred to when He said,

"*They will put you out of the synagogue; in fact, a time is coming when anyone who kills you will think that he is offering a service to God. They will do such things because they have not known the Father or me. I have told you this, so that when the time comes you will remember that I warned you*" (John 16:2-4).

When Southern Baptist missionaries are asked what more could have been done to prepare them for missionary service before they went overseas, almost without fail their answer is that they wish they had more training in spiritual warfare. Most of them say they had little preparation for the degree and kinds of spiritual opposition they face when they live and proclaim the gospel in countries outside of North America.

I don't consider coincidental the fact that just when spiritual opposition seems to heat up, the work of His Spirit grows more clearly into focus. Morris writes, "The Spirit is not a guide and a helper for those on a straight way perfectly able to manage on their own. He comes to assist men caught up in the thick of battle."[2] Light becomes most visible when it is placed against the black background of the darkest night. Jesus did not leave us to face alone the marauding hordes from Hell. Rather, He has sent us a *"Counselor to be with [us] forever—the Spirit of truth"* (John 14:16, 17).

The primary role of the Holy Spirit is that of *witness*. 1 John 5:6 makes this remarkable statement: *It is the Spirit who testifies, because the Spirit is the truth*. He is the *Spirit of truth* who guides us "*into all truth*" (John 16:13).[3] He does this by taking the truth of Christ and using it to penetrate human hearts that have been softened by the perils of life in an embattled world. Those who accept this truth and apply it to their lives experience its transforming power. The truth of Christ frees them (John 8:32) from the bondage they have been held in by Satan, the "*father of lies*" (John 8:44).

Jesus told his disciples that when the Holy Spirit fell on them, they would become witnesses for Christ (Acts 1:8). This not only was because the Spirit would empower the disciples to do the work that Jesus had called them to do. It also is because when the Spirit causes the light of truth to break forth from their changed lives, people become witnesses of that truth in an embattled world.The Spirit who bears witness to the truth becomes the "author of all witnessing."[4] As He calls people to go forth as witnesses, the Holy Spirit is ***the One*** who directs the assault on the powers of darkness. Those who respond to His call simply carry out the mission of the Spirit of Christ.

The Spirit of Christ

Jesus promised his disciples that He would not leave them alone when He returned to God the Father. "*I will come back,*" He told them (John 14:3). "*I will be with you always,*" Jesus promised them (Matt. 28:20). "*You will receive power when the Holy Spirit comes on you,*" He reassured them (Acts 1:8). "*I will ask the Father, and he will give you another Counselor to be with you forever—the Spirit of truth,*" Jesus said (John 14:16, 17). "*Unless I go away, the Counselor will not come to you; but if I go, I will send him to you,*" Jesus explained (John 16:7).

At first glance Jesus' words seem contradictory. Jesus promised to always be with us, but He also said that He must go away. Jesus must go to the Father in order to send the Spirit who will come in His name (John 14:26).

How can Jesus both go away and remain with us? Both of these statements cannot be true unless some sort of direct correspondence exists between the identity of Jesus and the identity of the Spirit whom Jesus sends.

In referring to the Holy Spirit, Jesus told his followers, "*I will not leave you as orphans; **I will come to you***" (John 14:18, emphasis mine). In other words, Jesus promised that through the Holy Spirit He will be with us continually. Paul confirms this when he writes,

If anyone does not have the ***Spirit of Christ,*** *he does not belong to Christ. But if* ***Christ is in you,*** *your body is dead because of sin, but your spirit is alive because of righteousness* (Rom. 8: 9, 10, emphases mine).

By means of the Holy Spirit Christ Himself dwells in the believer. As a result, we are able to experience life and righteousness now, even while the world around us is suffering death and decay as a result of sin. While our own bodies continue to bear the yoke of mortality due to the penalty of sin, our spirits already have been brought to life forever as a result of their communion with Christ's Spirit.[5]

The sending of the Holy Spirit in Christ's name (John 14:26) means that the Spirit arrives "in place of Jesus"[6] to "represent Him" and "to carry on His work."[7] This does not mean Jesus and the Spirit are separate persons who carry out the Father's will while working in partnership with one another. One God is, at the same time, Father, Son, and Holy Spirit.[8] Just as God once was present with us **physically** in the person of his Son, He now is present with us **spiritually** in the person of the Holy Spirit.[9]

The arrival of the Holy Spirit is tied to the completion of the Son's work on earth and His return to heaven. The salvation which the Spirit appropriates is based entirely on the atoning work of Christ.[10] Men and women could not be empowered to "preach the gospel until there was a gospel to preach."[11] The cross and the resurrection had to occur before Pentecost. Only the crucified and resurrected Christ "restored to the divine state" at the "right hand of God" could "pour out . . . the promised Holy Spirit."[12] This power to bestow the Spirit, Peter told the crowd on Pentecost, was proof that God the Father had made Jesus, *whom [they] crucified, both Lord and Christ* (Acts 2:33, 36).

This interrelatedness between God's Son and God's Spirit runs throughout John's Gospel. Jesus repeatedly said that those who believe in Him will receive spiritual life through the Holy Spirit (John 3:5-8, 16; 4:13-14; 6:63-64; 7:37-39). People receive spiritual life when they believe in God's truth which He has revealed to us through His Son. This truth has not come to us in the form of written words or rational assertions. Rather, God's truth is revealed to us through a person and what He has done for us. Because the Son of God came to earth to live among us as a man, to teach and to heal, to die on a cross and to rise again from death to life, we are able to understand the truth. Jesus Christ lived God's truth among us so that we clearly see both God's love for us and his power to set us free.

The role of the Holy Spirit is to take the things of Christ and *make them known* to us (John 16:14). The Spirit takes God's truth that has been revealed through Christ and brings it to life in the human heart. The Spirit takes the cold and lifeless heart of a spiritually dead human being and, to paraphrase Genesis 2:7, breathes the breath of life into it. When the Spirit is finished, what was cold is now warm; what was not moving now has a pulse; what was dead is now very much alive and will be alive for all eternity. The Spirit does all of this by using the truth of Christ to move the human heart. This is something that only God can do!

Often I hear a statement such as, "I led him to faith in Christ." These words are arrogant because they claim human credit for something that only God can do. Our best presentation of the gospel, spoken in the clearest, most persuasive manner, cannot save. While good human communication is a necessary part in sharing the gospel, it is only one part. No one has ever been reasoned into the Kingdom of God. No one ever has been talked into becoming a child of the King. Salvation does not occur only because a person hears and believes. Spiritual life only occurs when a spiritual birth happens. The only One who spiritually can beget anyone is God Himself.

A better way to express this would be to say, "I shared the gospel with Him. He believed in Christ. I am so exited that **God saved him. Praise the Lord**!" Seeing missions and evangelism primarily as **God's work to redeem His embattled world** is paramount. Our role of bearing witness for Christ is not what we do for God to bring others to Him—to grow His church and to honor Him. Rather, God glorifies Himself through us by calling and empowering us to be his witnesses. God accomplishes all of this through His Spirit, who through us bears witness to the world.

The Spirit's Witness to the World

Jesus said that the Spirit "*will convict the world of guilt in regard to sin and righteousness and judgment*" (John 16:8). The imagery here is that of a prosecuting attorney whose coordination of the testimony of witnesses in a trial brings about the conviction of a criminal.[13] The words of the Spirit's testimony all center on Jesus. The people of this world are convicted because they have refused to believe the truth of Christ and show themselves to be the children of the "*father of lies*" (John 8:44, 45). They have turned away from the One who is the only means of right standing before God in favor of the "*prince of this world*" (John 16:11).[14]

People are convicted of sin, Jesus said, because they do not believe in Him (John 16:9). While we usually think of sin in terms of moral evil, missing God's standard, and rebellion against God, Jesus emphasizes the sin of **not believing** in Him. When people reject Jesus, they put themselves rather than Christ in the center of their lives.[15] Consequently they live in accordance with their own desires rather than obeying Christ's will. When "there is no faith in Jesus, self-centeredness, hatred, and immorality, all concrete signs of unbelief, take over."[16] People only seek to gratify their sinful natures (Gal. 5:16-18) rather than trying to please God.

We increasingly hesitate to talk about the sin of rejecting Christ. We are afraid of being labeled as narrow and bigoted. We have been told that we must learn to see the value in other faith traditions and the possibility of salvation in other religions. We must begin to see Jesus, not as the only way of salvation, but as only one part of a wider spiritual truth that encapsulates all religious faiths. K. P. Aleaz explains that in this approach,

> we have a duty to identify the glorious ways in which God's revelations are available to us **in other religious experiences** which can help in our experience of **new dimensions of meanings of the gospel of God in Jesus.** Rather than evaluating other religious experiences in terms of a preformulated criteria, we have to allow ourselves to be evaluated by them in our understanding of the gospel. They, **in the Holy Spirit will provide us with new meanings of the person and function of Jesus,** rather if we dictate it to them always. **From the particular Jesus we have to come to the universal Jesus** (emphases mine).[17]

The problem with this way of thinking is that following the advice of Dr. Aleaz and, at the same time, believing the words of Christ is impossible. Jesus said that the people of this world will be judged guilty because they do not believe in Him. Furthermore, He said that the Holy Spirit would convict people of this sin. The Spirit continually will point people to the truth that Jesus is the only way of salvation. Since the Spirit's work is to point to this very particular truth regarding Jesus, He cannot also at the same time help people to arrive at believing in the kind of universal Jesus to which Aleaz refers. No doubt a spirit is at work in this formulation of theology, but He is not the Spirit of Christ.

Second, Jesus said that the Holy Spirit will convict people *"in regard to* ***righteousness****, because I am going to the Father, where you can see me no longer"* (John 16:10, emphasis mine). While

Jesus was on earth, He lived a perfect life. His disciples could look at Jesus and see God's righteousness embodied in the flesh. But after Jesus returned to the Father, this visible example of righteousness no longer was available. The Spirit's role was to help people understand God's righteousness which Jesus revealed while He was on earth.

By pointing to the righteousness of Christ, the Holy Spirit unmasks the unrighteousness, injustice, sin, and evil of the present world.[18] When the Spirit convicts people in accordance with Christ's righteousness, they are *cut to the heart* so that they cry out to those who bear witness to the gospel, "*What shall we do*?" (Acts 2:37). When people are convicted of their unrighteousness, they realize that they must "entrust themselves" to the righteousness of God accomplished on their behalf through the death, burial, and resurrection of Jesus Christ.[19]

We have a strong tendency to reduce Christianity down to a list of moral values that are to be followed in order to become a "good person." While this perspective often is identified with liberal theology, it is just as pervasive in Evangelical churches where preaching centers on the *do's* (go to church, tithe, love other people) and the *don'ts* (divorce, have an abortion, drink alcohol, use tobacco). This kind of thinking goes all the way back to the very beginning of Christianity. You might say that the very first heresy which Christianity had was the heresy of legalism. We have quit calling legalism a heresy because it has become so prominent in the life of our churches. But Paul warned, *"I do not set aside the grace of God, for if righteousness could be gained through the law, Christ died for nothing!"* (Gal. 2:21).

The problem with this moralistic approach to Christianity is that it causes us to trust in ourselves rather than in Christ. Righteousness cannot happen by following rules, even if these rules are based on Scripture. The purpose of the law, Paul says, is to *lead us to Christ* (Gal. 3:24). Once we have been justified through faith in Christ, his Spirit sets us *free from the law of sin and death* (Rom. 8:2). The moralistic approach to Christianity that I mentioned above misses this spiritual dimension. Rather than relying on the power of the gospel enacted within us by the Holy Spirit to make us righteous, we depend on our own strength. As a result, rather than being set free from the power of sin, we continue to struggle against it. We ignore the strength of Paul's reflection in Romans 7:24-25: "*What a wretched man that I am! Who will rescue me from this body of death? Thanks be to God—through the Lord Jesus Christ!*"

Third, the Holy Spirit convicts "*in regard to* ***judgment****, because the prince of this world now stands condemned*" *(John 16:11,* emphasis mine). Jesus is not talking about the final judgment at the end of the age when the devil will be thrown into the lake of fire (Rev. 20:10). He is referring, rather, to His judgment of Satan on the cross. We sometimes live as though the final results of history still are in doubt. We worry about whether, in the end, evil somehow might triumph over good. But the Holy Spirit is with us to remind us every day that this never could happen. "At the cross, the redemptive righteousness of God and the sin of the world met on a collision course." And Jesus was victorious![20] All of power of hell was forced to break loose from its stranglehold on the world when, in his final agonizing moment, Jesus cried out, "*It is finished!*" (John 19:30).

Just because the final outcome has been decided, however, does not mean that the war is over. While Christ's victory is secure, the battle still rages on. I cannot go along with the interpretation of Scripture that says Satan is bound in the present age (Rev. 20:2). If the dragon from hell has been bound, his chain is much too long! Satan is capable of reaping much destruction. Despite the fact that their doom is certain, Satan and his legions continue to fight on with great ferocity. Before the end occurs, they desire to inflict on God's Kingdom all of the damage possible.

The results of Satan's work are all around us. Many damaged people are in the world. In Tokyo I see them every day. People are caught up in habitual behaviors such as alcohol, drugs, and pornography. Women and children are abused by weak men who must dominate others to convince themselves of their own strength. Elsewhere, masses of this world are displaced by famine, pestilence, and warfare. Statistics are alarming, but they shield us from reality. Bringing ourselves to the realization that those masses are made up of millions of individual men and women, boys and girls. is much more difficult.

I can realize that the 10-year-old girl in Southeast Asia who is traded on the sex market today is someone's daughter, not unlike my own daughter. Both girls have thoughts and feelings; both of them have dreams; God loves both of them. Jesus died on the cross for each one of them to set them free from the power of sin and death.

The 8-year-old boy in Zambia is not unlike my own 7-year-old son—full of life and adventure. But the Zambian boy's life will be cut short because his father was sexually promiscuous and then brought AIDS home to his own marriage bed. Why does this boy have to die? Jesus loves him, too. God's Son died on the cross so that this son of Africa would not have to die because of sin.

We easily can point our fingers at the sinful, suffering, and dying people of our embattled world and say, "Your life could have been different." Admitting that we could have been where they are now save for the grace of God is far more difficult. Paul writes,

> *As for you, you were dead in your transgressions and sins, in which you used to live when you followed the ways of this world and of the ruler of the kingdom of the air, the spirit who is now at work in those who are disobedient. All of us also lived among them at one time, gratifying the cravings of our sinful nature and following its desires and thoughts. Like the rest, we were by nature objects of wrath. But because of his great love for us, God, who is rich in mercy, made us alive in Christ even when we were dead in transgressions—it is by grace that you have been saved* (Eph. 2:1-5).

When the Holy Spirit made his initial encounter with each one of us, we also were in the world. When the Holy Spirit first got our attentions, we were wandering in the wilderness of sin and death. We were like Moses following Jethro's sheep across the desert until Moses encountered the burning bush. When the Holy Spirit spoke to us, He took us by surprise. We were not looking for Him or expecting Him. The internal voice of the Holy Spirit, like Christ's work on the cross, is an act of God's grace. To have the Spirit descend on us—penetrating our hearts with the Word of the gospel and imploring us to be saved—is not a right. It is not a privilege that is bestowed on us by birth or a prize that we have won. The work of the Holy Spirit is, from first to last, God's unmerited gift to us.

While both the Son and the Spirit are gifts of God's grace, when a person responds to God out of the world, this person does so as a matter of human choice. God has done everything that is necessary to provide for the salvation of every human being. God woos people to respond to Him, but whether they actually do so depends *on their response*. When the Holy Spirit confronts people with the truth of the gospel, they must choose one way or the other.[21] If they respond with faith to the testimony of the Holy Spirit, they will be saved, but if they reject His words, then they are "already judged."[22] "*Whoever does not believe stands condemned already because he has not believed in the name of God's one and only Son*" (John 3:18). When a person does say *yes* to the Spirit's call, this is only the first step in a lifelong process of spiritual transformation that results from listening and responding to the Spirit's voice.

The Spirit's Witness to Believers

When we were lost in the world of sin, the Spirit's role was to bring us to Christ. Now that we have responded to His call and begun to follow Christ, the Spirit's role still is to bring us to Christ.

This is because Christianity is, from first to last, putting aside ourselves so that we can take up our cross and follow Jesus (Luke 9:23). After we begin with faith in Christ, we do not attain spiritual growth by human effort. Rather, we must continue to live by the faith in Christ to which the Spirit first called us (Gal. 3:3-4). The Christian life is a matter of faith in Christ *from first to last* (Rom. 1:17). The writer of Hebrews tells us, *Without faith it is impossible to please God, because anyone who comes to him must believe that he exists and that he rewards those who earnestly seek him* (11:6).

In following Christ, deal with the ambiguity of believing that some things are certain even though we *cannot* see them (Heb. 11:1). God calls us to believe that His promises are true even though we may not see their results in the present world. We believe, for example, that someday we will see Jesus and be with Him forever. We believe this because God's Word promises it. We are like the patriarchs *longing for a better country, a heavenly one*, which God has prepared for us (Heb. 11:16).

We also can exercise this same kind of faith in missions. We go to a new place in which few if any Christians are present. We begin to get to know the area, meet people, pray for them, and share the gospel with them. As people respond we gather them into the groups, teach them to follow Christ, and help them to form into local expressions of the Body of Christ. We do all of this because God has called us and given us a vision to carry out His mission in a new place. From the very beginning we *cannot* see what will become of our work with our physical eyes, but *we can see the results through the eyes of faith*. These days we sometimes refer to this as *vision*, but the Bible calls it *faith*. It is this kind of faith that enables us to glorify God by doing what pleases Him.

We can believe in what we cannot see because we trust the One who promised these things to us. We are like Abraham who *believed the Lord, and he credited it to him as righteousness* (Gen. 15:6; Gal. 3:6). Since Abraham trusted God, when God told Abraham to go to a new country, he packed up everything he had and went.

This is not unlike a husband and wife who sense that God is calling them to serve Him overseas in a country they never have seen. They sell their house and car along with most of their belongings. They pack up their kids and what few things they can take with them and go where God has called them. Even with the information overload available to us on the Internet these days, this husband and wife do not know very much about where they are going. They do not speak the language; they do not understand the culture; and they do not know everything that will happen to them and their family while they are in this land faraway from home. But ***they trust the One sending them,*** so they go in peace and believe in promises that they cannot see.

This brings us to the role of the Holy Spirit in the life of the believer. Jesus said when "*the Spirit of truth comes, he will guide you into all truth . . .. He will bring glory to me by taking from what is mine and making it known to you*" (John 16:12, 14). The truth to which the Holy Spirit guides us is "Christ Himself." The Spirit glorifies Christ. "He reveals Christ" and by doing so enables us to trust in Him.[23] As the Word of God, Jesus Himself is the text of the message which the Holy Spirit makes known to us.[24] The Spirit clarifies this revelation that God already has given to us through his Son. The Spirit helps us to know Jesus and to draw close to Him. As we begin to know Jesus, the Holy Spirit uses this opportunity to shape our characters so that we become more like our Lord. And through all of his activity the Spirit brings glory to Christ.

In trying to understand how the Holy Spirit works in the lives of believers, much has been said about the distinction between the *fruit of the Spirit* (Gal. 5:22-23) and the *gifts of the Spirit* (Rom. 12:6-8; 1 Cor. 12:4-11, 27-31; Eph. 4:11-13). The **fruit** of the Spirit are the character traits of Christ produced in us when we "walk" with the Spirit (Gal. 5:25). Those who act in conformity with the Holy Spirit's guidance produce spiritual fruit.[25] Spiritual **gifts,** on the other hand, are "tools" which the Spirit gives to us for building up the church.[26]

Since individual Christians serve on the basis of their spiritual gifts, by deciding what gifts to give to each person, the Holy Spirit exercises control over the spiritual life of each believer and the church as a whole.[27]

While spiritual fruit and spiritual gifts are to be distinguished, we also can recognize the close relationship between them. **First, the Holy Spirit is the source of both spiritual fruit and spiritual gifts.** Neither is the product of human ingenuity and strength. We do not force the Spirit's hand through what we do, whether it is praise, prayer, preaching, or practicing moral principles. No amount of human effort can cause a person or a church to become more spiritual, unless God's Spirit is in control of the human effort. The Holy Spirit is sovereign over both spiritual gifts and spiritual fruit.

Second, both spiritual fruit and spiritual gifts are related to spiritual maturity. The fruit are the result of the maturation process, as each believer attains the *whole measure of the fullness of Christ* (Eph. 4:13). Spiritual gifts represent the means which the Holy Spirit uses to mature Christ's whole body. As individual Christians serve according to their gifts, the church is *built up* spiritually (Eph. 4:12). As individual Christians mature, the Spirit works through the whole church to reveal Christ's glory to the whole world.

Finally, recognize that spiritual gifts and spiritual fruit represent the means the Spirit uses to achieve His ultimate purpose. That purpose is to bear testimony to Christ, to reveal the truth about Christ, and to glorify Christ. The Holy Spirit does not bring us to faith in Christ, assimilate us into the Body of Christ, and conform us to the image of Christ only for our own sake. Certainly, the results of all this activity by the Spirit does benefit us—we are saved from lostness, our sins are forgiven, and we receive the gift of eternal life. We become children of God and co-heirs with Jesus in the Kingdom of God. But, more importantly, we fulfill the purpose for which we were created in the first place. **As the Holy Spirit transforms us to the image of Christ, through us He bears witness to the truth.**

We Are His Witnesses

In Japan, if a Christian goes around her community inviting neighbors to participate in a Bible study at her house, she likely will have few positive responses. A few people will show up because they consider the inviter to be their friend and don't want to hurt her feelings. They will endure the Bible study time with carefully hidden disinterest. Participants will ask just enough questions so that they seem to be involved in the lesson but carefully will avoid any indication that they actually believe what they are hearing. Then they will participate with great enthusiasm in the conversation over coffee that follows the Bible study. This will give the Christian some measure of hope. "The ladies really seemed to enjoy our time together today," she will tell herself. "If we keep going, some of them eventually will believe in Jesus." This statement is true. Some of the women who continue to hear God's Word eventually do trust in Christ. But this is a small minority. Most of them eventually will drop out. They will wonder what the teacher was trying to say and what the Bible really has to do with them.

This situation is not unique to Japan. In the United States the lack of interest in Bible-based teaching by those outside of the church has given rise to seeker-sensitive worship services and study groups which attempt to address the *felt needs* of nonbelievers. Carl E. Braaten writes about this situation,

> As we enter the third millennium we are still the people elected to bring the gospel and build the church in this post-Christian, post-modern, post-communist, post-denominational, post-whatever kind of situation in which we find ourselves. It seems that the gospel is too weak a message to persuade the skeptics, critics and nihilists of the postmodern culture. So we often try to dress it up in the latest styles to appeal to the cultured despisers today.[28]

Standing in sharpest contrast to what I have just described is what now is taking place in many areas of the world that once were thought to be resistant to Christianity. In China, for example, between 1982 and 2000, the estimated number of Christians increased from 1.3 million to just under 90 million.[29] More than an estimated 30,000 new believers in China are baptized every day.[30] Between 1990 and 1992 the number of known Mongolian believers increased from only six to over 60,000![31] Similar examples of rapid growth in numbers of believers are reported in many places in Asia and Africa.[32] Even in the Muslim world, where conversion to Christianity is a capital offense, in some countries thousands of people have turned to faith in Christ.[33]

Many factors account for the rapid growth of Christianity which we now see in some areas of the world. One of the most significant has to do with the "messenger" who shares the gospel. David Garrison writes,

> True evangelism goes beyond proclamation to communication. Communication means that someone has to hear and understand what is proclaimed. Often times, the subtle shift from proclamation to real communication triggers a response that was previously absent. . . . Church Planting Movement practitioners typically achieve this same end through *indigenization*—transferring responsibility for gospel communication to those who naturally present it through their own worldview perspective. Though missionaries often begin the evangelization of a people group . . ., the primary evangelizers are always the new believers themselves, and they contextualize the gospel better than anyone else.[34]

Although I do not discount the importance which Garrison places on indigenization of the gospel message, this factor alone does not account for the present response to the gospel. When we only talk about contextualizing the gospel so that it fits the indigenous understanding of a culture, something is still missing. As we previously noted in our study of John 6, Jesus clearly communicated the gospel in a way that fit the cultural context of the Jews in first-century Palestine. But when they understood what Jesus was saying, they rejected Him. Understanding does not always bring conversion. ***More exists to being an effective messenger of the gospel than merely clarity of explanation***.

Numerous Japanese Christians, fervent in their faith, do quite well explaining the gospel so that anyone who hears could understand and believe. Yet, while the response is to the gospel in China is great, in Japan it is practically nil. For 150 years missionaries and Japanese Christians have continually asked *why*? Why doesn't God's Spirit move here and now?

This last question is crucial, because what we are talking about not only is the conversion of massive numbers of people to faith in Christ. We are talking about a movement of God's Spirit—something only He can do. More is at stake than culturally and linguistically appropriate communication.

Jesus said, "*I tell you the truth, anyone who has faith in me will do what I have been doing. He will do even greater things than these, because I am going to the Father*" (John 14:12). When He goes to the Father, Jesus sends the "*Spirit of Truth*" to be "*with*" us and "*in*" us (John 14:17). The Spirit empowers believers to continue and even exceed the work that Jesus accomplished while He was on earth. The Spirit does this by "t*aking what is* [Christ's] *and making it known to* [us]" (John 16:14).

I believe that ***when we see many people turning to faith in Christ, this indicates that people are following the leadership of the Holy Spirit.*** First, they have yielded to the Spirit's desire to transform them so that they reflect the image of Christ. They have said *yes* to the Spirit's impetus to use His sword to cut them to the heart, to remove sin, and to make them holy vessels fit for the King's service. They have been changed so that their own lives bear witness to the truth of the Gospel. When they, with Paul, say, "*I no longer live, but Christ lives in me*" (Gal. 2:20), no one can deny the truthfulness of their words.

When we fail to see a response to the gospel, I fear that in some cases this is because those who are trying to proclaim the gospel have not yet been transformed by its power. Rather than being "*streams of living water*" (John 7:38), they resemble dried up cisterns. Nothing about the way they live indicates that the gospel has any real impact at all.

Jesus already has provided the remedy for this situation. He is the Holy Spirit. The Holy Spirit is present to remake the believer so that he or she resembles Christ. But, in order for this to happen in accordance with God's will, we can develop a "no-holds-barred" attitude in our response to the Spirit's work. ***Be willing to open up every corner of your life to the Spirit's work.*** When He reveals any area of our lives that does not measure up to the standard of Christ, allow the Spirit to remove the blemish. The very sins we try to hold out of the Spirit's reach prevent us from being fully transformed by the Spirit's power. These sins prevent us from becoming effective witnesses for Christ.

Second, we must be willing to follow the Spirit's leadership regarding place of service. In the Scriptures we have many examples of people who gave up what they were doing to relocate to a new place because God led them to do so. Abraham moved to Canaan. Moses gave up following sheep to lead the Hebrews out of Egypt. Philip left a spiritual awakening in Samaria to meet the Ethiopian eunuch on the road to Gaza. Paul gave up his plans to go to Asia and went to Macedonia instead. The Lord Jesus left his carpenter shop to go by the way of the cross.

Be careful that we do not become so consumed with carrying out our own plans that we fail to discern the voice of God's Spirit. When I was in seminary, a friend of mine told me that he did not like to go to missiology class. When I asked why, he said he believed the professor was trying to make him feel guilty for not going to the mission field. I remember thinking that perhaps my friend was so consumed in his own plan to become a pastor that he was unwilling to make himself available to follow the Spirit's leading to serve overseas.

The truth is that in so many ways every day all of us miss opportunities for witness because we fail to follow the prompting of the Holy Spirit. How many times have we failed to lend a helping hand, to have a cup of coffee with a friend, to offer a word of encouragement, to visit the sick, or to run an errand because it seemed less important than the work that consumed our attention at the time? In God's economy no task is too small. How do we know when a seemingly small deed of service will open the door to share a word about the love of Christ? How can we measure the potential impact that the one to whom we have the opportunity to witness can have for the Kingdom of God? Only God knows the potential of any person. All that we know is every man, woman, and child is a person God loves—a person for whom Christ died. Every person is important, so every opportunity which the Spirit provides to share the gospel is of lasting, eternal importance.

If you want to become an effective witness for Christ, say *yes* to his Spirit. Allow the Spirit to fully transform you into the image of Christ. Be attentive to the Spirit's prompting so you can be at the right place at the right time to bear witness for Christ. Then what you do as well as the words you say for Christ will have the ring of truth.

Responding to His Voice

1. What role did the Holy Spirit play in wooing you to faith in Christ?

2. How has openness to the possibility of spiritual truth in other religions affected your own witness for Christ?

3. Do you have any areas of your life that you have not given over to be transformed by the Holy Spirit?

4. Are you sensitive to the Spirit's leadership when you share the gospel, or do you act tend to act on your own?

Chapter 12

When His Kingdom Comes

Jesus said, "My kingdom is not of this world. If it were, my servants would fight to prevent my arrest by the Jews. But now my kingdom is from another place."

"You are a king, then!" Pilate said.

Jesus answered, "You are right in saying I am a king. In fact, for this reason I was born, and for this I came into the world, to testify to the truth. Everyone on the side of truth listens to me" (John 18:36-37).

Words and Actions that Tell Others that Jesus is King

In 1942, 120 Holiness pastors in Japan "were arrested on the charges of 'disseminating statements which reject the national structure.'" Specific charges related to their belief in the second coming of Christ which was considered incompatible with the divinity of the Japanese emperor. Seven of the pastors eventually died as a result of their imprisonment. All 270 Holiness churches in Japan were closed.[1]

More recently, in China numerous house church leaders have been arrested, their members scattered, and their churches closed. In most cases the charges leveled against these Christians had to do with sedition and other crimes against the state.

In Islamic countries, where the *Sharia* legal code is strictly enforced, a Muslim breaks the law if he or she converts to Christianity. Christian believers routinely are beaten, jailed, and even killed if they refuse to recant their faith in Christ.

In Western democracies, where some degree of religious freedom exists, many people have difficulty understanding why a government's response to a person's belief in Christ would be so extreme. "People should be able to believe whatever they want," people reason, "as long those beliefs do not impinge on the rights of others." This view fails to recognize that genuine faith in Christ cannot merely be a private matter. When a person experiences the spiritual transformation that results from faith in Christ, it will impact the way he or she interacts in every other sphere of life, including the political, the social and the economic.

Christians from other countries often cringe when they walk into an Evangelical church building in the United States and see the Stars and Stripes hanging from a pole in one corner of the room. For American Christians this is almost a matter of course, because in our hearts love for country is so closely related to faith in God. The reaction of Christians from abroad to this American custom is not based on any dislike of America. They love the United States and the freedom for which it stands. Given the opportunity, many of them would choose to immigrate to the United States and put down new roots. What troubles them is the tying together of Christian faith and patriotism in any way that subsumes belief in Christ under loyalty to one's country. This emerges from their own experience of putting Jesus first, even when this means saying that their own nation will have to take second place. For taking this stand they have paid a heavy price—sometimes even shedding their own blood.

When rulers call for absolute obedience, a man is a threat if he says he will obey Christ. A woman who gives her life to Jesus rather than to the state is disloyal. A person who says, "I will follow my Lord, even if it means disobeying my earthly ruler and his decrees," is the potential leader of a seditious movement who must be put out of the way before he gets out of hand.

When a nation or its ruler denies to the citizens of that land the opportunity to believe in Christ, this action has spiritual as well as political significance. Not only is this a political act done by a government against its citizens. It also is a spiritual act done by Satan against the subjects of the Kingdom of God. As political authorities carry out their plans, the prince of darkness also is moving in the shadows and working out his own sinister designs. As Peter Beyerhaus has written,

> Behind the hatred of the world stands the primeval hatred of the prince of this world who rebelled against God. He wants to subdue the world to his rule. He knows, however, that this usurped position is going to be taken away from him by God's own Son, whom God has appointed to be the Redeemer and real Ruler of the world. Satan reacts to this in fury! His hatred is directed primarily against Jesus Christ himself. He wants to crush him in order to prevent his work of redemption from taking place. But he cannot succeed in this, so his wrath turns against the followers of Christ. They still live in the world; they are sent into it in order to bring all nations under the authority of Christ by proclaiming to them the gospel of his atoning death and glorious resurrection. Therefore, they become the new target of Satan's fierce attacks.[2]

Whenever Christianity moves into a new territory to claim it for Christ, "religious and political authorities [see] their power endangered."[3] As the Kingdom of God advances through the proclamation of the gospel, it never moves into neutral territory. Rather, God's Kingdom always advances at the expense of Satan's dominion. The result is not peace on earth. Rather, a "growing polarity" between those who submit to the rule of Christ and those who refuse Christ and remain under Satan's domination.[4] Evil persons working under the influence of the evil one create evil social structures to carry out evil deeds in a fallen world. That is why something is identifiably demonic in "oppression, cruelty . . . racism, nationalism, totalitarianism, terrorism, torture, war, scientism, depersonalizing technocracy, waste and pollution."[5]

Remember that Satan is at work "through social structures, ideologies, movements and persons." Never forget the evil one who works behind all of this evil. Otherwise we will aim our attack at the wrong enemy. We will attack communism or global capitalism, Hinduism or Islam.[6] We will blame the people who are a part of these social, economic, political and religious systems for the evil that these systems cause. Personal accountability for individual actions is a factor. But if we reduce responsibility for these evil acts only to their human perpetrators, we will miss the point that **the people who take part in these systems are enslaved by them as well**. As Satan's emissaries of death, they are themselves under the sentence of death. They have only one hope to set them free. It is the same hope they share with us. True liberation only occurs when the power of Jesus Christ frees people from the bondage of sin.[7]

As long as a person resides in an oppressive kingdom, he or she cannot be free. Freedom only occurs either when the person relocates to another kingdom with a benevolent ruler or the old totalitarian monarchy is overthrown and a new kingdom is set up in its place. In John 18, we find out that this is why Jesus was sent to earth. This is what the gospel is all about. **Jesus was sent from outside of this world to set people free from the oppressive rule of the dark prince. Jesus brought freedom, light, and life to all who are willing to trust in Him. This is the power of the gospel!**

"My Kingdom Is Not of this World"

Pontius Pilate served from A.D. 26 until A.D. 36 as the prefect of Judea. During that time, Pilate's actions on behalf of the Roman Empire resulted in repeated threats of insurrection by the Jews. Near the beginning of his administration, for example, Pilate had military standards which bore the image of the emperor brought into

Jerusalem. The Jews saw this as idolatry and threatened a massive revolt. Pilate gave in to the threat and had the images removed. Later, Pilate tried to have golden shields inscribed with his own name and those of Emperor Tiberius placed on the walls of Herod's palace in Jerusalem. A letter of complaint was filed by leading Jewish citizens who saw the shields as a "violation of the religious sanctity of Jerusalem." The emperor ordered Pilate to have the shields moved. On a third occasion Pilate used money from the temple treasury to build an aqueduct to bring water into Jerusalem. When Pilate used troops to squelch the resulting demonstrations, numerous Jews were killed.[8]

Against this background the dialogue in John 18 between Pilate and Jesus occurred. When the Roman prefect asked Jesus, "*Are you the king of the Jews?*", (John 18:33), Pilate acted on the basis of his own volatile experience of dealing with the Jews. Perhaps he was playing a hunch that Jesus was a zealot who was planning to launch some kind of Jewish rebellion to attempt to overthrow Roman rule.[9] Pilate went on to point out that Jesus' "*own people*" had handed Him over for trial (John 18:35). Clearly Jesus had done something to "arouse the hostility of the chief priests." Pilate needed to get to the bottom of it. In this environment in which religion became so easily intertwined with politics, Pilate wondered whether this only was a Jewish religious matter or whether Jesus actually had done something to offend Roman law.[10]

In the world in which we attempt to live and proclaim the gospel, religion and politics continually are interwoven in such a way that they are difficult to distinguish much less separate. E. Stanley Jones articulates the degree of this problem in Christian history,

> Take the Crusades—men of violence tried to take that kingdom by force and succeeded in laying the foundations of hate and conflict through the centuries. Take Genghis Khan's suggestion through Marco Polo to the Pope: "Please

> send us a hundred teachers, well learned in the seven arts and well able to prove that the way of Christ is best." Marco Polo, seeing that the request was of great significance, hastened back to the Pope. Two years later, two teachers instead of a hundred were sent with this message, "Become politically and ecclesiastically attached to Rome." They didn't bother to offer the kingdom of God, a universal kingdom; they offered political and ecclesiastical attachment to Rome. Genghis Khan turned it down, accepted Islam, and spread blood and fire and a hating faith through Asia and Europe.[11]

Although many will take exception to Jones's characterization of Islam, we cannot fail to see his point that at least some of Islam's furor is the result of the untidy mixture of Christianity with politics in the West. This has not been limited to Catholicism. When Protestant missionaries fanned out across Asia and Africa in the 19th century, they were so closely linked with colonial authorities that the local populations often viewed them as advance agents for their governments. The local response to Protestant missionaries was not too far afield. This is because, as Bosch writes, many missionaries during that period operated on the basis of "manifest destiny"—

> the conviction that God, in His providence, had chosen the Western nations, because of their unique qualities, to be the standard bearers of his cause even to the utmost ends of the earth.[12]

Little wonder that during the Boxer Rebellion, which arose in China in 1900, in their attempt to expel all foreign influence, the Chinese killed 189 Protestant missionaries and their children. A large number of Chinese Christians, who were regarded as the "running dogs of imperialism", also lost their lives.[13]

Despite these warnings from the past, the attempt to infuse the gospel with political content still is with us. One can look no further than the various political theologies now being advocated as indigenous Christianity—Liberation Theology in South America, Black Theology and radical forms of Feminist Theology in North America, and Minjung Theology in Korea are only a few examples. In all of these, the transcendent aspect of God and His kingdom is lost.

Rather than a **person** with whom we can have a relationship, God is reduced to an **impersonal spiritual force** which energizes people to bring about equality and justice in the present world.[14] The result is a single-minded focus on human reconciliation in which the "vertical dimension" of Christianity, the human need for God's forgiveness and new life through faith in Christ, is completely lost.[15] This never was what Jesus intended when He preached the kingdom of God. Jesus said, "***My kingdom is not of this world.*** *If it were, my servants would fight to prevent my arrest by the Jews*" (John 18:36, emphasis mine). Jesus was not sent to recruit an army of fighting men to set up a worldly kingdom.[16] Jesus' followers did not display military resistance when the armed guard arrested Him in the garden.[17]

Every political, economic, and social system ever devised by human beings is "shakable."[18] The Roman Empire, which Pilate represented before Jesus, looked rock-solid in the first century, but eventually it crumbled and fell apart. In his response to Pilate Jesus Himself alluded to this limitation of Roman power, "*You would have no power over me if it were not given to you from above*" (John 19:11).

In our day the United States is considered the world's only superpower. But the fragileness of American power was exposed to the whole world on September 11, 2001. As a result, we now have a power vacuum, as the United States labors to rebuild its status as the world's political, economic, and military leader. Radical Islamicists, on the other hand, long for a new center of the world order built around those who bow their knees to Allah. They are working to extend the sphere of Islamic influence and power throughout the world. These are two models of kingdom building—one secular and economic, the other religious and moral. But neither of them is in line with the kingship of Jesus Christ.

When He spoke of His kingdom, Jesus had something else in mind than what we usually reference as power. Jesus was talking about the "unshakable kingdom of God."[19] He was talking about a spiritual kingdom that God Himself would set up as men and women bow their hearts to Him. In this kingdom God does not need to use political, economic, or social means to gain control over people. God has a much more powerful means at his disposal than politics and social action. It is the **power of the gospel** lived and proclaimed by Christians in an embattled world. And the power of the Holy Spirit is at work in those who yield to Him.

Even Evangelical Christians tend to underestimate the gospel's power to transform the world. We try to help the gospel along by advocating change through the political process and social service. Don't get me wrong. I believe in Christians being politically and socially active. To me, this is a part of what being salt and light in the world means. Only I think that we take care not to allow these other priorities to overshadow our first priority, which is to make Christ known. Only the message of Jesus, received and trusted in, has the power to change people. Only through the changed lives of individuals who have placed their faith in Christ will the nations of the world be transformed as well.

The kingdom which Jesus rules over is not worldly, but it is **in the world.** It is here because Jesus Himself brought His kingdom into the world *"from another place"* (John 18:36).

"My Kingdom Is from Another Place"

Pilate was the emissary of a powerful earthly empire whose mindset decidedly was this-worldly. He was concerned with advancing his own career in the present world by elevating the prestige of his emperor among the subjugated Jews of Palestine. In his way of thinking, little room existed for spiritual matters. Pilate had very little patience, for example, with religious issues related to Judaism. We see this in his initial response to the Jewish leaders when they brought Jesus to Pilate. "*Take him yourselves and judge him by your own law,*" Pilate said (John 18:31). Only when he heard that Jesus might be guilty of a crime requiring the death penalty did Pilate agreed to hear the case.

With a view of life so focused on the present world, Pilate must have had difficulty understanding what Jesus meant when He said that His kingdom was "*from another place*" (John 18:36). Pilate hardly could have understood that Jesus' words included His claim to be the pre-existent Son of God[20] whom the Father sent to re-establish His authority on earth. Pilate must have wondered how this traveling teacher from Galilee who now stood before him could have been a king at all. Doubt was in Pilate's words, "*You are a king, then!*" (John 18:37). Perhaps placing a question mark at the end of this sentence best would capture the meaning of what Pilate said: "Are you a king, then?" He was like Thomas who, on hearing of Jesus' resurrection, wondered, "How can these things be?" Unless Pilate could see some evidence that Jesus really was a king, he had no reason to believe what Jesus was saying was true.

The people of the world in which we live and proclaim the gospel look at things from the perspective of Pontius Pilate. They tend to look at Jesus from the vantage point of His life on earth before the crucifixion and ask, "Who was this carpenter from Galilee who became an itinerant preacher and went about doing good?" Was He a prophet? So say the Muslims. Was Jesus an ascetic who helped us to see beyond ourselves into the realm of the supernatural? That is what some Hindu mystics would like us to believe. Was He a revolutionary who was here to found a movement for freedom from oppression and equality for all? That is the Marxist ideology that underlies political approaches to theology and mission. This question of Who Jesus is and why He was sent is the fundamental question we face when we bear witness for Christ.

In responding to this issue, bear witness in light of the New Testament. God's Word tells us that Jesus brings God's kingdom into the world in three stages. The first stage was the "incarnation of God's Son in the person of Jesus Christ."[21] The culmination of Jesus' first appearance on earth was his death and resurrection. As a result Jesus broke the stranglehold which Satan, through the power of sin and death, exercised over the world.

At the time that Jesus stood before him, Pilate had no way to know what would transpire in the next few hours, the next three days, or the 2,000 years that have since passed. Pilate could not have realized his own central role in this decisive event in world history. Although I am certain that Pilate heard rumors about Jesus' resurrection and the subsequent, rapid growth of Christianity throughout the Roman Empire, Pilate probably went to his grave without ever having fully understood the king that he had nailed to the cross.

On the other hand, Jesus' own understanding of the reason He was sent to the earth centered on the kingdom of God.[22] As Jesus itinerated from place to place, the message He taught had one main theme, "*The kingdom of God is near. Repent and believe the good news!*" (Mark 1:15). God's kingdom advanced as Jesus overcame the power of evil in whatever form He found it, "pain, sickness, death, demon-possession, personal sin and immorality, the loveless self-righteousness of those who claim to know God, the maintaining of special class privileges, the brokenness of human relationships." Jesus was saying, "If human distress takes many forms, the power of God does likewise."[23] Jesus was not sent to earth only to preach, teach and heal. Jesus was here to re-establish God's divine rule on earth over which He Himself would reign as king!

The second stage of God's kingdom entering the world commenced with Christ's ascension to sit at the right hand of the Father. From this position, Jesus presently exercises his authority over all the nations of the earth. He carries out his plan to bring people of all nations under His authority through the work of the Holy Spirit, the ministry of the church, and the proclamation of the gospel.[24] As Christ's people proclaim His good news and serve those who have physical, emotional, and spiritual needs, God exercises his caring authority over all of life. The resulting transformation becomes a sign that God's kingdom already is present in the world.[25]

At the same time, God's kingdom also has a "not-yet" aspect to it. The prince of this world "still exercises power over all those who have not accepted the redemptive love of God in Jesus Christ."[26] The deep polarity, which now exists between the kingdoms of God and Satan, results in a "time of intense conflict, struggle and suffering."[27] At a rather high cost God's kingdom progresses in the face of stiff opposition. If the foundation of the church is the death and resurrection of Jesus Christ, then the framework on which it is built is the sacrifice of those who have laid down their lives for their faith in Christ. Revelation 12:11 tells us that Satan has been overcome "*by the blood of the Lamb and by the word of* ***their testimony****; they did not love their lives so much as to shrink from death*" (emphasis mine).

We now wait for the third, future stage of God's kingdom. That stage will arrive with the return of Jesus Christ. Jesus finally will defeat and banish from His realm "every hostile force that counteracts his holy will."[28] It will have *a new heaven and a new earth* in which *there will be no more death or mourning or crying or pain, for the old order of things has passed away* (Rev. 21:1, 4).

We live and proclaim the gospel at the junction of two worlds. We live in an age when God's kingdom already has arrived but is **not yet** present in its final perfected form. Those who live only in the present world tend to see only the **not yet**. They do not see Jesus ruling as king. They see only a world ravaged by the effects of evil. In this situation, they have no choice but to reduce Jesus to a category that fits their own worldview. That may mean making Jesus into a great teacher, a supernatural apparition, or a gunslinging liberator. They must do this because they lack the spiritual framework they need really to understand who Jesus is.

If the world's peoples are to develop a renewed understanding of Who Jesus is, they are going to have to **catch it** from us. People need not only to **hear** about Jesus being king. They also need to **see** what the rule of Jesus looks like through watching a life that has been given to Him. Talking about the kingship of Jesus or the Lordship of Christ will do little good if we also do not live lives that are yielded to His rule. This is why living in the light of the kingship of Jesus is essential. We must endeavor to yield to Christ's rule over every area of our lives. We need to speak and act in a way that proclaims "Jesus is Lord"—not only of His people and His church but also of the whole earth. When we who claim to serve Jesus remain unwilling to submit to His authority over our own lives, the reality of His Kingship is impossible for those around us to grasp.

"I Am a King"

The interview of Pilate with Jesus was a confrontation between two views of "kingship"—one a worldly kingship directed by force and terror, and the other a spiritual kingship expressed by the power of grace and truth.[29] In the **light of the cross** we best see this contrast between worldly and spiritual power. The worldly king displays his power by using the cross as an instrument of punishment and death. The spiritual king displays His power by using the cross as instrument of grace and life. The worldly king uses the cross to accomplish the purposes of Satan; the spiritual king uses the cross to fulfill the will of God.

When Jesus said to Pilate, *"I am a king"* (John 18:37), He was speaking of a kingship that was rooted deeply in God's personal relationship with His people. In Exodus 19:5-6 God told Israel that although all the nations belonged to Him, Israel was His **"treasured**

possession" by virtue of the people's covenant relationship with Him. On the other hand, Israel had to recognize God's rule if the people were to be blessed. If they failed to obey God, they would be punished (Deut. 30:11-20). As a nation Israel never reached its God-given potential, because the people continually disobeyed God.[30]

Rather than completely rejecting Israel, however, God chose to fulfill his plan for the nation as a whole through only one man, a descendant of David. The Lord promised David,

> "*I will raise up your offspring to succeed you, one of your own sons, and I will establish his kingdom. He is the one who will build a house for me, and I will establish his throne forever. I will be his father and he will be my son . . . I will set him over my house and my kingdom forever; his throne will be established forever*" (1 Chron. 17:11-13, 14).

In the Old Testament understanding, a son through obedience fulfilled his obligation to his father. Through acting as God's obedient Son, Jesus fulfilled both God's purpose for Israel and his plan for the Davidic kingship.[31]

Everything that Jesus did was an act of obedience to God the Father. As Jesus said, "*I always do what pleases Him*" (John 8:29). As such, **Jesus' life on earth became the perfect example of what a life that is totally yielded to God looks like**. Through the cross we see this most clearly. On the night before Jesus was crucified, He prayed, "*Father, if you are willing, take this cup from me; yet not my will, but yours be done*" (Luke 22:42). As a human being Who loved life, Jesus recoiled from the idea of death. Jesus was not afraid of death. His perfect love for us drove out all fear (1 John 4:18). As a human being, Jesus did not want to die. Yet Jesus, for the sake of life, was willing to walk the path to death. Through this act of complete obedience, Jesus became the means by which God's grace could be poured out on all people. As a result of His death and resurrection, Jesus made forgiveness of sin and new life available to all. The only thing that is necessary to receive these gifts is to trust in Him.

To bless the people of all nations God the Father established an eternal kingdom through His Son. The results of God's rule through His Son impact every area of life. Peace, justice, and prosperity exist among the nations (Isa. 2:1-5; 9:1-7; 11:1-16). God's people are redeemed from the spiritual captivity that occurred because of their own defilement. Where God reigns, the result is salvation which leads to shouts of joy (Isa. 52:1-8). God provides freedom instead of bondage, *gladness instead of mourning*, *praise instead of . . . despair.* The *righteousness* which the Lord bestows displays *his splendor* (Isa. 61:1-3).[32]

Every kingdom set up by a creature is limited in time, space, and power. Take, for example, the kingdoms created by people. No human kingdom will last forever. No human kingdom controls the whole world. And no human kingdom has absolute authority. Perhaps this is best illustrated by Alexander the Great who, on reaching India, is said to have wept because he had no more worlds to conquer. Soon thereafter Alexander died suddenly; his empire ended abruptly.

Satan, who is not a human being but who is a creature, also finds himself in this same predicament. Satan longs to rule the universe. He longs to "*raise [his] throne above the stars of God* and to make himself *like the Most High*." But instead, Satan shares the destiny of the people who serve him. He will be "*brought down to . . . the depths of the pit*" (Isa. 14:13, 14, 15). Although he is the prince of this world, **Satan does not and cannot rule the universe forever, because it belongs to God.** Satan "*is filled with fury, because he knows his time is short*" (Rev. 12:12).

In contrast, God's kingdom is eternal—not only in duration, but also in breadth and in power. Christ rules with all power and authority over an eternal kingdom that includes the whole universe. The kingdom Christ rules is not limited to only redeemed human beings. Since God is the Creator, the whole universe rightfully belongs to

Him (Isa. 66:1). As we have seen, God's authority over heaven and earth now is placed in the hands of His Son (Matt. 28:18; Col. 1:15-17). The Father's will is to redeem the whole physical universe from the results of sin (Rom. 8:19-21) by bringing *all things in heaven and on earth together under one head, even Christ* (Eph. 1:10). Jesus began to assert the authority necessary to bring this about when He was raised to the right hand of the throne of God.[33] And the culmination of his redemptive work will be the creation of *a new heaven and a new earth* (Rev. 21:1-4). In this way, the kingdom which Christ brings fulfills the purpose of creation. As Boyd Hunt writes, "Left to itself creation destroys itself. Redeemed it learns to sing again!"[34]

This divine kingdom has a breadth and depth and concreteness to it that cannot be found in worldly kingdoms. A stability found under the rule of Christ is not available anywhere else. E. Stanley Jones states this so beautifully,

> Man needs nothing so much as he needs something on which he can put his whole weight down in time and eternity, something which will not turn sour or stale through sickness, old age, or death and which will give Him something about which to sing when there is nothing outwardly to sing about, nothing except the fact of an Unshakable Kingdom and an Unchanging Person.[35]

Human participation in God's kingdom, like Jesus' own participation, takes place through obedience to the Father's will. Jones notes that in the Lord's Prayer "*your will be done*" explains how "*your kingdom come*" (Matt. 6:10) takes place. When individuals and whole societies act in obedience to God's will, this brings about God's rule on earth as well as in heaven.[36]

When we live in submission to God's will, "every work becomes God's work."[37] We do not follow Christ by our own initiative. We do not serve God by our own strength. Only when God intervenes to bring a miraculous change in our hearts can we acknowledge His rule in our lives.[38] *For we are God's workmanship, created in Christ Jesus to do good works, which God prepared in advance for us to do* (Eph. 2:10). Apart from this transforming work of God in us, we cannot do what He desires. Unless Jesus enters and re-creates us (2 Cor. 5:17), we are incapable of following Him.

This is why we avoid proclaiming a gospel that says salvation occurs as a result of giving mental assent to the teachings of Christ. Also avoid restricting the meaning of Christian faith to belief in the historicity of Jesus' virgin birth, life, death, resurrection, and ascension. While believing in these events is necessary, their reality must trigger a realization that Jesus Christ is Lord, king, and the rightful ruler of our lives. When we acknowledge the authority of King Jesus, we entrust both our present lives and our eternities to Him. When the New Testament writers speak of faith in Christ, they mean **trusting** in Jesus enough to follow Him. This is the only kind of faith that brings about forgiveness of sin and eternal life.

"Everyone on the Side of the Truth Listens to Me"

When we share the gospel, we often talk about Jesus as Savior. Of course we have strong, biblical support for this emphasis. Acts 4:12 tells us, "*Salvation is found in no one else, for there is no other name under heaven given to men by which we must be saved.*" Paul and Silas told the Philippian jailer, "*Believe in the Lord Jesus, and you will be saved—you and your household*" (Acts 16:31). And in Romans 10:9 we read, "*That if you confess with your mouth, 'Jesus is Lord,' and believe in your heart that God raised him from the dead, you will be saved.*"

Notice these passages do **not** teach that people only must believe in Jesus as Savior in order to be saved. Rather, they must both "*believe*" (Acts 16:31) and *confess* (Rom. 10:9) that "***Jesus is***

Lord. " For such a confession to be true, however, it cannot be only verbal. People who say, "*Jesus is Lord*", also obey Jesus and do His will. Otherwise their confession is meaningless. Salvation is the result of making Jesus Lord—of accepting His authority to rule over us and doing His will.

Reading the Great Commission (Matt. 28:18-20) from this perspective is instructive. Jesus has "*all authority in heaven and on earth*" (28:18). The purpose of the Great Commission is to extend **Jesus' authority** to the ends of the earth. Of course, the whole world already belongs to Him. But Jesus wants people to recognize His authority. He wants people to bow their knees before Him and to confess that *Jesus is Lord* (Phil. 2:10-11). This is why Jesus sends out his followers to "*make disciples of all nations*" (Matt. 28:19). The basic meaning of a *disciple* is **not** a believer. A disciple is not someone who trusts in Jesus. While faith in Jesus is necessary, **a disciple of Christ is, rather, someone who brings himself or herself under Jesus' authority and commits to do his will**. Jesus instructs those He sends out to teach "*them to* ***obey*** *everything I have commanded you*" (28:20, emphasis mine).

The goal of gospel proclamation is not to encourage people to make a one-time confession of faith in Jesus as Savior. The goal is, rather, to encourage people to commit the remainder of their lives on earth to following Jesus as Lord. It is, in a word, **to make disciples**. As Howard Snyder writes,[39]

> An evangelism which focuses exclusively on souls or on an otherworldly transaction which makes no real difference here and now is unfaithful to the gospel. An evangelism of cheap grace which does not call for true, present allegiance to Jesus as Lord is not true evangelism.[40]

During the present period, Christ has commissioned the church to proclaim his "kingship" among the nations. By bringing the people of all nations under allegiance to Christ, their spiritual bondage to "Satan's power structures" can be broken.[41] But this proclamation of Christ's authority makes no sense if it proceeds out of the mouths of people who have not yielded their own lives to Christ. For this good news to have its maximum impact, those who proclaim Jesus also must obey Him. People see the gospel's power by watching the life of a person who says *yes* to everything that Christ has commanded.

Since the gospel of Jesus Christ is everything that we say it is, it has the power truly to transform the lives of men and women—to remake them into new human beings who are in the image of Christ. But how can people know that this is possible unless they see that we who say we believe in Jesus **already** have been changed? Our own, personal transformation by the gospel—the life we are able to live because Christ's Spirit is at work in us—convicts the lost of their need for Jesus. When we **live** as those who no longer are under the yoke of sin, caught in the grasp of Satan, and limited by the fear of death, we bear witness to the truth that those Christ set free really are free!

Jesus said to Pilate, *"Everyone who is on the side of truth listens to me"* (John 18:37). This is the basis for living and proclaiming the gospel in an embattled world. In order to live and proclaim the words of Jesus, **listen to Him**. Merely hearing us is not enough for those with whom we share the gospel. Let them also **hear Jesus' voice** through our words and our actions. Only when people hear Jesus' voice do they turn away from their own way and begin to follow Him. They forsake all for the sake of the cross. They say *no* to self and *yes* to Jesus as Lord. They are set free from sin and death for salvation and receive new life through faith in Jesus Christ.

Responding to His Voice

1. If you were arrested and put on trial for obedience to Jesus, would your opponents have enough evidence to convict you?

2. Jesus has rightful authority over all of heaven and earth. Are you attempting to limit Jesus' rule by reserving some areas of your life for your own control?

3. Do you believe in the gospel's power to transform those who believe in Christ?

4. Can other people see in your life the results of the gospel's transforming power?

Epilogue

Do They Hear His Voice through You?

To this John replied, "A man can receive only what is given him from heaven. You yourselves can testify that I said, 'I am not the Christ but am sent ahead of him.' . . . He must become greater; I must become less" (John 3:27-28, 30).

At the end of a hot summer day a missionary serving in a Muslim country was traveling home by rickshaw when he encountered a young man making his way to a bus stop. The young man appeared lonely and dejected. He was amazed when the missionary asked him, "Hey, brother, do you want to get up in this rickshaw and ride with me?" As they rode together in the rickshaw, they talked. Eventually the missionary asked the young man to stop by his house to meet his wife. When they arrived at the missionary's house, his wife gave the young man coffee and chocolate-chip cookies. After they talked for a while, the couple sent the young man on his way with a New Testament.

The young man stayed up all night and read the words of the New Testament. On the second night as he continued to read, the Holy Spirit took hold of his life. Years later the young man, now a mature Christian leader, recounted the story in his own words,

> "I was reading the Gospel of John, chapter three. When I got to verse 17, it hit me. John says, 'Jesus did not come into the world to condemn the world, but that the world through him might be saved.' . . . You see, I wasn't just a sinner boy. Jesus had come into the world to save me."[1]

This story from David Garrison's book, *Church Planting Movements*, illustrates what can happen when a person who **proclaims** the gospel also **lives** the gospel. Before this Muslim young man ever **heard** a word of the gospel from the missionary's mouth, he **experienced** the gospel through the actions of this missionary couple. The young man was drawn to the gospel because he witnessed the results of its transforming power in the lives of two people who, through simple acts of kindness, shared Christ's love with him. Then when the young man opened the New Testament, his heart already was prepared to receive its words. As a result of experiencing Christ's love, this young Muslim had become fertile soil for the seed of God's Word to be implanted and to bear fruit. Here was a life that was open for the Holy Spirit to do His work. As a result the young man turned to faith in Jesus Christ.

This is only the beginning of this man's story. The best evidence of genuine conversion is spiritual growth to mature discipleship. In this case what began as a divine appointment between a missionary in a rickshaw and a young man waiting for a bus grew into a movement with thousands of new churches and tens of thousands of Muslims turning to faith in Christ.[2]

Living and proclaiming the gospel begins with *hearing Christ's voice*. When we hear Christ's voice, we can acknowledge who He is. As a result of listening to Christ's voice, we bow before Him as the one true God in worship. We commit each day of our lives to serve Jesus as Lord. That commitment impacts what we do as well as what we say.

Hearing Christ's voice causes us to remove ourselves from the center of our lives. We realize that the only proper occupant of that position is Jesus Himself. This transition from living for self to living for Christ is not instantaneous. Some time must pass for us to give everything over to Him. Our hearts have many quiet corners that we try to keep for ourselves. But the Lord approaches, one by one, each of these doors. First He knocks on the door. Then He tries the doorknob. Finding it locked, Jesus turns and says to us, "What have you been keeping from Me here? When I paid the price for you on the cross, don't you know I bought everything? I am the Lord of this part as well." Then when we open the door, Jesus cleanses another corner of our lives that sin stained. He breathes in new life where before only was death and destruction.

Listening to Jesus' voice allows the Holy Spirit to do His transforming work in us. The Spirit helps us to make Christ's truth our own. Through the Holy Spirit's instruction we realize that not only does God love the whole world, but He also loves us. Not only did Jesus die on the cross to save sinners, but we can confess, "I am a sinner for whom Christ died." The Holy Spirit uses God's Word as His sword (Heb. 4:12) to cut away the cancerous sin that drains the life out of us. He remakes us into God's new creations (2 Cor. 5:17) who are destined to live forever as children of the Heavenly King.

Finally, listening to our Lord's voice beckons us to participate in His work in the world. We realize that everything we do in ministry, whether sharing the gospel, caring for the needs of people, or starting and growing churches, really is *His work*. We quit expending so much effort trying to do *for Him* and begin the much tougher task of walking *with Him* day by day in ministry and service. This is difficult, because we still tend to want to call all of the shots. We want to run ahead with our plans so we can brag about what we *have done* for Jesus. But to do Jesus' work we have to reign in our own will. When we listen to Jesus' voice, rather than proclaiming the gospel for Him, *we allow Him to proclaim the gospel through us*. Rather than trying to live for Him, we allow Him to live and carry out His purpose in the world through us. Like Paul we say,

> "*I have been crucified with Christ and I no longer live, but Christ lives in me. The life I live in the body, I live by faith in the son of God, who loved me and gave himself for me*" (Gal. 2:20).

This is what John meant when he said, "*He must become greater; I must become less*" (John 3:30). When Jesus becomes greater and I become less, Jesus takes control; I relinquish command. Jesus walks ahead; I follow in His steps. Jesus empowers for ministry; I serve with the power that He provides. Jesus receives the glory; I do not. This is difficult to do, because we are accustomed to using Christian service to build our own kingdoms so that others will exclaim our greatness. But it is absolutely essential for Jesus to "*become greater*" if we are to live and proclaim the gospel in an embattled world.

Our relationship with Jesus must take precedence in everything we do, whether we preach, disciple, train leaders, or minister to human needs. This list is much too narrow, because it only includes what we tend to think of as "Christian activities." To this list we add law, medicine, politics, teaching, waiting tables, selling shoes, and any other possible work that Christians may do in the "secular" realm.

When we labor for Christ, He moves into every corner of our world so that the distinction between sacred and secular is removed. With our feet, we carry Christ into every sphere of life. With our hands, Christ reaches out to meet the needs of a hurting world. With our tongues, Christ confounds the darkness of the satanic lie with the truth that has the power to set men and women free.

To illuminate a dark world Jesus even wants to use our play. At the end of the 2002 World Cup in Japan the members of Brazilian national team, which just had won the championship, began to peel off their jerseys. I watched in amazement as many of the team members ran around the field showing off their T-shirts which proclaimed their faith in Jesus Christ. I thought, *Here we are struggling to get a hearing for the gospel in Japan. Despite all of the efforts of missionaries and Japanese Christians, we have not been able to raise the Christian percentage of the population in Japan to more than one percent. But in this act of personal testimony that took all of five minutes, the Brazilian soccer team may have done more to get the attention of Japanese people than anything else that has been done during the last five years.*

Bill Easum is right on target when he writes,

> The challenge of working with [people in the contemporary world], then, is to get them to experience the healing, liberating presence of God in Jesus Christ. The only way this happens is if Christians learn how to walk among pagans as Christians who imitate Jesus. . . .. They must discover Jesus in us and see the connection to their life situation. What they so desperately seek cannot be imposed on them. It must be witnessed and experienced. . . .. It is all about our relationship with Jesus that makes us different. Jesus is all we have to offer the world. Nothing more or less.[3]

In the end, living and proclaiming the gospel is all about hearing Christ's voice. Not only do those who live and proclaim the gospel need to hear His voice. Let those who see our lives and hear our words hear Christ's voice through us. Unless those with whom we share the gospel see the results of the gospel's transforming power by watching the way we live, they are unlikely to stake their lives in the present world, much less their eternal destinies on the carpenter from Nazareth who died on the cross. The lost world says to those who claim to follow Christ, "Never mind the resurrection! What proof do we have that Jesus lives unless we see that He lives in you?"

Through your words and actions let the world hear Jesus' voice. His voice brings light and life to a dark, embattled world.

Notes

Chapter 1

[1]Oscar Cullman, *The Christology of the New Testament* (Philadelphia: Westminster, 1959), 251.

[2] Ibid., 254-55.

[3]F.F. Bruce, *Hebrews* (Grand Rapids: Eerdmans, 1964), 3.

[4]Ray Summers, *Behold the Lamb* (Nashville: Broadman, 1979), 22.

[5]C.K. Barrett, *John* (London: S.P.C.K., 1965), 130.

[6]Gordon H, Clark, *The Johannnine Logos* (Phillipsburg, NJ: Presbyterian and Reformed, 1972), 21-22.

[7]Leon Morris, *John* (Grand Rapids: Eerdmans, 1971), 82-83.

[8]Barnabas Lindars, *John* (Grand Rapids: Eerdmans, 1972), 85.

[9]"Neshama" in *Theological Word Book of the Old Testament,* ed. R. Laird Harris, Gleason L.Archer, and Bruce K, Waltke (Chicago: Moody Bible Institute, 1980), 605.

[10]Morris, 81.

[11]Roger L. Fredrikson, *John* (Waco: Word, 1958), 35.

[12]Ibid., 36.

[13]Ibid., 40.

[14]Lindars, 90.

[15]Clark, 27.

[16]Lindars, 78-79.

[17]Frederic Louis Godet, *John* (Grand Rapids: Kregel, 1978), 265.

[18]Gregory A. Boyd, *God at War* (Downers Grove, IL: InterVarsity, 1997), 230.

[19]Peter F. Ellis, *The Genius of John* (Collegeville, MN: Liturgical, 1984), 24.

[20]C.S. Lewis, *Mere Christianity,* reprint (London: Fontana, 1960), 52-53.

[21]Alister McGrath, *Understanding Jesus* (Grand Rapids: Academie Books, 1987), 96-97.

[22]Fredrikson, 46.

[23]Morris, 104-105.

[24]Godet, 272-74.

Chapter 2

[1] Tom Wright, *Bringing the Church to the World* (Minneapolis: Bethany House, 1992), 36.

[2]Morris, 192-93; Fredrikson, 73.

[3]Fredrikson, 73

[4]Morris, 193-94.

[5]Fredrikson, 73, notes that the fee for exchange was equivalent to another day's wages.

[6]Morris, 195.

[7]William Dyrness, *Themes in Old Testament Theology* (Downers Grove, IL: InterVarsity, 1977), 146.

[8]Ibid., 146-47.

[9]Ibid., 145.

[10]Calvin J. Roetzel, *The World That Shaped the New Testament* (Atlanta: John Knox, 1985), 56-57,

[11]Ibid., 57-61.

[12]Fredrikson, 74.

[13]Ibid., 75.

[14]Ravi Zacharias, *Jesus Among the Gods* (Nashville: Word, 2000), 67.

[15]Morris, 838-39.

[16]William L. Banks, *In Search of the Great Commission: What Did Jesus Really Say?* (Chicago: Moody, 1991), 22-23.

[17]Gordon Fee, *God's Empowering Presence* (Peabody, MA: Hendrickson, 1994), 116.

[18]Zacharias, 73.

[19]Fee, 118.

[20]Wright, 150.

Chapter 3

[1]Barrett, 171.

[2]Fredrikson, 83.

[3]Morris, 219.

[4]Barrett, 175.

[5]Bernard Ramm, *The Witness of the Spirit* (Grand Rapids: Eerdmans, 1960), 47.

[6]Godet, 381-82.

[7]C.R. Vaughan, *The Gifts of the Holy Spirit* (Edinburgh: Banner of Truth Trust, 1975), 172.

[8]Ibid., 173.

[9]Fee, 48.

[10]Lindars, 156.

[11]Dorothy A. Lee, *The Symbolic Narratives in the Fourth Gospel* (Sheffield, England: JSOT, 1994), 46.

[12]The words translated "born again" in verse 3 also may be translated "born from above." While John's intention is unclear, we perhaps best understand this phrase as having both of these meanings. Through faith in Christ and the resulting work of the Holy Spirit, believers experience a new birth that comes down from heaven as God's gift to us. Lindars, 150-51.

[13]Fredrikson, 83.

[14]Morris, 215.

[15]Godet, 381.

[16]R.A. Torrey, *The Holy Spirit* (n.p.: Fleming H. Revell, n.d.), 76-77.

[17]Godet, 382.

[18]Ramm, 48.

[19]Torrey, 79-81.

[20]Ellis, 51.

[21]Billy Graham, *The Holy Spirit* (Waco: Word, 1978), 55.

[22]Lindars, 154.

[23]Fredrikson, 84.

[24]Barrett, 176.

[25]Ellis, 56.

[26]Barrett, 179.

[27]Fredrikson, 86.

[28]Ellis, 57.

Chapter 4

[1]Dean Nelson, "Do Drink the Water", *Christianity Today* (September 2003), 38-39.

[2]Ellis, 69.

[3]Summers, 76.

[4]Ibid., 74.

[5]Torrey, 89.

[6]Morris, 261.

[7]Fredrikson, 97.

[8]Morris, 261.

[9]John Wimber, "Spirit Song", Mercy Publishing, 1979.

[10]Barrett, 191, 195.

[11]Summers, 111; Godet, 634-35.

[12]Morris, 422; Summers, 111-12; Godet, 635-36.

[13]Summers, 112.

[14]Barrett, 272.

[15]Morris, 427-28.

[16]Lee, 73.

[17]Torrey, 90.

[18]Summers, 79.

[19]Torrey, 91-92.

[20]Fee, 178.

[21]Summers, 112.

[22]Morris, 263.

[23]Fredrikson, 95, 96.

[24]David Mark Ball, *"I Am" in John's Gospel* (Sheffield, England: Sheffield Academic, 1996), 178-80.

[25]Ibid., 65

[26]Ibid., 66-67.

Chapter 5

[1]William Byron Forbush, ed., *Fox's Book of Martyrs* (John C. Winston, 1926; repr., Grand Rapids: Zondervan, 1967), 7-8.

[2]Ibid., 9.

[3]Ruth A. Tucker., *From Jerusalem to Irian Jaya* (Grand Rapids: Zondervan, 1983), 90-93.

[4]John Piper, *Let the Nations Be Glad* (Grand Rapids: Baiker 1993), 73.

[5]Elisabeth Elliot, *The Savage My Kinsman* (Ann Arbor: Servant Books, 1961), 1-2.

[6]Ibid., 29.

[7]Gracia Burnham and Dean Merrill, *In the Presence of My Enemies* (Wheaton: Tyndale House, 2003), passim, 307.

[8]Ibid., 262.

[9]David B. Barrett and Todd M. Johnson, "Annual Statistical Table on Global Mission: 2002," *International Bulletin on Missionary Research* (January 2002), 22-23.

[10]Jeff M. Sellers, "Crushing House Churches", *Christianity* (January 2004), 63.

[11]"Al Qaeda Targets Christians in Kingdom", *Christianity Today* (February 2004), 24.

[12]Piper, 111-12.

[13]John 5:4, which most scholars consider to be a later addition to the text, provides useful information on the thinking of the people at that time about the Pool of Bethesda: "From time to time an angel of the Lord would come down and stir up the waters. The first one into the pool after each disturbance would be cured of whatever disease he had." If this was the common belief among the people at the time, it explains why so many disabled people were gathered at Bethesda as well explains the lame man's response to Jesus in verse 7.

[14]Fredrikson, 112.

[15]Morris, 303.

[16]Ibid., 303-04.

[17]Yechiel Eckstein, *What You Should Know about Jews and Judaism* (Waco: Word, 1984), 83.

[18]Ibid.
[19]Ibid., 82-83.
[20]Ibid., 88-89.
[21]Ibid., 91.
[22]Ibid., 90.
[23]Ibid., 89.
[24]Ibid., 86-87.
[25]Fredrikson, 114.
[26]Eckstein, 261-62.
[27]Morris, 313.
[28]Fredrikson, 115-16.
[29]Cullman, 327.
[30]Ibid., 300, 301.
[31]Morris, 308, 309.
[32]R.V.G. Tasker, *John*, (Grand Rapids: Eerdmans, 1960; repr. 1986), 87.
[33]Ibid., 88.
[34]Fredrikson, 117.

Chapter 6

[1]Summers, 102.
[2]Lee, 144.
[3]Ball, 77.
[4]Summers, 99.
[5]Ball, 73.
[6]Lee, 146.
[7]Morris, 366.
[8]Lee, 148.
[9]Zacharias, 93.
[10]Morris, 378.
[11]Ibid., 378.
[12]Dunn, 185.
[13]Godet, 601. "This mystery of our complete union with His person, which in this discourse is expressed in *words*, is precisely that which Jesus desired to express by an *act*, when He instituted the rite of the Lord's Supper. We need not say, therefore, that this discourse alludes *to* the Lord's Supper, but we must say that the Lord's Supper and this discourse refer to one and the same divine fact, expressed here by a metaphor, there by an emblem."
[14]Ibid., 596.
[15]Lee, 151.
[16]Morris, 380.
[17]Fredrikson, 137.
[18]Summers, 102.
[19]Ibid., 102-03.
[20]Morris, 387.
[21]Lee, 156.
[22]Fredrikson, 140.
[23]Barrett, 249.
[24]Summers, 100.
[25]Godet, 590.
[26]Morris, 367.
[27]Barrett, 253.
[28]Ibid., 251.
[29]Morris, 385.
[30]Summers, 104.

Chapter 7

[1]William J. Bennett, ed., *The Book of Virtues*, (New York: Simon & Schuster, 1993), 572, 576.
[2]James E. Tull, *The Shapers of Baptist Thought*, (Valley Forge, PA: Judson, 1972), 217.
[3]Martin Luther King, Jr., *Strength to Love*, (New York: Harper & Row, 1963), 125; quoted in Tull, 217.
[4]Peter P.J. Beyerhaus, *God's Kingdom & the Utopian Error* (Wheaton, IL: Crossway), 93-122.
[5]David Hesselgrave, *Communicating Christ Cross-Culturally* (Grand Rapids: Academie, 1978), 199.
[6]Ibid., 219.
[7]Godet, 658.
[8]Ellis, 152; Lindars, 320.
[9]Ball, 85.
[10]Fredrikson, 162.
[11]Morris., 463-64.
[12]Erwin Lutzer, *The Serpent of Paradise* (Chicago: Moody, 1996), 42, 43.
[13]Ibid., 43, 44.
[14]Stephen F. Noll, *Angels of Light, Powers of Darkness* (Downers Grove, IL: InterVarsity, 1998), 99, 106.
[15]Lutzer., 45, 46.
[16]Ibid., 55.
[17]Ibid., 56-57.
[18]Ibid., 58-59.
[19]Roetzel, 50-51
[20]Winfried Corduan, *Neighboring Faiths* (Downers Grove, IL: InterVarsity, 1998), 196-99.
[21]Ibid., 223-24.
[22]Lutzer, 60, 61.
[23]Corduan, 198-99.
[24]Lutzer, 61.
[25]Ibid., 61-62.
[26]Vinoth Ramachandra, *Gods that Fail* (Downers Grove, IL: InterVarsity, 1996), 72.
[27]Lutzer, 63-64.
[28]Barrett, 286.
[29]Ball, 193-94.
[30]Lindars, 320-21.

[31]Ball, 190-91.
[32]Ibid., 88.
[33]Morris, 456.
[34]Ellis, 153.
[35]Morris, 447.
[36]Ibid., 225.
[37]Ibid., 452.
[38]Godet, 663.
[39]Bennett, 574.
[40]Barrett, 285.
[41]Morris, 457.
[42]Fredrikson, 161.
[43]Morris, 457.
[44]Godet, 668.
[45]Neil T. Anderson, *The Bondage Breaker* (Eugene, OR: Harvest House, 1990), 23.
[46]Godet, 666.

Chapter 8

[1]Tasker, 129.
[2]Ibid., 128.
[3]Fredrikson, 181.
[4]Morris, 505.
[5]Ibid., 505-08.
[6]Ibid., 512.
[7]Tasker, 130.
[8]Wright, 196.
[9]Wolfgang Simpson, *Houses that Change the World* (Emmelsbull, Germany: C&P, 1999; repr. Carlisle, Cumbria UK: OM, 2002), 262, 263.
[10]David J. Bosch, *Transforming Mission* (Maryknoll, NY: Orbis Books, 1991), 76.
[11]John Ortberg, *Love Beyond Reason* (Grand Rapids: Zondervan, 1998), 190-191.
[12]Ibid., 186-87, 188.
[13]Morris, 502, 503.
[14]Ibid., 511.
[15]Andy Stanley, *Visioneering* (Sisters: OR: Multnomah, 1999), 63.
[16]Rick Ferguson, *The Servant Principle* (Nashville: Broadman and Holman, 1999), 97-99.
[17]Ibid., 99-100.
[18]Ibid., 100-102.
[19]Ibid., 102-03.
[20]Ibid., 103.
[21]Morris, 509-510.
[22]Ibid., 510.
[23]Fredrikson, 182.
[24]Ibid., 183
[25]Ortberg, 20, 21.
[26]Wright, 92, 93, 94.
[27]Stanley, 192.
[28]Morris, 513.
[29]Fredrikson, 185.
[30]John R.W. Stott, *The Cross of Christ* (Downers Grove, IL: InterVarsity, 1986), 323.
[31]Ortberg, 126-27.

Chapter 9

[1]See Chapter 8, "The Shepherd's Love", 156.
[2]Stephen F. Noll, *Angels of Light, Powers of Darkness* (Downers Grove, IL: InterVarsity, 1998), 103.
[3]Much is to be commended about the "warfare worldview" set forth by Gregory Boyd in his two books, *God at War* (Downers Grove, IL: InterVarsity, 1997), and *Satan and the Problem of Evil* (Downers Grove, IL: InterVarsity, 1998). I differ with Boyd, however, in that I believe maintaining that the present universe is in a state of spiritual warfare is possible without diminishing belief in God's sovereignty.
[4]Ortberg, 209.
[5]Ball, 104.
[6]Summers, 134.
[7]Ellis, 185.
[8]Roberta Stephens and Ann Borquist, "Blood of Martyrs: From Suffering and Sacrifice Comes Joy: The Story of the Covell Family", *Japan Harvest* (Winter 2004), 2-4.
[9]Morris, 558; Fredrikson, 199.
[10]Ball, 105.
[11]Barrett, 332; Lee, 211-12.
[12]Lee, 202.
[13]Godet, 739.
[14]Lee, 203.
[15]Ball, 109-110.
[16]Lee, 204-05.
[17]Barrett, 329.
[18]Lindars, 395.
[19]Timothy C. Tennent, *Christianity at the Religious Roundtable* (Grand Rapids: Baker Academic, 2002), 239-240.
[20]Lindars, 392-93.
[21]Summers, 139.
[22]Ibid.
[23]Lee, 225.
[24]Summers, 137.
[25]Corduan, 223.
[26]Summers, 139.

[27]Morris, 550.
[28]Boyd Hunt, *Redeemed! Eschatological Redemption and the Kingdom of God* (Nashville: Broadman & Holman, 1993), 347.
[29]Barrett, 329.
[30]Godet, 740.
[31]Ibid., 741.
[32]Fredrikson, 196.
[33]Morris, 551-52.

Chapter 10

[1]Corduan, 287.
[2]Ian Reader, *Religion in Contemporary Japan* (Houndmills, England: MacMillan, 1991), 124.
[3]Ueda Kenji, "Shinto", in *Religion in Japanese Culture,* ed. Noriyoshi Tamura and David Reid (Tokyo: Kodansha International, 1996), 27-32.
[4]David C. Lewis, *The Unseen Face of Japan* (Turnbridge Wells, Kent, England: Monarch, 1993), 47-51, 87-90.
[5]Ibid., 98-109.
[6]Ibid., 33-34.
[7]Morris, 636-37.
[8]Lindars, 470.
[9]Neill T. Anderson, *Victory over the Darkness* (Ventura, CA: Regal Books, 1990), 57.
[10]Summers, 178.
[11]Lindars, 470.
[12]Ibid., 470-71.
[13]Morris, 638-39.
[14]Barrett, 381-82; Lindars, 471; Summers, 179.
[15]Barrett, 382.
[16]Summers, 179.
[17]Ibid., 179-80.
[18]Fee, 545.
[19]Barrett, 382; Lindars, 471.
[20]Fredrikson, 229.
[21]Lindars, 473.
[22]Godet, 832; Barrett, 382; Lindars, 126.
[23]Morris, 641.
[24]Ball, 127-28.
[25]Summers, 181.
[26]Morris, 641.
[27]Ball, 127.
[28]Summers, 181.
[29]Lindars, 473.
[30]Lindars, 472; Barrett, 382.
[31]Summers, 181.
[32]Ball, 128.
[33]Bill Bright, *Have Your Heard of the Four Spiritual Laws?* (San Bernadino, CA: Campus Crusade for Christ International, 1965).
[34]Ball, 123-24.
[35]Clark, 67-68; quotation from Johannes Climacus, *Concluding Unscientific Postscript*, 179-80.
[36]Morris, 644.
[37]Lindars, 475.
[38]Summers, 182.
[39]Godet, 833.
[40]Ronald Allen and Gordon Borror, *Worship: Rediscovering the Missing Jewel* (Eugene, OR: Wipf and Stock, 1982), 18.
[41]Piper, 12.
[42]Ball, 125.
[43]While many books have been written on this topic, perhaps the best-known are John Dawson, *Taking Our Cities for God* (Lake Mary, FL: Creation House, 1989), and Peter Wagner, *Warfare Prayer* (Ventura, CA: Regal Books, 1992).
[44]David Garrison, *Church Planting Movements* (Midlothian, VA: WIGTake Resources, 2004), 172-77.
[45]Morris, 646.
[46]Fredrikson, 230.

Chapter 11

[1]Donald Bloesch, *The Holy Spirit* (Downers Grove, IL: InterVarsity, 2000). 19.
[2]Morris, 692.
[3]Ramm, 72.
[4]Ibid., 72-73.
[5]Fee, 545-52.
[6]Summers, 200.
[7]Walter Thomas Conner, *The Work of the Holy Spirit* (Nashville: Broadman, 1940) 90.
[8]Summers, 200-01.
[9]Conner, 91.
[10]Morris, 697.
[11]Ibid., 86.
[12]Godet, 868.
[13]Morris, 697.
[14]Conner, 87-88.
[15]Morris, 698.
[16]Fredrikson, 244.
[17]K.P. Aleaz, "The Role of Asian Religions in Asian Christian Theology", *Asian Journal of Theology* (October 2001): 280-81.
[18]Fredrikson, 244.
[19]Lindars, 502-03; Morris, 698-99.
[20]Summers, 204.
[21]Lindars, 503.

[22]Godet, 869.
[23]Conner, 88, 89.
[24]Godet, 873.
[25]Fee, 444.
[26]Charles Stanley, *The Wonderful Spirit-Filled Life* (Nashville: Thomas Nelson, 1992), 127.
[27]Fee, 174.
[28]Carl E. Braaten, "The Future of the Apostolic Imperative: At the Crossroads of World Evangelization" in *The Strange New World of the Gospel*, ed. Carl E. Braaten and Robert W. Jenson (Grand Rapids: Eerdmans, 2002), 174.
[29]Garrison, 52.
[30]Ibid., 54.
[31]Ibid., 65-68.
[32]Ibid., 68-97.
[33]Ibid., 99-122.
[34]Ibid., 179, 180, 181.

Chapter 12

[1]Carolyn Bowen Francis and John Masaaki Nakajima, *Christians in Japan* (New York: Friendship, 1991). 31.
[2]Beyerhaus, 165.
[3]Ibid., 166.
[4]Ibid., 30, 31.
[5]Hunt, 115.
[6]Howard A. Snyder, *Community of the King* (Downers Grove, IL: InterVarsity, 1977), 109.
[7]Ibid., 108.
[8]James S. Jeffers, *The Greco-Roman World of the New Testament Era* (Downers Grove, IL: InterVarsity, 1999), 131.
[9]Fredrikson, 270.
[10]Morris, 769.
[11]E. Stanley Jones, *The Unshakable Kingdom and the Unchanging Person* (Nashville: Abingdon, 1972; repr. Bellingham, WA: McNett Press, 1995), 18.
[12]Bosch, 298.
[13]J. Herbert Kane, *A Global View of Christian Missions* (Grand Rapids: Baker, 1971), 216.
[14]Beyerhaus, 115, 121-122.
[15]Ibid., 125-26.
[16]Morris, 769.
[17]Fredrikson, 270.
[18]Jones, 32-33.
[19]Ibid., passim.
[20]Morris, 171.
[21]Beyerhaus, 15.
[22]Bosch, 31.
[23]Ibid., 32-33
[24]Beyerhaus, 15.
[25]Bosch, 34-35.
[26]Beyerhaus, 17.
[27]Hunt, 114.
[28]Beyerhaus, 15.
[29]Tasker, 201.
[30]Beyerhaus, 22.
[31]Christopher J.H. Wright, *Knowing Jesus through the Old Testament* (Downers Grove, IL: InterVarsity, 1992), 109.
[32]Beyerhaus, 23.
[33]Snyder, 46-47.
[34]Hunt, 96.
[35]Jones, 31-32.
[36]Ibid., 28.
[37]Hunt, 96.
[38]Beyerhaus, 25.
[39]Snyder, 104.
[40]Ibid., 102.
[41]Beyerhaus, 63.

Epilogue

[1]Garrison, 112-13.
[2]Ibid., 115.
[3]Bill Easum, *Leadership on the Other Side* (Nashville: Abingdon, 2000), 76, 77.

Hannibal Books

is an Evangelical Christian book-publishing company

To order more copies of *Hearing Christ's Voice* at $19.95 each plus shipping

Call us toll free:

1-800-747-0738

Write us:

P.O. Box 461592
Garland, TX 75046

Visit our web site:

www.hannibalbooks.com

FAX us toll free:

1-888-252-3022

Email us:

orders@hannibalbooks.com

Order directly from Hannibal Books

It's a Jungle Our There! by Ron Snell. Book One of the Rani Adventures. Ron's life and adventures begin in this fast-paced, hilarious romp through the Amazon jungle.

____Copies at $7.95 =_______

Life is a Jungle! by Ron Snell. Book Two of the Rani Adventures is full of the exhilarating escapades of Ron's high-school years.

____Copies at $7.95 = ______

Jungle Calls by Ron Snell. Book Three of the Rani Adventures. Ron returns to the jungle during his college years and finds even more adventures.

___Copies at $7.95 = ______

The 3-volume Rani Series. Order all three of the Jungle adventures by Ron Snell and save. Volumes 1, 2 and 3 sell as a 3-volume series for the special price of $19.95.

____ Sets at $19.95 = ______

The Man in the Green Jeep, by Viola Palmer. If you liked the Jungle books, you'll also enjoy this captivating glance into children's lives and culture in Central America.

____Copies at $9.95 = _____

Add $3.00 postage and handling for first book, 50 cents for each additional book.

Shipping & Handling: ___________

TX residents add 8.25% sales tax: _______

Total Enclosed
(check or money order) ___________

Name ____
Address____
City_________________State______________Zip__________
Phone _____________________ Email ______________________

See address and other contact information on page 253.

CPSIA information can be obtained at www.ICGtesting.com
Printed in the USA
LVOW081312210312

274006LV00001B/35/A